THE NO-RISK SOCIETY

Chatham House Series on Change in American Politics

edited by Aaron Wildavsky
University of California, Berkeley

The
No-Risk
Society

YAIR AHARONI
Issachar Haimovic Professor of Business Policy
Tel-Aviv University

CHATHAM HOUSE PUBLISHERS, INC.
Chatham, New Jersey

THE NO – RISK SOCIETY

CHATHAM HOUSE PUBLISHERS, INC.
Post Office Box One
Chatham, New Jersey 07928

PUBLISHER: Edward Artinian
DESIGNER: Quentin Fiore
COMPOSITION: Chatham Composer
PRINTING AND BINDING: Hamilton Printing Company

LIBRARY OF CONGRESS CATALOGING IN PUBLICATION DATA

Aharoni, Yair.
    The no-risk society.

    (Chatham House series on change in American
politics)
    Includes bibliographical references and
index.
    1. Social security.   2. Welfare state.
3. Insurance.   4. Risk.   I. Title.   II. Series.
HD7091.A4   368   81-6144
ISBN 0-934540-07-1   AACR2
ISBN 0-934540-06-3 (pbk.)

Manufactured in the United States of America

10 9 8 7 6 5 4 3 2 1

Acknowledgments

I am indebted to many for ideas and assistance in the long process of collecting the data for and the actual writing of the many drafts of this book.

The idea for the book originated in 1975 during a truly enjoyable sabbatical at the University of California at Berkeley. I benefited from many lively discussions with Edwin M. Epstein, Dow Votaw, and several doctoral candidates at the school of business. Paul A. Tiffany provided me with able assistance. A special thanks goes to Aaron Wildavsky for many stimulating discussions.

Work continued at the Graduate School of Business at Harvard University (where I studied state-owned enterprises) and of course at my home campus, Tel Aviv University.

At Harvard, Professor Richard Rosenbloom, former associate dean for research, provided continuous encouragement and assistance. Professor Raymond Vernon helped me immensely with his thorough review of several drafts of the manuscript. My thanks also to Brian Levi, a Harvard doctoral candidate, Professor Seev Hirsch, my colleague at Tel Aviv University, and Ted Lang, professor emeritus, New York University, for helpful comments.

A word of thanks is also due to several editors who did a wonderful job in making my language much more precise, and to several anonymous reviewers who criticized and commented on the manuscript, and to the many secretaries who patiently labored through piles of illegible notes to process the many versions of the draft.

During the last year, several staff members at the Tel Aviv Faculty of Management worked with me to help this book come to fruition. My appreciation to Orly Cohen, my secretary, and to Hannah Zohar, my research assistant, for the painstaking job in preparing material, proofing, and typing, and for their stamina in meeting innumerable deadlines. My thanks to Elvira Moisa for her editorial assistance and to Gila Rubin for her willingness to pitch in and lend a hand during the preparation of the final manuscript.

I wish to note my particular appreciation for Ed Artinian. I have worked with several publishers over the years, but the personal involvement and car-ing that Ed exhibited made working with him a particularly rewarding experience.

Finally, I acknowledge my special debt to my wife, Nili, and my daughters for accepting a rival for their time and for their belief in my ability to do the job.

Tel Aviv

Contents

1. The New Social Order   1

Increasing Demands for Protection   3
The Evolving Social Order   6

2. The Individual, Society, and Social Choice   13

Individuals and Society   13
Individuals and Markets   15
Markets and Ethics   17
Market Failures   20
The Broker State: Interest Groups and Elites   24
Bureaucrats   26
Social Choice and Uncertainty   27
Models of Humanity and Social Choice   30
The Insurance State   32

3. Shifting the Risk   39

Risk: Meaning and Measurement   39
Decision Process under Risk   41
Forms of Risk-Avoidance   44
Intensified Demands for Protection   46
Risk-Reduction by Government Decree   50
Unknown Events   53
Shifting Responsibility for Risks   61
The Increasing Umbrella of Insurance   65
Inflation   69
The Impossible Dream   70

4. The Insurance State   76

The Social Security System   78
Health Insurance   85
Property Insurance   90
Insurance Against Crime and Civil Disorder   94
Rationale for Government Insurance   96
Increased Expenditures   98

5. The Invisible Government 110

Quasi Property Rights and Disguised Taxes 111
State-Owned and Government-Sponsored Enterprises 115
Off-Budget Items 118
Contracting 121
Forced Costs of Compliance 124
Cross Subsidization 133
Tax Expenditures 133

6. Risk in International Perspective 140

Independence: A Constraint on Risk Reduction 140
International Trade and International Production 143
The Pains of Adjustment 144
Industrial Policies 148
"Orderly Adjustment" 152
Subsidies and Other Invisible Protection 158
The Dangers of a New Mercantilism 160

7. The Limits to the Public Interest 169

The Delusion of a No-Risk Society 169
Moral Hazard 173
Dependency 177
Rigidities 180
Short Time Horizon 182
Delays 183
Inefficiencies and Increased Risks 185
Economic Change without Risk? 187

8. Toward an Age of Humility 193

Have We Gone Too Far? 195
The Need for Balance 196

Appendix 211

Index 219

The No-Risk Society

1. The New Social Order

In all countries of the developed world, government is being used to reduce or shift the risk borne by individuals. A new social order has evolved that started with a reliance by citizens on government for the solution to certain economic, social, and cultural problems and has grown to include pressures on government to mitigate almost every risk any individual might be asked to bear. The costs of many of the new government protection programs, as well as some of the old ones, are not covered by taxation, nor are they shown in a government budget, nor, often, even in any official report or document. Rather, governmental objectives are often achieved through laws, regulations, and licenses. As a result, government is much bigger than most people realize. Its ability to disguise its vast size is partly what makes the new social order work.

The expanding role of the government started from moral and equity considerations: the recognition that an unfettered market might lead to what was considered socially unacceptable income and wealth distribution. These considerations were reinforced by a gradual shift in the distribution of political power. This power is less concentrated among a few aristocrats and property holders. The combination of moral considerations and the increasing political power of the poor created the welfare state: redistribution of income through high taxes on the rich and governmental supply of subsidized houses, free education, welfare, and health. The richer the countries became, however, the louder the demands for an expanded role of government.

In the last few decades the rapid rise in both the size and impact of the public sector can no longer be explained away as the legitimate functions of a welfare state. The welfare state has been turned into an insurance state, as all individuals are protected against a whole array of risks by shifting the burden of their consequences to a larger group or the whole community or simply by eliminating them. We are insured against a variety of mishaps that range from earthquakes and other natural disasters to poor health, unemployment, and the infirmities of old age. Safety in terms of workplace and working hours is regulated; ailing firms are supported, research and development subsidized by guarantees and grants; quality is controlled, information and social insurance supplied, foreign competition checked, extreme weather conditions and technological changes insured against, and even social status protected.

The movement is away from a reliance on the rational individual as a decision maker and a bearer of the consequences of his choice to a socially determined allocation and distribution of resources, much of which is designed to shift the responsibility for both new and existing risks from individual to society.

The redistribution is achieved in many cases by indirect means. A person who buys a steak may not be aware of it, but the price he pays is affected by a "voluntary" agreement negotiated by the U.S. government with Australia and New Zealand to curb the importation of beef to the United States. The consumer may not know even a small proportion of the myriad regulations that affect the production of beef, the tax loopholes that affect the flow of capital into this particular industry, or the subsidies airlines are forced to grant for those flying to some small cities in the Midwest where beef production is centered. He may well believe that the price of beef is dictated solely and exclusively, as the standard textbook in economics tells us, by the law of supply and demand. A young man who buys his first car may not be aware of the regulations that affect its cost except perhaps for those involved in recent debates on mileage and safety features. The consumer seems to know, at most, the amount he pays directly. He probably does not know the amount he pays indirectly. It is almost certain that he does not recognize inflation as a tax (although he should), nor that he pays for the myriad government regulations through the price of goods and services he buys.

In point of fact, in all developed countries, decisions in the private sector are based to a large extent on appeal, pressure, and manipulation by government. A web of taxes, legal restrictions, subsidies, quotas, regulations, standards, licenses, purchase orders, and guarantees ensure results, allegedly "in the public interest," that are essentially enforced for political reasons. The profitability of private firms has become at least as much a function of the way managers react to government as it is a result of efficient management and superior innovation. Market demand is also affected by government, both in its aggregate and in specific areas of the economy and specific products. The direction of technological change and the creation of new technologies are largely determined by governmental decisions about which project will or will not be financed or encouraged. The choice is most often based on arguments referring to national security or prestige and glory. The recipients grow to depend on government, and their managers are often recruited for their ability to negotiate with the government bureaucracy, a talent altogether different from those needed to compete successfully in the marketplace. The relations between managers of large business firms and the government bureaucracy are sometimes symbiotic, sometimes parasitical, and always different from those assumed in standard economics textbooks.

Increasing Demands for Protection

As is the case with most social phenomena, this new social order did not come about abruptly. It grew out of a combination of change in values and expectations and a shift in the balance of political power. The belief in the supremacy of the individual and the efficacy of market forces so characteristic of the nineteenth century dwindled in the course of the twentieth to be replaced by an equally firm belief in the supremacy of society and the efficacy of planning. "Society," conceived as more than the sum of the individuals composing it, was construed as having a significance of its own, with needs and desires peculiar to it.

The notion that the individual is not always the best judge of his or her own interests combined with changing definitions of justice and fair play has brought about some significant changes in government's role in the Western nation-states. Government has long been expected to protect the poor, the weak, and the unfortunate against misfortune. But as political power has spread from a few aristocrats and property holders, with the advent of universal suffrage, to take in—at least potentially—the entire adult population, the relative power of propertyless workers, women, and minority groups has increased, and they have learned that they can achieve more for themselves using the political clout available to them than they would if they relied solely on the market. The result has been growing demands on government, no longer simply to protect the poor and the unfortunate or to supply free education or subsidized transportation, but for a complete array of insurance services to all citizens against almost every hazard.

In the 1930s, governments assumed the responsibility for the total management of the economy; then they added insurance against unemployment, against the vicissitudes of the business cycle, and against the crises of economic recession. Later, they took on minimum standards of income, nutrition, health, and housing, "assured to every citizen as a political right, not a charity,"[1] equitable distribution of income, and economic and social opportunity. By now equality includes, not only formal political equality or equality of opportunity, but equality of results as well. Over time, demands for social justice and equity have turned into calls for more insurance and fewer risks. Individual responsiblity for the consequences of a growing array of risks is diminishing, and the role of government is increasing dramatically.

Today, the government is forced to protect its citizens from many economic and social problems, immunize them against almost any change, and insure them against almost every conceivable hazard. The state has become a huge insurance agency seemingly trying to guarantee a no-risk society. Government insurance covers not only natural disasters but risks stemming from political or technological changes, lack of information, and even individual folly. Both the old privileged classes, who feel their rights are threatened, and the emerging masses seeking additional rights attempt to shift the burden of risk-bearing from themselves to the other group. If there is one point on which almost everyone can agree it is that risks are intolerable and must be shared either by all members of the society or by some groups within it. The cynic may describe this as a belief that while the benefits of high-risk ventures should accrue to me, the costs should be borne by someone else or, more often, by government. Since government as such does not have any resources of its own, what this actually means is that risk-bearing shifts from individuals to everyone.

The term "risk" involves a potential harm, injury, damage, danger, or loss to the individual or to his or her property or social status. The potential harm could be to human health, as in the familiar cases of saccharin, DDT, birth-control devices, air pollutants, noise, drugs, asbestos, or vinyl chloride. Risk could also be a probability of disability experienced by victims of violent crimes, medical malpractice, bad products; or that of loss of employment, income, status, freedom, or dignity. It is often subjective, being the result of an assessment of consequences that exist in the minds of the choosers.

If an efficient and just system for distributing the incidence of risk could be devised and agreed on, this redistribution would often rigidify the economy and make any adjustment difficult or impossible. For example, if employment were guaranteed in a workplace, its owner would feel within his rights to demand a guarantee for the prosperity of his firm through tariff protection or a halt in technological change. Still, if this state of affairs were the result of a consensus, there would be no logical objection to it. Unfortunately, in reality there is no such consensus. Instead, aggregate demand for public insurance is high, but the collective willingness to pay the insurance "premiums" is not. Most people cry for lower taxes and at the same time increase their demands for both government services and risk reduction. In a private market economy, demands mean nothing if they are not backed up by willingness and ability to pay. In the public arena, these same demands can be turned into legislation, and government then has to face a gap that cannot be closed between vociferous public demands for reduction of risks and equally loud outcries for reduction of taxes. This gap is a major reason for inflation and its many attendant ills, not to mention social and political tensions.

Faced with an insoluble problem, government resorts to invisible methods of redistribution. It exerts its influence on allocation and distribution of resources nominally owned, managed, financed, and controlled by the private sector. To do this, it has all sorts of mechanisms at its disposal, none of which need be recorded in the official statistics. Most of their impact is seen instead in the changing nature of private property rights—an array of restrictions on discretionary decision making by owners and the creation of property rights through government largesse. Invisible methods enable the government to hide most of the mounting costs. Because they are not registered in the budget, legislative scrutiny is reduced and public debate often avoided.

As a result, Western nations are gripped by roaring inflation and stagnant growth. Inflation is primarily caused by increasing costs of overregulation coupled with mounting governmental expenditures financed by budgetary deficits. The public that has been turned off by ever proliferating government is the same public that demanded the government assume vast new responsiblities, which imply a commitment to increased spending. As a result, while in the past the budget was balanced most of the time, it is now in a continuous state of deficit: the 1980 U.S. federal budget was labeled austere because it called for "only" a more than $30 billion deficit. The financing of these deficits and the increasing costs of production caused by regulation are two of the main reasons for the continuous inflation. Stagnant growth is partially caused by turgid productivity that is largely a result of attempts to protect individuals against risks—including those of technological innovation or economic change. Many nations have been mortgaging their future, shifting capital away from productive investments to protection of the environment, of employment in obsolete and noncompetitive firms, or of the real and even imagined risks caused by new technologies. As a direct result of attempts to mitigate risks or insure people against them, less money is available for investment to create jobs. Thus the Western world faces both inflation and stagnation.

Government also faces a gap between the demands for action on behalf of genuinely worthy causes and the limited supply of workable and manageable solutions. Its ability to act effectively is limited by its administrative capabilities, by the willingness and the ability of the population to comply with its edicts, and by the weakening of various policy tools, resulting in part from the sharp rise in the volume of international transactions and the accelerated development of multinational organizations. Governmental action is also thwarted by unintended and undesirable consequences that swamp many worthy intentions. Despite popular belief, government cannot eliminate all problems, and government is not economically omnipotent. When government reduces risk for some people, it increases it for other people. Those who already have more than enough attempt to safeguard what they have, and the costs are often paid by those who cannot afford to pay. In the new social order, the distribution of risk has become political, and government is expected to protect its citizens against risks or insure them against the consequences. Costs of protection and insurance are not covered by those receiving the benefits. If these costs are not covered by taxation, they have to be met through one of the most inequitable taxes of all: inflation.

The Evolving Social Order

In this new social order many questions arise. Are there limits to the demands people place on government? How is the class struggle affected by conflicts over the payment of taxes and receipt of benefits from government? What is the proper balance between the public and private sectors and the appropriate activities and domain of each? If the idea of distribution to each according to his needs is rejected, what is the criterion for a just and equitable distribution? In a world marked by an interdependence within nations and among them, what are the basic rules of moral behavior, especially in the international arena? How far and to what extent should governments attempt to alleviate economic adjustments by subsidizing "lame ducks" or financing their deficits? How far should the government go in eliminating or mitigating which risks, and when should risks be socially insured?

Whether one assumes the conservative attitude that the functions of government should be limited, or the liberal approach that government intervention is necessary to preserve freedom, greater understanding of public sector operations and their interaction with individual behavior is required before any of these questions can be answered.

This book is an attempt to explore the major reasons behind the swelling of the public sector and its invisible operations and to suggest some lessons to be drawn from the experience of the last three decades. It does not mean to preach the evils of big government, nor is it another polemic on the physical or social limits to growth. Instead, it is an attempt to describe and analyze the major characteristics of the new social order and the way that this order has evolved.

No solutions are suggested, nor are rules for "how much government" or "how much market" prescribed. At this stage prescriptions are probably not even possible. Instead, some limits to socioeconomic systems and organizations are pointed out.

Several characteristics of the evolving social order are emphasized. First, the growing reliance on government is the result of pragmatic responses to social problems and not of a waning faith in individual freedom. The importance of the individual, the rejection of the notion that one set of beliefs has any greater claims to truth than any other, the emphasis on the right of the individual to be different and on the right to private property continue to be regarded as fundamental—at least in theory. At the same time, the contrary trend toward requiring government to supply an expanded array of services, fueled by demands for equality in more and more areas of human activity, accompanied by an unwillingness to suffer the consequences of rapid technological change and interdependence, results in many demands for reallocation of costs and shifting of roles that end in greater and greater state control over our lives, higher inflation, and less productive investments for the creation of future jobs.

Power in society has shifted and parliamentary control has been reduced. The case for liberty, equality, fraternity has become in this century a call for higher wages, better working conditions, and social welfare. Unions have abandoned revolutionary phraseology and have concentrated on collective bargaining, using their political power to obtain security and redistribute income. In 1925 Rudolph Hilferding, the leader of the German Socialist party, coined the term "political wage." The power of employers is curbed by law and by the power of strong labor unions at the bargaining table. Despite a variety of setbacks, the working class as a whole on both sides of the Atlantic has improved its income, its working conditions, and its social status.

Suffrage gave organized labor the political power to ensure benefits and reduce the risk of unemployment and work-related hazards. The rise of big industrial organizations and urbanization combined with universal suffrage resulted in a new concept of government as one that would bring a better life and a better world free from abuses, excessive power, and poverty. Later, many of these demands turned into calls for protection against risks, mitigation of uncertainty, and social insurance against the consequences of risky events. To a large extent, all these demands call for a preservation of the status quo: the government is expected to protect its population not only against physical harm but (mainly) against such social risks as change of social status or loss of employment in an existing job. This protection is costly, and less money is available for investment in the creation of new jobs. The ability of the individual to make choices at the risk of suffering the consequences has been curtailed. Reward-seeking individuals are forced to accept preventive, safety-conscious collective choices. The development of new technologies is arrested by attempts to achieve a risk-free, predictable society.

The new social order is partly a result of greater interdependence within society, which became apparent just as interdependence among nations was reducing the power of each sovereign government to control the destiny of the nation. Any single decision is seen today as both influenced by and influencing other decisions. Interdependence in a national economy is the result mainly of urbanization and technological complexities. In these close quarters anything done by one individual creates "externalities" by affecting others.

World travel and a surge in international production controlled by a few hundred huge multinational (or transnational) firms, successive international agreements formally establishing free convertibility of currencies and reducing tariff barriers, vast sums moving across borders with every shift in interest rates or any change in governmental policies—these are all part of this global complexity. While governments assume more and more responsibility for the economic, social, and cultural well-being of their citizens and attempt to protect them against most risks, they grow more vulnerable to economic forces from distant lands. The quadrupling of oil prices in 1973 was for some the beginning of a massive effort to reap economic benefits in the world and for others the signal to impose protectionist measures to transfer the risk of unemployment to other countries. Since then, increasing government intervention focused on safeguarding jobs, using formal and informal restrictions on imports, subsidies, and other means. Governments tried to conserve existing industrial structures rather than attempt structural adjustments.

The new social order is impatient for immediate social results and fears the consequences of technological changes and the ramifications of scientific discovery. It is legitimized by calls for equity, justice, and fair play. It sees equitable solutions as requiring that risks borne by individuals or businesses be shifted to society. In extreme cases, such as the development of life-prolonging devices (an artificial heart or an organ transplant), the impossibility of equitable distribution hindered the development of new techniques. In many more cases, attempts to prevent risk actually resulted in increasing risk: resistance to nuclear power did not reduce the demand for energy; it may have caused increasing risks of lung cancer to coal producers. The more stringent conditions of certifying drugs in the United States caused firms to make their tests on foreigners less able to alleviate any unfortunate consequences. The calls to reduce risks on equity grounds often caused the risk to be borne by those least able to afford the contingencies. As one example, product liability insurance may have helped certain individuals, but the additional costs of doing business may have impoverished others, mainly small firms. Attempts to mitigate a wide variety of risks reduced the amounts of funds available for investment in future jobs, and the maintenance of jobs in obsolete technologies reduced the incentives for the creation of new technologies. Being cautious can be a very risky policy. Any mitigation of risks through social prevention means that restrictions on individual freedom must be used, and people must live differently from the way they would have liked.

While people continue to proclaim their belief in individualism, they do not necessarily practice what they proclaim. Instead, pragmatic responses to problems result in the public sector's involving itself in economic, social, and cultural activities to an ever greater extent. Individual freedom is restricted by rules and regulations designed for a "public good" that is rarely defined but usually reflects the individual analyst's judgment of what constitutes social justice and fair play. "Needed in whose view?" "Fair in what terms?" or "Needed for whom?" are questions rarely asked.

Many argue that individual freedom must be curtailed because there is no other way to solve problems in a society where an act by any one individual affects some other. Society should protect the individual (even the individual who does not want to be protected) and prohibit him or her from taking unacceptable risks. A person who is willing to take risks to earn more money often finds that it is against the law. Those who enjoy taking risks find that a paternal society compels them to pay, directly or indirectly, for a large and growing catalog of compulsory insurance schemes to protect themselves.

The free-enterprise market economy was based on an economic theory bolstered by doctrinal and religious justifications. Politically determined allocation and distribution of resources has no comparable theoretical underpinnings, either in economics, sociology, or any other field. Groups whose wealth or status seems threatened by the new demands for equality and redistribution react by lobbying for benefits from government policies. Most of these benefits are achieved through means not usually subject to legislative or public scrutiny. The class struggle is transformed into a debate over the distribution of costs of both visible and invisible government programs and over who should profit from its benefits and largesse.[2] All this results in increased public insurance and protection. Profits no longer result solely from success in undertaking a risky project but also from negotiations with government on the reduction of risks. Workers who strike for higher wages are often protected from losing income; consumers are insured against misrepresentation; farmers are protected against crop failure, and citizens against flood and other disasters.

The growth of the public sector involves an ambiguity: on the one hand, most people seem to want both more social services and less risk; on the other, they are afraid of a "big government" that they see as inefficient, interfering, and corrupt. The feeling that loss of freedom and independence is the price to be paid for social insurance, justice, and equity is not often clearly articulated. Sometimes it simply comes in the form of claims by the middle class that their share of the price is too high.

For each individual, risk is minimized by spreading it among a large group. But when every individual receives protection, the cost of the various insurance schemes still mounts and must be met. Individuals then try to use whatever economic or political power they have to increase their benefits and reduce their payments. Governments respond by making some payments less visible, putting them in the form of inflation or hidden costs rather than taxes. The massive bureaucracy and limits on indvidual discretions then lead people to feel hemmed in and disenchanted.

The fear of big government is more common in the United States than in Europe, and so the U.S. government more often resorts to invisible methods, carrying out public programs through the private sector. In Europe after the Second World War, those industries considered to be on "commanding heights" were nationalized. In the United States, they were regulated and their discretion in many decisions restricted. In both cases, the firms are shielded against competition. Europe protects workers from losing their jobs by ac-quiring certain ailing firms (or, as the British call them, "lame ducks"). In the United States, these firms are aided through subsidies, through governmental purchases of their output, or through loans; but they are never purchased outright. The so-called military-industrial complex in the United States (and in some cases in Europe) is composed of nominally private firms, but their dependence on government for contracts is almost complete.

In all Western countries, the risks of developing new technologies has largely been absorbed by governments through state ownership, subsidies, or government contracts. Although the organizational methods used to reduce risks, to sponsor certain business activities and restrict others, vary, and although these differences are by no means unimportant, the trend is un-mistakably clear. The market economy is no longer a free-enterprise econ-omy. Each firm operates under governmental restrictions, regulations, and rulings and benefits from government's largesse. Profits depend more on this largesse, these restrictions, and this protection than they do on taking risks in the marketplace. The line of demarcation between the public and the private sector blurs, and the interdependence between them increases.

In the 1960s, people believed that government could solve any problem. A nation that could reach the moon ought also to be able to control pollution, increase safety, abolish crime, find a cure for cancer, develop an artificial heart, and relieve all citizens of risk and uncertainty. In the 1970s, red tape, mistrust of public servants as corrupt or corruptible, and a growing feeling that most government-initiated programs fail, undermined this conviction. Today, governments feel more and more impotent. They are expected to reach any number of often conflicting goals and at the same time have lost many of the policy tools once at their disposal. National jurisdictions have eroded in the international arena, partially as a result of the growth of multi-national enterprises. Governments are unable to insulate their economies from outside economic forces; thus their ability to protect their citizens diminishes as well, while the demands for protection keep growing. On the domestic front, attempts to develop a coherent and consistent set of policies are frustrated by the conflicting demands of many strong interest groups, including those within the government bureaucracy.

For some, this state of affairs is proof that any government intervention is deplorable. They see the difficulties as yet another indication of the internal contradictions of capitalism and recommend a complete abandonment of the system in favor of some other, more society-centered ideology. Others see the same difficulties as a proof that government intervention must end. Still others feel that the more science and technology advance and the more the gross national product grows, the more vile, nasty, brutal, and precarious human existence will become; these people see the remedy in zero growth and a stationary state. They would rather see no growth and no scientific discovery than face the awesome consequences and Faustian choices produced by them. Some see the trend as unavoidable: "As the perils loom closer, and as men come to apprehend their increasing vulnerability, the instinctive desire for self-preservation—found in organized societies as well as individuals—will prompt them to cede to governments far greater powers of surveillance, control and repression than are compatible with contemporary notions of personal liberties."[3]

While the days of individualism are certainly over, extreme solutions are not the answer. We must examine the basic premises of all systems, determine the limits of each, and then see how far we should go in any direction. All socioeconomic systems and organizations are imperfect. A perfect system is impossible simply because the human beings that run it are imperfect. We are selfish, but sometimes altruistic; we would like to achieve equality, but also like to be better than the rest; although we may recognize that markets are efficient, we sometimes find them unfair. Our beliefs and preferences are inconsistent, making it almost impossible to reach an agreement on what the best methods might be for solving many fundamental issues.

Analysis cannot produce miraculous solutions to the ills of the modern world because such solutions do not exist. Any solution to any problem always generates additional problems. In the social sciences, problems can only be reduced to manageable proportions. "One-shot" solutions based on declarations of "war" on poverty or cancer are not the answer, nor is blind reliance on self-regulating free-market economic forces, nor futile attempts to plan every step in life. All these simple solutions are symptomatic of fear of the unknown. What we need instead is a stoic acceptance of inevitable conflicts, of the inherent limitations of human beings and their world, and of the inconsistencies in human motivations, desires, and goals.

One reason for failure is that our expectations are often too high to begin with. Stopping economic growth does not solve problems of distribution; it can, in fact, aggravate them. Shifting a problem to the public sector does not guarantee a successful solution and is certainly far from being an optimal way of answering the distribution questions: who gets what? when? and who pays?

It is impossible to achieve a no-risk society. Shifting risks from individuals to groups sometimes results in increasing the burden of risks even for the same individual. The worker who calls for protection at his place of employment is also a taxpayer sharing the higher costs of government, a consumer paying inflated prices, and a shareholder suffering the risks of lower profits. If he relies on government to support him in his old age or to pay for his health insurance, he faces the risk that these programs might any day be voted out of existence. Reducing risks is not riskless. The mitigation of any one risk may cause other risks to increase; and social insurance against many risks is extremely costly, causing inflation with all its ugly consequences. Attempts to reduce risks are often made by those who already have more than enough. In the name of social justice and equity they may force those unable and unwilling to bear the costs of the social insurance to change their way of life. In the new social order the level of risk is not individually determined. Rather, it is politically allocated.

NOTES

1. Harold L.Wilensky, *The Welfare State and Equality: Structural and Ideologcal Roots of Public Expenditures* (Berkeley: University of California Press, 1975), p. 1.
2. Cf. James O'Connor, *The Fiscal Crisis of the State* (New York: St. Martin's Press, 1973).
3. E. J. Mishan, *The Economic Growth Debate: An Assessment* (London: Allen and Unwin, 1977), p. 247.

2. The Individual, Society, and Social Choice

Individuals and Society

The increasing protection of individuals by government is characteristic of all industrialized countries. Nevertheless, there are differences in the extent to which governments protect individuals and in the tools employed by them in supplying insurance. These differences are at least partially explained by the way individual citizens perceive their roles in society.

Points of view differ widely about the role of individuals relative to society. At one extreme are those who passionately believe in the supremacy of the rights of the individual; for them, individual wants are the only criterion for social action. At the other extreme are those who claim that the supremacy of society is the only guide for human conduct. These two viewpoints also differ in the way they portray human motives: one sees people as basically selfish and greedy, aspiring to maximize their benefits; the other sees people as altruists whose highest achievement is aiding others. Two other related groups are the proponents of self-regulating markets and those who call for detailed planning. Finally, some see a world order based on continuous conflict; others believe in at least the possibility of harmony.

These various beliefs and value systems are to a large extent interrelated. If society is basically a loose combination of individuals, then the market system is preferred; under this system each individual decides and chooses according to his or her own beliefs, wants, and desires, selfish as they may be. Any conflict among these various wants is resolved through the mechanism of the market whereby allocation is based on individual transactions and avoids any need to impose values, views, or preferences on others. If, on the other hand, humans are social animals, if they prefer working for the good of the community and to sacrifice for communal aims (i.e., if the community is the supreme value), then society can dictate a life style to each indivudal. Society must plan the individual's work, life, habits, consumption, and values; and it must eradicate any values it finds morally offensive. Of course, if every human being is basically altruistic, then through additional knowledge, continuous dialogue, and a search for the imminent truth, people will find a harmonious coexistence.

If one believes in the supreme value of individual choice, then social choices can be only the summation of individual wants. Such choices can ideally be based on social interaction in a market where each individual makes personal, private decisions. Government derives from consent of the governed, to freely assign to it the execution of certain acts. Government action is needed if, and only if, there is a market failure, and it can be guided only on the basis of a minimal agreement. The way such minimal agreement is manifested is through participation in the political process of individuals enjoying equal rights. The methods of participation and the meaning of equality have long been debated. The great difficulty, as James Madison observed in the *Federalist #51*, "lies in this: you must first enable the government to control the governed; and in the next place oblige it to control itself." The precise desirable balance between authority and democracy, as well as between power and liberty, has been achieved in different ways. In many democracies, and mainly in the United States, it was achieved through the interplay and social interactions of organized interest groups.

If, on the other hand, the individual is, above all, part of a much bigger entity called society, if he or she finds the greatest achievement in working for the common good, if happiness is based on sharing, giving, and serving the public, then there is no problem of revealed preferences because individual preferences do not count. Society will plan to achieve what is in the public interest, will arrive at the greatest possible public good, and will eliminate the vicissitudes of the market. In short, it will tell us what is good for us. The individual members, in this extreme view, bear the same relation to society as children do to their parents. They may not like what the parents direct them to do, but they are told that parents know best.

In a strange way, the belief in individualism leads to a solution of the problem of choice through a vast system of social interactions: goods, services, even values are exchanged in the market according to the value placed on them by each individual. At the other extreme, society is composed of individuals, but these individuals are either all exactly equal or else believe so much in a common cause and a common destiny that they accept one solution. Planning is possible in this case because the planner knows best. The planner does not have to take into account different tastes because taste is a societal value shared by all. The planner does not have to compensate human beings for their contributions, or create incentives, because all human beings are ready and willing to accept the planner's ruling of what is good for society. Those whose values are basically individualistic may wonder how the planner will know what is good for society. Those who view society as an entity above all individuals do not have this problem since they are sure that societal decisions are the best guides for human behavior.

The belief in the importance of the individual is a basic tenet of Western civilization. If the individual is entirely selfish and knows best what is good for him or her, then it follows that all interactions among individuals must be based on free choice. Each individual has equal rights to pursue happiness as he or she defines it, based on a personal understanding of what is good for him or her. Each individual is guaranteed God-given equality of rights: the right to free expression, the right to choose a place to live, the right to change his or her mind, and the right to hold property. Certain rights are recognized to have a superior position. In the United States, the First Amendment provides that "Congress shall make no law respecting an establishment of religion, or prohibiting the free exercise thereof; or abridging the freedom of speech, or of the press; or the right of the people peaceably to assemble, and to petition the Government for a redress of grievances." The free exercise of religion and freedom of speech cannot be changed by law or through the exercise of any other rights. Freedom of press and religion cannot be denied "because a single company has a legal title to all the town."[1] Other rights are also inalienable, that is, cannot be taken away without due process of law, and the law must defend and protect the individual from being deprived of them. Because every individual has the same rights, the purpose of the law is to reconcile them in such a way that their exercise by someone will not reduce the rights of others.

Individuals and Markets

The notion of individual rights is also at the root of classical economics and much of economic theory today. Every individual has the right to define his or her own wants, needs, and desires. The individual will achieve more of what he or she wants by exchanging goods and services with others. Since human beings are rational maximizers of their own self-interest, institutional arrangements must be based on voluntary exchanges in which individuals can act voluntarily, depending on self-interests as they see them. Since each individual defines his or her own goals, classical economics did not recognize national goals; they were simply assumed to be based on the consent of all citizens. Economists were not concerned with why a goal was chosen but with how it could be achieved once it was formulated.

The market system and capitalism are rooted in the belief that, in the oft-quoted words of Adam Smith, economic activity is motivated by "the uniform, constant and uninterrupted effort of every man to better his condition."

Therefore "it is not from the benevolence of the butcher, the brewer, or the baker that we expect our dinner, but from their regard of their own interest." Many find it hard to accept a theory based on the human being as a selfish maximizer of self-interest; they claim instead that many people are or should be willing to sacrifice self-interest for the common good. Humans are social animals; they live in a community and strive to achieve what is best for the community as a whole.[2] If necessary, a person is willing to sacrifice even life itself in defending some community ideal, such as the country's independence. Humans can also be benevolent and kind, and can achieve self-fulfillment by working for the benefit of the whole community. Therefore, it is claimed, a society can be built that will be much more moral, much better to live in, with a much higher quality of life, and in which all persons will be equal; alternatively, as in an Israeli kibbutz, each person will receive his or her needs and serve to the best of his or her ability. It is sometimes added that even if most people today are guided solely by self-interest, this is not a biologically determined trait but the fault of the educational system and the false values implanted in pupils during their formative years. Schools, it is argued, are based on competition for grades rather than on teaching students to help one another. A different educational system will provide a different outlook. Self-interest will be replaced by seeking and achieving a much higher quality of life on "spaceship earth." As Paul Baran puts it: "A society can be developed in which the individual would be formed, influenced and educated . . . by a system of rationally planned production for use, by a universe of human relations determined by and oriented toward solidarity, cooperation and freedom."[3]

The arguments of both the proponents and opponents of "free market" solutions are largely emotional ones; market solutions are basically heartless and inhumane. The market degrades and mutilates human beings and ignores many important human values and motivations. The use of market mechanisms is alleged to be a cynical and wrong way of achieving any social goals. A person made in the image of God cannot be reduced to a faceless, mindless atom. People are not purely materialistic, and they are not always (or they should not be) motivated by self-interest.

The market system is an excellent mechanism of efficient allocation, that is, the parceling out of resources to produce maximum amount of products using minimum resources. The resulting distribution or command over resources for use by different segments of the population is sometimes objectionable on moral grounds.

Since all human beings are equal, they all have the same rights. Market transactions, however, are based on property: the more property one has, the more "votes" one can cast in the marketplace. Therefore, the market might work well for the able, gifted, and privileged and for those who inherit wealth, but it does not take into account the plight of the poor and the weak. Is this unequal distribution of wealth the right one? For the classical economist, the answer is yes; the distribution of wealth is based on the contribution of each individual. In the marketplace, each individual receives an amount equal to his or her marginal contribution. The alleged reason a man is poor is that he is lazy. A person who wants more should simply work harder. Today, this point of view is less popular than it once was, and government is expected to redistribute costs and benefits.

The problem, again, is how costs and benefits should be distributed. Market solutions give one answer, based on the power of the purse. Bargaining solutions give another answer, based on political power. Still another possibility is distribution based on need or on some vague notion of equal sacrifices—the notion is necessarily vague because sacrifices cannot be distributed equally. An equal tax on the poor and the rich does not constitute equal sacrifice.

Each one of these distribution methods is possible, and each will have some effects not only on choices but also on incentives. The less an individual benefits from his or her own effort, the less he or she may be willing to work hard. The more the individual receives through political bargaining, the more time will be spent to achieve political power. Further, in a market system, rewards and benefits are at least partially a result of risk-taking. In a politically determined distribution, the distribution of risks is an object of political contention. Distribution, however, should be based on ethical norms.

Markets and Ethics

Blood, for example, cannot be produced artificially, and transfusion is sometimes essential to save human lives. For some, a blood transfusion may be regarded as any other voluntary market transaction; donors of blood are paid by those in need of the blood, at a price established in the market. In those cases in which processed plasma can be used instead of whole blood, there is even an international trade in plasma. Others passionately argue that blood should be donated rather than sold, and they view the international trade in blood with anguish. To them, the sale of blood is immoral and symbolic of the total absence of community bonds and of the heartless exploitation of human misery. In the United Kingdom, for example, both blood donations and transfusions are given free of charge.

Emotional reactions to the existence of a market in blood sometimes lead to further accusations about the quality or adequacy of the service. According to Titmuss,[4] in the United States, both blood shortages and a much higher level of death caused by transfusion-induced hepatitis are the result of reliance on the profit motive for the supply of blood, a situation that is both medically and socially unhealthy. Available tests of potentially fatal hepatitis infections are less than 50 percent effective. When blood is sold, donors have an incentive to conceal the real state of their health. If donors are carriers of hepatitis and lie about the quality of their blood, they can cause death.

In this example, as in many other cases, the desires and needs of some individuals come into conflict with what other individuals regard as immoral. If indignation is sufficiently strong, laws are passed that forbid certain private exchanges on moral grounds. Sometimes an illegal market is created. Prostitution and gambling continue even though they are illegal, and blood is sold even where it is forbidden by law. Attempts to eliminate other immoral behaviors simply continue on the grounds that because they cannot be eliminated, this does not mean that they should be condoned. No one suggests, for example, that murder should be legalized on the grounds that the police fail to catch all murderers.

Taboos are as ancient as the world in which we live. Cain killed Abel because he envied him, but envy was a taboo, and Cain was severely punished. It has always been recognized that a government is needed to maintain law and order and protect property, since greedy individuals may decide that theft is a better way to get wealth than exchange. In fact, a market exchange system presupposes both moral behavior and the enforcement of law and order. Certain taboos are enforced for ethical or moral reasons. The right of an individual to do as he or she pleases is restricted not only by the right of other individuals but also by their moral indignation.

Immorality can jeopardize a society's existence. Society, therefore, has the right to enforce a moral code to preserve itself. Others would say that practices condemned by some members of society on moral grounds but which are not harmful to others should be outside the realm of law.[5]

Moral rules change with time and are sometimes inconsistent. For example, during the Middle Ages, usury laws, based on moral grounds and on specific citations from the Bible, made the charging of interest illegal. Yet, at the same time, the church freely sold indulgences to mitigate punishment for sins.

Gambling is illegal on moral grounds in many states. In a few states, however, it is permitted as a "free enterprise"; and in others, it is forbidden in private but allowed and even promoted in the form of state-owned and managed lotteries.

In all Western societies, it is illegal to buy a wife or, for that matter, to be married to more than one woman at a time. In other countries, bigamy is perfectly legal and wives are for sale in the market; the investment in human capital made by the parents of a lady are recouped through this arrangement.

Theoretically, it is possible to create a market for punishment of crimes instead of standing trial: an individual may simply pay for the right to avoid trial. Such a system would save a nation the costs of the judicial system, but is rejected on moral grounds. Yet, in the case of minor traffic violations, a person is allowed to pay a fine instead of facing trial.

In many cases, government intervention is justified on moral gounds. At the extreme, these justifications become ridiculous. Thus, in April 1977 *Fortune* magazine reported that the Federal Trade Commission called on Professor Charles J. Fillmore, a linguistics expert from the University of California at Berkeley, to testify as a theoretical linguist whose expert advice was called on as a part of the committee's efforts to grapple with some problems of deceptive advertising of over-the-counter drugs. The FTC, *Fortune* reported, "is considering a regulation that would, among other things, require advertising copy-writers to use only certain government-approved words when they say what the drugs are for."

Whatever the causes of moral rules, "once there is a consensus on a moral order, this determines, within wide limits, the way a community experiences physical conditions: this perception is then enforced by methods of social control."[6] If it is believed that risk-taking in one area or another is immoral, it will be forbidden. If it is immoral to spoil golden nature by the noxious fumes of industrial pollution, then pollution must be prevented—not on the basis of any cost-benefit calculation but at all costs! For those who see the reduction of a certain risk as an ethical problem, essential for the maintenance of the structure of society, no monetary limits exist.

The market system, some vigorously claim, is ethically wrong. It creates limits that are socially intolerable because the costs under the system are borne by those least able to bear them: "Abolition of luxury and waste, or obviously harmful forms of expenditure, would by itself be sufficient to make possible a doubling of useful public consumption in the Western world, that is, in particular, expenditure on education, health, public transport, conservation of natural resources, etc."[7] Advertising increases waste and encourages materialistic values. Government intervention therefore is needed to increase production of "socially desirable" goods and services. The production of wealth, according to this view, cannot be based on economic criteria alone, but must take social, ethical, and political considerations into account as well. In the

1960s, it was believed that social programs could be financed through so-called fiscal dividends, that is, the automatic increase in governmental tax revenue that results from economic growth. In the 1970s, however, scarcity was rediscovered. Since there were not enough resources to do everything, it was claimed, one should increase the production of socially desirable goods at the expense of wasteful products. Big cars use too much gasoline, so why not have small cars? Color televisions and the electronic gadgets now found in nearly all American homes cannot possibly be more important than having enough for the poor.

In sum, market systems are said to create an ethically unacceptable distribution of wealth, income, and economic power; consumer preferences are alleged to be wrong and based on the wrong education and on wasteful and damaging advertising. Today it is generally accepted that government should redistribute income on ethical grounds. Government is expected to help the poor, the aged, and the needy to have a minimum standard of living. Some economists, notably Milton Friedman, while accepting the need for redistribution, call for money transfer payments that allow individual recipients complete sovereignty over the way the money is being spent. Most of us would not go that far. It is strongly felt that money given to the poor should be used for socially acceptable consumption, not for horse betting or booze. For example, ". . . prenatal and early childhood malnutrition have irreversible effects on the mental capabilities of victims. Society may thus legitimately demand that some portions of transfers be spent on food for mothers and children."[8]

The right of society to enforce a moral code for its preservation is a notion out of favor today. Instead, individual freedom is constrained by practices designed to protect a totally different "public interest." The belief that the individual is solely responsible for his or her own fate has been replaced by the notion that society is responsible for the welfare of all its citizens. Gordon Bjork goes so far as to maintain that "the absolute sanctity of private property, individual freedom, and the impersonal self-regulating market were classical myths designed to prevent political interference in the status quo."[9] For him, individual freedom, even freedom of expression, must be balanced and checked against the effect of each action on the rest of society. Rights are not "natural" and inalienable but socially created and enforced, and "no sacred and inviolable contract exists between a government and its people to maintain the purchasing power."[10] Therefore, the problem of when public interest should be preferred to individual choice becomes much more important.

Market Failures

Government intervention is said to be needed for efficiency reasons, too, because of "market failures." Market solutions may not work, for example, when the goods are "pure public goods," that is, those goods (e.g., defense) in which the consumption of a good by one individual does not preclude its consumption by another. The increasing complexity of technology and the growth of urbanization have vastly increased the number of public goods. In addition, an exchange between two persons may, favorably or adversely, affect a third person who is not a party to the exchange. This is called a positive or negative "externality." If the smoke from a factory's chimney dirties someone's laundry, the person who washed the clothes suffers from a negative externality; if the view of flowers blooming in the garden of Mr. A. increases the happiness of Mr. B., then Mr. B. enjoys a positive externality. In economic theory, externalities must be internalized to achieve optimal solutions to the problem of market exchange. If the factory owners do not pay for the right to emit smoke, they do not have any incentive to reduce the smoke. Therefore, either the person whose laundry is covered with soot should pay a subsidy to the factory to reduce the smoke, or the factory should pay the person compensation to cover losses or permit the purchase of a dryer. Economic theory demonstrates that these tax-subsidy schemes will be carried out to the point where the marginal cost to the launderer and the cost to the manufacturer will be equalized.

It is also acknowledged that many problems with this kind of bargaining crop up between individuals. When they do, each of the parties has an interest in concealing true preferences and true costs, either to gain additional compensation or to reduce the amount to be paid. Transaction costs are, as a result, very high; and when considerable numbers of people are involved, bargaining becomes tedious if not impossible. Consider, for example, the problem of a real estate developer who tries to purchase 500 plots of land to build a shopping center. Once the shopping center is built, the income from the land will be considerably higher, and the value of the total area will be higher than the total of the current market values of the individual plots. In other words, there is an externality. To realize these future gains, however, the developer must first negotiate with each of the 500 owners, and any one of them can block the whole deal by refusing to sell. Further, each of the present owners knows that he or she will gain by holding out a little longer. Under the circumstances, the deal becomes almost impossible to close. In cases of urban redevelopment, this reasoning is used to justify governmental intervention to eliminate externalities that are difficult to resolve through the private bargaining process.[11]

According to this view, the government is part of a contractual arrangement whereby citizens delegate to the government certain coercive mechanisms, which are then used to satisfy their desires. The government is responsible for the preservation of institutional arrangements that allow the market to operate. In addition, the government is expected to intervene in many cases of market failure.

One reason behind the increase in the role of government according to this theory of social choice is that a larger number of goods and services partake of the nature of public goods. Economies of great scale are achieved when such public goods as defense of the country, provision of a legal system, or control of contagious diseases fall within the public domain. In a technologically complex society, the number of such goods increases, and with them the role of the government. Another reason for the increasing role of the government is the growing number of market failures and externalities. Fewer externalities occur in largely agricultural societies than in highly urbanized communities. Geographical contiguity implies greater externalities; hence, many more services have to be supplied by a governmental authority. In an urban society, services like sewage disposal, road cleaning, or garbage collection must be supplied to the whole community. This state of affairs can produce "free riders": people who refuse to pay for services, claiming that they do not want them, but knowing full well that when the services are supplied, they too will benefit. Political leaders, according to this line of reasoning, do not lead their constituents in new directions but simply react to their aggregate wishes. If public expenditures grow, it is because citizens want more services to be supplied by government. The increase in public expenditures is assumed to be a result of structural changes in society, of technological complexity, of urbanization, and of similar variables, all of which are exogenous to the political system.

Yet the theory of social choice based on maximization of individual welfare has not been very successful in explaining the rise of public expenditures, though many have tried, and people still try, to explain governmental actions as based on contractual theories or transaction costs.

The problem of "free riders" raises a broader question of morality. Economists dealing with social choice generally claim that they are not concerned with morality, with what people do in their own homes, as long as their activities do not cause externalities. Drinking at home without disturbing anyone is no reason for intervention. If, however, a person chooses to drive a car "under the influence," all kinds of externalities are generated. Thus there are laws that prohibit drunken driving but few that restrict private drunkenness.

Questions of ethics and morality are not always so simple. Since every individual is assumed to be both rational and a selfish maximizer, we should expect every individual to maximize his or her own benefits. When this happens, and there are no moral restrictions in the system, the government must intervene and enforce "law and order." In the case of a simple exchange, the alternative to market transaction is theft. A person who believes that God commanded "Thou shalt not steal" and wants to obey God probably will not steal. If all individuals, knowing that they are thieves by nature, agree to have a government that will hire policemen and try to enforce laws that make theft illegal, they also will probably not steal. Of course, a system relying on God is much cheaper to operate, since in God's kingdom one does not need policemen. Whenever morality is thought to be weak, however, policemen are regarded as necessary. The less the belief in morality as a restraint, the greater the belief in the need for policemen. In the extreme case where there is no morality, one is faced with a dilemma: the policeman may (because of self-interest) join the thief by accepting bribes or a share in the booty, and the judges may maximize their incomes by auctioning decisions at trials. If all individuals are maximizers of their self-interest, this same principle should logically be applied to their elected representatives and other government officials because politicians must be assumed to be maximizers of their self-interest. They will be greedy, take bribes, and, in thus advancing their self-interest, neglect the public good. Even the most ardent believers in humans as selfish egoists would not go so far. The question of who controls the controllers is generally not faced by most economists. Many of them are willing to assume that once an individual becomes part of the government, he or she changes behavior and becomes an unselfish worker on behalf of the public interest.

This somewhat naive assumption, based largely on the British tradition of public service, is part of British economic theory from John Stuart Mill to John Maynard Keynes. Most British economists since Adam Smith despised businessmen and abhorred their greedy behavior. Though they accepted it as an unavoidable part of the economic system, a number of economists preferred to identify with the "real gentlemen," those who served their country, rather than with those who maximized profits. It was only a short step from there to the view of "the government" as regulator in controlling monopolies or employing monetary and fiscal policies (as advocated by Keynes) for the benefit of the nation. In the world of the Keynesian economist, government officials are not selfish and work only for the public good: fiscal and monetary policies and any other instruments of the economy are used to achieve the best results without regard either for votes or for possible benefits to the bureaucracy.

Some American economists reject this view, maintaining that the regulators are captured by the regulated, for this is in their best interest,[12] and that government employees are inflators of their budgets. This view that politicians and public servants are invariably guided by self-interest has some serious consequences, since without self-restraint no politico-economic system can work. Many problems cannot be reduced to merely legal dimensions, and laws are not always a substitute for old-fashioned standards of integrity.

The Broker State: Interest Groups and Elites

In the American political system, individuals attempt to maximize benefits for themselves through social interactions. These interactions take place not only in the economic markets but also in the political ones. The state is portrayed by American political scientists as an agent, promoted to further individuals' *nonsocial* interests. There is no agreement on social goals common to all. Instead, public policy is the result of an interplay of organized interest groups. Each one of these groups attempts to further its own interest and its own cause through the use of the state machinery. The result is what John Chamberlain called "the broker state":[13] a government intervening in ad hoc and piecemeal fashion on behalf of organized interest groups of sufficient economic or political power to use the political machinery to achieve assistance for their own interests. In this system, administrators, organized interest groups, and legislators bargain continuously on public policies. And "any institution that is large enough to be of a significant factor in the community shall have its existence underwritten."[14] The government dispenses favors unto these groups, and in effect socializes their risks.[15]

To be sure, equality is considered a major goal of political and social life. The exact meaning of "equality" and the best means to achieve it became a major topic of debate in the 1960s.[16] Whether equality should be defined in terms of opportunities or results, one thing is clear: the number of interest groups and "cause" organizations mushroomed in the American political structure during the 1960s. "Previously passive or unorganized groups in the population now embarked on concerted efforts to establish their claims to opportunities, positions, rewards, and privileges, which they had not considered themselves entitled to before."[17] Many of these demands were legitimized as necessary for the public interest. However, "community needs" and "public interest" are vague and undefinable terms. Different individuals find different things to be in the public interest. For some, it may be reduction of the rights of criminals to make it easier for the police to catch them. For others, it may be that contraceptives should not be used; still others, disturbed by earth's limitations, would like to make sterilization compulsory.

The concept of the public interest plays a central role in discussions of public policy and public choice, even though no two people totally agree on the meaning of that term. It is vacuous, deceptive, confused, and not very useful in explaining the social order. It is questionable whether the public interest could even be reduced to the sum of the pressures of all the conflicting, vociferous, contending interest groups on the government to follow their own interests, or to what extent individuals can be relied on to decide their own destiny. The definition of the "public interest" is thus both nebulous and changing with changing values.

The radical economist would rather rely on the judgment of the community "guided by reason and science."[18] Radicals all agree with the view represented in the *Communist Manifesto*, that the government in a capitalist system is "the executive committee of the bourgeoisie," totally dominated by the ruling class, whose economic power enables it to appropriate political power for its own uses and divert a disproportionate share of the social product to itself. It is therefore also to its interests to maintain the status quo.

In the Marxian view of society, the increase in public expenditures is a response to the growing internal contradictions of the capitalist system. Capitalism, being inherently destructive, resorts to public expenditure as an investment in social control. O'Connor points out, quite correctly, that public expenditures can be viewed as a system of conflict. The political system that faces demands based on high expectations on one hand and scarcity on the other cannot meet all expectations. Instead, it needs to devise means either to reduce them or to decide on priorities.[19]

As already observed, others see the public interest as a result of a process of bargaining among large and powerful elite interest groups. For them, democracy consists of competition among these organized elites for benefits and lower costs. Farmers try to increase farm subsidies, families with many children strive for more benefits for children. To some, these elites are responsible and farsighted and, therefore, lead the country toward higher goals rather than simply reflecting short-term interests. The mass of the electorate is neither interested nor informed about the complex maze of problems facing society. It is the function of the elite to guide them and make a better world for them. Most people do not really know what their best interests are, and the public interest is of a much higher order than a mere summation of individual wants.

Other theories stress the structure of power. Public expenditures result from a power play between large organizations, each one of which tries to get as much as possible from the state. In its extreme form, the maintenance of power by the elite can become an end in itself and lead to a totalitarian state. In less extreme forms, these elite organizations control the political machinery to achieve ends they regard as important.

The common denominator in all elite theories is that the elite knows best what the public expenditures should be and to what ends public revenues should be devoted. Some put their faith in rational, coordinated planning, which they regard as one of the major duties of a responsible government.[20] For them, government expenditures grow both because government planning is preferred as against market forces and because the benevolent and paternalistic elite supply to the masses more social services.[21]

One corollary of the elite theories is that the very existence of state-sponsored programs creates additional and powerful interest groups. State action creates groups of welfare recipients, subsidized tenants, health-care beneficiaries, veterans, and so on. Each of these groups then exerts pressures on the government to continue and increase the benefits it receives.

If the elite is supposed to understand the public interest better than the public does, then the degree to which their decisions respond to the need of the people is irrelevant. The response of the elite to the extension of suffrage was to work toward a decline in the importance of the electorate, "leaving the basic decisions to a bargaining process between interest organizations, parties, agencies and departments of the national bureaucracies."[22] A principal consequence of the democratization of the electoral process, according to this view, may have been that political and economic elites developed mechanisms to neutralize or cancel out the consequences of this democratization.[23]

Bureaucrats

In a democracy an organized minority group can have an influence on government out of all proportion to its actual share of the population. One such minority group is the government bureaucracy itself. If one assumes that all individuals try to maximize their own utility, then so do government employees. For them, according to Niskanen,[24] success is measured by the ability to increase the size of the budget for which they are responsible. Therefore, different agencies of the civil service consistently and persistently demand increases in public expenditures independently of voters' preferences, the need to win elections, or the pressures of other interest groups. In other words, the civil service itself consists of a strong and substantial interest group that has to be taken into account.

If administrative agencies press for additional funds and seek to control extra resources, then the budgets of government will continue to grow whatever the voters' preferences happen to be. Public policy programs will be better financed the older they are, and new programs will have to be adjusted to fit constraints created by old programs. As the working space of government programs becomes congested, it will be more difficult to add more programs.

The civil service will continually increase its own pay scale and better its conditions of work. Government civil servants are the most secure elite group in all Western societies. Reducing the size of the civil service is an almost impossible task. Nor can one gauge the output of most of its workers. Classical economic theory is based on the notion that the remuneration of the worker is a function of his or her marginal contribution. Since there is no known way to measure the marginal contribution of most civil servants, their salaries cannot be based on this standard, and pressures to raise it are often difficult to counter. Many civil service employees find it hard to believe that their salaries cannot be raised; some think governments have an unlimited ability to pay, either by raising taxes or by borrowing. A few also enjoy strategic importance and enormous disruptive power in the economy; if they go on strike, the costs to the economy can be very severe. In small countries certain groups can even bring the economy to a halt. Port workers, telephone operators, flight controllers, income tax collectors, drivers of public vehicles, and garbage collectors fall into this category.

While bureaucrats are important, budgets must be approved by legislators, and their goals cannot be ignored. According to economic models of political behavior pioneered by Anthony Downs and further elaborated by Albert Breton,[25] shifts in government expenditures can be explained by pressures generated by the political system—that is, government expenditures are the result of party competition to attract votes. Since politicians need to be elected and reelected, expenditures and taxes are allocated to guarantee political support. If voters are more conscious of taxes than they are of government benefits, the rational behavior of a politician is to minimize taxes. Downs argues that this is indeed the case—voters are more aware of costs than of benefits, and as a result government budgets in a democracy are smaller than they would have been if all citizens had perfect information. On the other hand, if voters were more aware of benefits than of costs, taxes would indeed grow.[26]

If politicians are only concerned with trying to gather more votes, then "invisible government" is a more efficient way of achieving that goal than a visible budget. For example, while the specific groups who gain from administrative regulations or tariff protection are fully aware of the benefits, voters are ignorant of the invisible costs involved. Thus, if Downs' hypothesis is correct, one would expect greater government intervention through invisible than through visible means—as this book suggests.

Social Choice and Uncertainty

If individuals are the best judges of their own welfare, decentralized decision making is preferable, since information on preferences is extremely fragmented and dispersed.[27] This argument assumes that information is freely available. In many cases, however, the individual making a decision may not know the results of that decision. If he did, he might decide differently. Take the case of traffic congestion: the more people use their private cars (and ignore the pollution problem created), the more traffic congestion results. In technical economic terms, the right of every individual to use a car was utilized in a way that did not take into account all the costs and all the benefits. One important cost not taken into account when the use of a private car is contemplated is that the use of a car by any one individual imposes additional costs on the community. For example, since the size of the road is limited, the use of any one car lengthens the time it takes anybody else to arrive from any one point to another.

Theoretically, a solution might be reached by which each person has to purchase the right to drive in traffic. But since there is no conceivable way for each driver to negotiate with the thousands of other drivers for the right of way, the economist then suggests, subject to the size of the transaction costs, that local government representing all citizens should intervene by imposing additional charges in the form of tolls or stiff fees for downtown parking.

In other cases, the problem is one of irreversibility. One justification for the imposition of social security is that the young are improvident. By the time they realize the importance of taking care of themselves when they will become old, it is too late.

An individual may also be unaware of hazards that can cause severe losses because they occur infrequently or because of the complex technical nature of the hazard. For example, a person may not fully appreciate the contingency of building a house in a flood-prone area and thus fail to take out adequate insurance.[28] Some claim that in such cases the government should require individuals to purchase comprehensive disaster insurance.[29] The Flood Disaster Protection Act of 1973 has as its principal provision that no federal financial assistance will be made available for construction purposes to any flood-prone community unless it is participating in the National Flood Insurance Program. In other cases, the magnitude of the hazard may not be known for a long time; the dangers of exposure to asbestos or lead are two obvious examples. A compulsory safety program to reduce the risk may be called for. Alternatively, since no private insurance can be available, a government compulsory insurance such as workmen's compensation may replace it.

Once uncertainty is introduced, there are many problems in defining "efficiency"; in a world of uncertainty, efficiency involves accuracy of prediction as well as production efficiency. An error in predicting demand may cause bankruptcy, educating oneself in a profession that becomes obsolete after one graduates may cause loss of income, inability to predict weather conditions may cause crop failure, and an unexpected illness may cause severe hardships. In all these cases, rational individuals may prefer to insure themselves against some unfortunate consequences. In so doing, individuals pay a premium in order to diversify or shift the risks that may be borne by them. However, diversification of risks among a large group through contingent markets, the simplest example of which is insurance, is not always available. One reason for such a "market failure" is that events are not always verifiable by both parties to the insurance. There may be many false claims, increasing the insurance costs. Another is that only high-risk individuals will buy the insurance; therefore, the premium that has to be collected would be too high for those perceiving themselves as facing a lower risk. In many cases, the inability of individuals to buy protection against risk gives rise to a loss of welfare.

It is common in economic literature to argue that individuals tend to display aversion to the taking of risks. If individuals are risk averters, they will tend to prefer a perfectly certain outcome to an equal but uncertain one. The degree of aversion to risk is often measured by the difference between the certain amount an individual is willing to accept and the expected value of a random income. This difference might be interpreted as an insurance premium.

Again, insurance is one way of shedding some of the risks borne by an individual. Premiums are collected and then used to accumulate funds to pay unfortunate victims. Thus, the risk is spread over a large number of individuals, each one of which pays for the divestment of risks. Other institutions for risk-shifting have emerged. One of these has been the corporation—and the later development of capital markets. Through incorporation, the owner of a business firm could share the risks and benefits with others. In the stock market, each individual can diversify his or her portfolio and own shares with different risks attached, thus deriving the benefits of a reduced aggregate risk through pooling. But, again, the market for insurance is limited and imperfect. Some economists contend that individuals would choose to avail themselves of publicly provided insurance. An increase in public insurance is justified by these economists because they claim that individuals would have bought the insurance had they known the hazards. A compulsory insurance is also justified in order to minimize the potential political pressure to aid citizens after they become victims of disaster. Further, it is claimed that since a lack of a private insurance market stems from market failure, there is a cause for government to step in. Government insurance or regulation against hazards has been recommended in such areas as safety of products, drugs, and labor; licensing of professionals; and insurance against major hazards.

Several economists are also of the opinion that risks associated with a public project are distributed over the entire population of the country. Therefore, assuming new project yields are independent of national income, the government should be risk neutral. To quote Samuelson: "Often, government is one of the 'cheapest' ways of providing insurance against important risks."[30] Since government is able to average out the risks among all its citizens, then social risks are zero. Of course, if perfect markets for risks could exist, any individual could diversify risks by holding a portfolio of assets (or buying into a mutual fund that owns such assets). Since such markets are imperfect because of indivisibility and other reasons, a case for government intervention is said to exist.

The crux of the matter again lies in our assumptions about the nature of the state and of individuals and the relations between them. If the state is authoritarian, as it is in the Hegelian view of an organic state, then state insurance is preferable. If, however, the state has a fiduciary role, that is, if social choice expresses individual choice, then the risk of the portfolio controlled by the government is irrelevant. What matters is the portfolio of each individual household. Government financing of projects and government insurance give benefits to certain households and increase costs to those who pay for them—either directly or through taxes. Neither the benefits nor the costs are distributed over the entire population, nor are the risks inevitably pooled and averaged over the entire population of the country. A project risk is not borne by those who receive the uncertain benefits. In this case, some agreed method of distributing the costs and the benefits must be found.

Models of Humanity and Social Choice

Most theories of social choice provide explanations based on the human being as individualist. Some stress maximizing rational behavior through the market, others the political bargaining process. At one extreme, humans are basically good, benevolent, kind, and see the utmost achievement not in self-realization but in service to society; their self-interest is subservient to that of society as a whole. At the other extreme, planning of all activities is possible, even easy, because the planner knows best what is good for society. Everyone will accept the planner's verdict because they recognize his or her ability to know what is good for them. One great mind tells us all what to do, and all (knowing how great this mind is) agree to follow. People conform to social anticipation, and individual behavior is totally determined by society.

The believers in society as a supreme value and those who believe their interests can be promoted demand more and more government action to cater to urgent and worthy needs. For those who cherish individual rights, the swelling size of the government is alarming. They feel government intrudes unnecessarily, exercises authority capriciously, often chooses improper means to achieve desired goals, and fails to do the job effectively. Although they may recognize some of the goals as worthy, they question government's ability to cope with them. Government action causes too many undesirable consequences. The preservation of individual rights requires constraints on governmental size and scope, and the avoidance of indiscriminate use of power.

While these two views have been held by many, most of us tend to feel that the truth is somewhere in between. People are complex: they can be greedy and selfish, but they also can be part of a community for which they are sometimes willing to make sacrifices. They have moral codes and values that lead them to reject certain actions. They are selfish but also willing—sometimes—to sacrifice for their families or the nation, especially in times of crisis. They are basically creatures of their culture; their behavior is, to some extent, a product of the customs, mores, and taboos of the society in which they were born and educated.

Human beings are certainly more complicated than they are portrayed by those who believe them to be motivated by self-interest and greed; or by those who see people as social animals; or by those who believe individuals want only power, prestige, status, or wealth. Humans are all that—and more. Some people are extreme risk-averters, others love risks. Some like to climb mountains, others suffer from a fear of heights; some want more money, others would rather read books; some think black is beautiful, and some prefer blondes. Human beings are all different—in height, appearance, intelligence, emotions, behavior—and social choice is dictated not only by self-interest but also by ambition, by a variety of moral codes and values including love, honesty, integrity, truthfulness, dignity, self-restraint, and pride.

Many of the clashes described above between various moral and ethical norms and the self-interest of the individual are based in the belief that the human being is weak and wicked and must be defended from himself or herself. The Protestant ethic preached that man demonstrated his "elect" status only through hard work, moral diligence, and thrifty accumulation; he was thus encouraged to forego the more socially pleasurable callings in this life in order to seek salvation in the next. The blue laws in the United States were enacted to ensure that people would not work on Sunday. Laws were presumably needed to protect people from their own greed; they might wrongly interpret their self-interest and work on Sundays in disregard of their spiritual safety and social taboos. For the same reason, governments enact laws making safety belts in cars mandatory instead of allowing each individual to decide whether or not he or she is willing to pay the price for the additional security afforded by the belts. Governments also enact various safety regulations to protect workers who might otherwise agree to do a more dangerous job for additional remuneration.

Once it is agreed that society has a right to preserve individual freedom on moral grounds, once it is accepted that society should protect the individual from himself or herself, then many rules are possible, and limits must be established.

The Insurance State

More and more people feel the balance is now tilted toward government and not citizens. In all Western democracies, there is a growing fear that government has become "too big," a loss of trust in leadership and a delegitimation of authority. All over the world, people are less and less satisfied by the way in which their country is governed.[31] At the same time, more people have escalated their demands on government. Thus, the pursuit of the democratic virtues of individualism and equality led to an escalation of aspirations and expectations. At the same time, it led to a loss of trust in leadership, a decline in public confidence, and a reduced compulsion to obey those previously considered superior in age, character, talent, expertise, or rank. The emergence of the insurance state has not been the result of a strong government attempting to increase its controls. Rather, it resulted from the basic weakness of political leaders to reject the many demands made upon them by more and more groups. "The democratic idea that government should be responsive to the people creates the expectation that government should meet the needs and correct the evils affecting particular groups in society."[32] Confronted with all these demands, governments had no choice but to expand.

The world would certainly be a much nicer place to live in if people would live in harmony and if we could rely on human cooperation and a sense of community. Unfortunately, they don't and we can't. Witness the amounts different countries spend on armaments. According to Seymour Melman, "by any reasonable reckoning, the United States and the Soviet Union both have much more nuclear hardware than needed for the destruction of each other's main population and industrial centers." Yet each of these two countries annually spend many billions of dollars on armaments. Melman goes on to show that in 1968 alone, the Vietnam war cost almost twice the amount needed for serious worldwide economic development efforts; and in 1966–67, developing countries were spending more on their armed forces from their own budgets than their combined spending on education and health.[33]

Thus, anarchy is not a feasible solution, and some resources must be allocated by government, at least for public goods such as defense and for cases where market failure can be shown. In reality, the market-failure argument fails to explain the zooming of public expenditures; nor are "imperfections" and "failures" confined to private enterprise.

Government has been growing not only because of the complexity of society caused by technology and interdependence. At least as important has been universal suffrage, a power that, over time, people have learned to use well. Since the majority is rather risk-averse than risk-loving, most of the new demands on government have been for protection, reduction of risk, and mitigation of its consequences.

In a democratic society, individual voters try to maximize their individual benefits from the public domain and at the same time attempt to minimize the costs of what they gain. Therefore, everyone tries to minimize the taxes levied on them and maximize their use of publicly supplied goods, services, and insurance. Once insurance is publicly supplied, the demands for insurance are much larger than the willingness to pay the costs. A private insurance firm cancels the insurance policies of individuals who refuse to pay the premiums. In the public domain, demand for protection is made effective through political pressures. These demands are often justified by moral reasons and calls for equity and equality. Second, one problem in any insurance is that the insured may modify their behavior: they may become careless, they may even attempt to cause the event against which they are insured to happen. For example, once a person is insured against fire, he becomes less careful not to cause fire, and in extreme cases, may even resort to arson. This so-called moral hazard factor is at least as evident in publicly supplied compulsory insurance as it is in private insurance schemes. Private insurance companies attempt to fight the moral hazard by increasing their supervision on the insured. Governments are doing the same. The requirement of safety belts in cars is sometimes justified because it is the public that will have to pay for the cost of hospitalization in case of accident. The more people are insured by government, the more government has to restrict their freedom in order to cover itself against the moral hazard.

In many cases, the calls for governmental intervention have not been expressed as demands for insurance. Rather, they were legitimized by lofty ideals, such as equity or equality, in the name of which more benefits and more insurance were pushed for. Farmers demand higher prices for their products, workers want more wages and fringe benefits, women press for more rights, and business firms seek higher profits. Yet many of the benefits called for lately are of the nature of risk-shifting: farmers want protection against unpredictable weather conditions and support for the prices of their major crops; workers call for increased work safety and for protection against unemployment; women want to be insured against pregnancy; and business firms want their profits to be protected against such market conditions as foreign competition or technological change. Demands for publicly financed health benefits are actually calls for moving the risks of falling sick from the individual to a larger group. Calls for the reduction of product hazards are in effect calls for reduction of risks. Claims that government should guarantee employment (and profits) or finance research and development outlays are claims that the government should become an insurance agency. Calls for protecting the consumer against fraudulent advertising are calls for risk-shifting.

Less privileged members of the society must have a stake in its maintenance; otherwise they may use their collective power to destroy it. Long ago, individuals refused to be considered a mere commodity whose price was determined in the market; and since then the variety of demands they have made upon society has increased dramatically. It now includes protection against hunger, unemployment, and a change in workplace; against fraud and false advertising; against unemployment hazards and unsafe cars; and most of its protective mechanisms are enforced not by individuals but by society. A worker cannot decide that he or she would rather take a dangerous job for higher pay; a driver cannot buy a new car that is below legal standard requirements in order to save money; a manufacturer cannot reduce quality standards in order to sell a product for a lower price. All these cases can be seen as a kind of compulsory insurance intended to reduce the risk to the individual; but this adds to its costs.

The immediate cause of the surge in governmental activity, therefore, was the higher level of participation of a larger number of people in the political process. More and more people demanded more for themselves or for causes they cherished. Once the participation increased, it caused mainly calls for more insurance, less risks, and more protection. These demands for reduction of risk came about because of a combination of several reasons. First, rising levels of general affluence led to changes in attitudes. For those who do not have enough to support themselves, monetary benefits may be more important than insurance. Those who are very rich can usually afford the risks. The incorporation of a substantial proportion of the population to the relatively affluent middle class meant that risk reduction became at least as important as increased income. Second, the increased participation of the post–World War II "baby boom" youth supplied activists to different causes perceived as just and equitable, and many of these causes were perceived to call for more insurance and protection, in particular for the needy and the aged. Third, as pointed out by Nie and Andersen, "the political events of the last decade, and the crisis atmosphere which has attended them, have caused citizens to perceive politics as increasingly central to their lives."[34] More generally, the more government grew, the more salient became the size of its largesse or the perceived costs to any one group. Racial discord, general alienation, and activist calls for environmental protection caused demands for increased income redistribution and changes of priority. Other groups, in turn, pressed for assistance to protect their previous achievements and sought haven in public laws that will protect the status quo.

To be sure, government has always supplied some insurance to at least a few of its members. The supply of police protection may be seen as a means to insure the propertied against the hazard of robbery, and the law of contracts insures to some extent lenders against default of borrowers. In fact, it is sometimes argued that when the state fails to provide effective police protection, it should compensate the injured party.[35] Recently, however, demands for protection and insurance have come from more people claiming more causes. The immediate result has been an enormous increase in the size of governmental expenditures and change in the composition of these expenditures. Government expenditure as a percent of GNP has been growing, and the percent of insurance programs within the budget has zoomed.

The availability of insurance tended to change people's behavior, increasing costs even further: flood victims who received governmental aid learned that private insurance against flood risk is not the best way to increase their welfare; workers found that industrial disputes and the occupation of a factory by its workers may cause the government to acquire the firm and guarantee their employment;[36] and many other groups have learned that demonstrations and political pressures provide cheaper insurance than that available in the market.

Demands for more protection and increased benefits to the less privileged members of society have sparked pressures from the established members of society to be protected against a change in their position or loss of their power and prestige. Today, society is expected to insure its members not only against major catastrophes or severe loss of income. Those who have power exert pressures to avoid change.

Yet, in many cases, demands for protection and insurance are contradictory, since reducing a risk for one group often increases it for another. Reduction of risk also brings along a shift in the distribution of income and wealth, since the cost of shielding a very large number of persons from a variety of risks has to be borne by someone. Paradoxically, while the demands for protection mount, the willingness to pay the costs of these protections wanes. Faced with the impossible task of achieving more than it can and with so many contradictory demands from so many quarters, government has promised more than it can deliver. One result of this situation has been frustration and a feeling of crisis. Another is inflation.

The hopeful vision of a no-risk society has proved to be little more than a fragile illusion. There is no way to guarantee a world without risks. In reality, attempts to reduce risks always increase other risks. Paradoxically, demands on government to insure against risks came at the same time that the belief in the ability of the government to deal effectively with these and other policy problems was waning. The challenge to authority caused another difficulty, since expert views on the size of risk have become less acceptable. To understand the nature of the problem, let us proceed by elaborating on the nature of risk.

NOTES

1. The words are taken from a decision of the Supreme Court in the case of *Marsh* v. *Alabama*, 326 U.S. 505 (1946). In this case a company-owned town, Chickasaw, owned and operated by the Gulf Shipbuilding Corporation, had an ordinance making it a crime to enter or remain in the premises after being warned not to do so. Grace Marsh, a Jehovah's Witness, came into the town, stood near the post office, and distributed religious literature. Grace Marsh was asked to leave, warned that soliciting is illegal and that the town was private property. When she did not leave, she was charged with violation of the statute. The Supreme Court decided that the statute violated the First and the Fourteenth amendments. For a discussion, see Adam Carlyle Breckenridge, *The Right to Privacy* (Lincoln: University of Nebraska Press, 1970). The specific case cited is discussed on pp. 62-63.
2. For a theoretical elaboration of this assumption, see David Collard, *Altruism and Economy: A Study in Non-Selfish Economics* (Oxford: Martin Robertson, 1978).
3. Paul Baran, *The Political Economy of Growth* (New York: Monthly Review Press, 1968), p. xvii.
4. R. Titmuss, *The Gift Relationship* (London: Allen and Unwin, 1970).
5. For the first point of view, see Patrick A. D. Devlin, *The Enforcement of Morals* (London: Oxford University Press, 1965). For the second, see H. L. A. Hart, *Law, Liberty and Morality* (Stanford: Stanford University Press, 1963).
6. Mary Douglas, "Environments at Risk," *Times Literary Supplement*, 30 October 1970, pp. 1273-75.
7. Ernest Mandel, *Marxist Economic Theory* (New York: Monthly Review Press, 1968), 2:616. See also John Kenneth Galbraith, *The Affluent Society* (Boston: Houghton Mifflin, 1958).
8. Robert A. Levine, *Public Planning: Failure and Redirection* (New York: Basic Books, 1972), p. 177.
9. Gordon Bjork, *Private Enterprise and Public Interest: The Development of American Capitalism* (Englewood Cliffs, N.J.: Prentice-Hall, 1969), p. 234.
10. Ibid., p. 231.
11. For an elaboration, see Gordon Tullock, *Private Wants, Public Means* (New York: Basic Books, 1975).

12. See, for example, George J. Stigler, "The Theory of Economic Regulation," *Bell Journal of Economics* 2 (Spring 1941): 3-21; and Paul MacAvoy, ed., *The Crisis of the Regulatory Commissions* (New York: Norton, 1970).

13. John Chamberlain, *The American Stakes* (New York: Harper & Row, 1941). See also Otis L. Graham, Jr., *Toward a Planned Society: From Roosevelt to Nixon* (New York: Oxford University Press, 1977).

14. Theodore Lowi, "Permanent Receivership," *The Center Magazine* 7 (March-April 1976): 36.

15. Ibid., p. 37.

16. See, for example, Dow Votaw, "The New Equality: Bureaucracy's Trojan Horse," *California Management Review* 20, no. 4 (1978): 5-17; S. M. Miller and Pamela A. Roby, *The Future of Inequality* (New York: Basic Books, 1970); Christopher Jencks, *Inequality* (New York: Basic Books, 1972); Herbert J. Gans, *More Equality* (New York: Pantheon, 1973); Lee S. Rainwater, *Social Problems: Inequality and Justice* (Chicago: Aldine, 1974); and Edward C. Budd, *Inequality and Poverty* (New York: Norton, 1967).

17. Samuel P. Huntington, "The United States," in Michel J. Crozier, Samuel P. Huntington, and Joji Watanuki, *The Crisis of Democracy* (New York: New York University Press, 1975), pp. 61-62.

18. Baran, *Political Economy of Growth*, p. 42.

19. James O'Connor, *The Corporation and the State* (New York: Harper & Row, 1974) and *The Fiscal Crisis of the State* (New York: St. Martin's Press, 1973). See also Daniel Bell, *The Cultural Contradictions of Capitalism* (New York: Basic Books, 1976).

20. Andrew Shonfield, *Modern Capitalism: The Changing Balance of Public and Private Power* (New York and London: Oxford University Press, 1968), p. 122.

21. John Kenneth Galbraith, *Economics and the Public Purpose* (Boston: Houghton Mifflin, 1973).

22. Stein Rokkan, *Citizens, Elections, Parties* (New York: McKay, 1970), p. 43.

23. Robert R. Alford and Roger Friedland, "Nations, Parties and Participation: A Critique of Political Sociology," *Theory and Society* 1 (Fall 1974): 307-28; and "Political Participation," *Annual Revue of Sociology* 1 (1975).

24. William A. Niskanen, Jr., *Bureaucracy and Representative Government* (Chicago: Aldine/Atherton, 1971).

25. Anthony Downs, *An Economic Theory of Democracy* (New York: Harper & Row, 1957); and Albert Breton, *The Economic Theory of Representative Government* (London: Aldine Treatises in Modern Economics, Macmillan, 1974).

26. See Samuel Brittan, "The Economic Contradictions of Democracy," *British Journal of Political Science* 5 (1975): 129-59.

27. For the argument, see F. A. Hayek, "The Use of Knowledge in Society," *American Economic Review* (1945): 519-30.

28. See Gilbert White, ed., *Natural Hazards, Local, National and Global* (New York: Oxford University Press, 1971); and Ian Burton, Robert Kales, and Gilbert White, *The Environment as Hazard* (New York: Oxford University Press, 1978).

29. See Howard Kunreuther, *Recovery from Natural Disasters: Insurance or Federal Aid* (Washington, D.C.: American Enterprise Institute, 1973).

30. Paul A. Samuelson, "Principles of Efficiency: Discussion," *American Economic Review* 54 (May 1964): 95.

31. By 1958, more than three quarters of the American people felt their government was run for the benefit of the people, and only 17.6 percent thought it run by a few big interests looking out for themselves. These proportions changed during the 1960s and '70s. The percentage of those believing that the government was run for the benefit of all the people grew steadily lower: 64.0 percent in 1964, 53.2 percent in 1966, 51.2 percent in 1968, 50.1 percent in 1972, and 37.7 percent by the end of 1972. On the other hand, the percentage of people believing the government was run by a few big interests looking out for themselves increased from 28.6 percent in 1964 to 33.3 percent in 1966, 39.5 percent in 1968, 40.8 percent in 1970, and 53.3 percent by the end of 1972. See Huntington in Crozier et al., *Crisis of Democracy*, pp. 78-85.

32. Ibid., p. 164.

33. Seymour Melman, *Pentagon Capitalism: The Political Economy of War* (New York: McGraw-Hill, 1970), pp. 109, 199, 200.

34. Norman H. Nie and Kristi Andersen, "Mass Belief Systems Revisited: Political Change and Attitude Structure," *Journal of Politics* 36 (August 1974): 570-71.

35. For a historical account, see Stephen Schafer, *The Victim and His Criminal: A Study in Functional Responsiblity* (New York: Random House, 1968).

36. Such was the case, for example, in Val-Saint Lambert, a Belgian firm that was hard hit by the economic recession. The government acquired the firm after it was occupied by its workers. In the 1970s European governments acquired many firms for similar reasons.

3. Shifting the Risk

Risk: Meaning and Measurement

According to the National Center for Health Statistics, an average of 46,000 Americans have died annually from traffic accidents over the last few years. The population of the United States is about 230 million, and so the average risk to an individual of being killed in a road accident is approximately 1 in 5000. Obviously, the risk to any specific individual depends on his or her proclivities: the amount of time spent on the road, driving habits, regional location, and so on. A better measure of risk is to calculate the probability of death from automobile accidents per hundred million vehicle miles, because the more time one spends on the road, the higher the probability of a fatal accident. By this reckoning, the rate of fatal accidents per hundred million vehicle miles was estimated in 1975 at 17.0 for motorcycles, 1.4 for cars (drivers and passengers), and 0.09 for scheduled airplanes. Using this criterion, airline travel is the safest mode of transportation.

This statistical illustration is an attempt to capture the sometimes elusive term "risk" in more concrete terms. Risk can be measured by the probability that a certain mishap, injury, or other phenomenon considered undesirable will occur. When we measure risk, we do not usually measure (with any degree of certainty) what will happen to particular individuals. The probabilities show only what the hazards are, on the average, to a large group of people in certain situations. An insurance company, for example, uses mortality statistics to arrive at decisions on what premiums to charge for its life insurance. More commonly, the behavior of individuals under conditions of uncertainty is not based on such "objective" data, and the calculation of insurance premiums is exceedingly difficult. In fact, the meanings of probabilities, the ways of measuring them, and their interpretations are endlessly debated.[1] For example, experiments that involved administering doses of saccharin to rats no doubt proved that the rats contracted cancer as a result, but did they necessarily prove anything about the incidence of cancer in human beings? This problem of inferring correlations from scientific experiments on animals to results in human beings arises constantly because experiments using human beings to assess risk factors create a host of difficult ethical questions. One of the many criticisms leveled against the Nazis was their use of human beings in scientific experimentations. A line must often be drawn beyond which one may not step; the indiscriminate use of people as guinea pigs is generally condemned by the scientific community and forbidden by law.

When social and economic problems are involved, the problem is infinitely more complex. Scientific experiments require controlling for a myriad of environmental factors. While these controls are possible under laboratory conditions, they are impossible in society. When social and economic phenomena are studied, there is no scientific way to determine whether inflation can be reduced by increasing unemployment because one would first need to know the pure effects of devaluation on exports, for example, and there is no objective way of finding out. Social scientists are forced to infer risks and their effects from historical precedent, statistical studies, or mathematical models. None is an adequate method; historical observations involve many interrelated events, and it is virtually impossible to establish without any shade of a doubt cause-and-effect relationships between any two of them. Statistical studies and theoretical models, on the other hand, are based on many simplified and often unrealistic assumptions.

To measure risk one has to assign probabilities to future events. Since the future is unknown, the probabilities for the occurrence of an event must be based on expectations. Expectations, in turn, are based on the information available today, and inferred from knowledge of the past and the present. They can change with additional knowledge and experience, and with them the assessment of risk. At any one time, there is no way to gauge all possible risks simply because there is no way to know all the possible side effects. Industrialization was a policy adopted by numerous nations in the nineteenth and twentieth centuries. In the early stages of the industrial revolution, some of the disruptive effects that it caused on society were the hardships of wage labor and the alienation of workers. Only recently have adverse effects such as pollution been added to the list of public concerns. As scientific knowledge grows, the number of known causal connections between certain environmental factors and hazards to human beings also increases. Additional information, for example, made us aware of the adverse effects of DDT. The possibility of a causal connection between the release of fluorocarbons in the air and the destruction of the protective ozone layer in the outer atmosphere was not even suspected a few years ago. Today, scientists are sure that this erosion is occurring, though they are still uncertain about the extent of ozone depletion that might be expected, or about the impact on human beings that might result from the increased exposure to ultraviolet light. With such increased knowledge, many people decided that the specific risk they had been made aware of should be prevented, even if their attitudes and preferences toward risk did not necessarily change. Many have also become more suspicious of any technological innovations.

In scientific literature the term "risk" is sometimes used to describe a situation in which an array of alternative consequences and their probabilities are known. The expectation of the occurrence of a specific event can be calculated mathematically; some theorists claim that under such conditions, rational people will try to maximize the mathematical expectations of the utilities of the gains. Risk is then measured by the variation from the mathematical expectation—usually the standard deviation. Uncertainty, on the other hand, is not quantifiable. It arises when one has incomplete information on the basis of which to act. In some cases, we might know that one of several outcomes will occur, but not know which one; in others, the outcomes themselves might not be known. Uncertainty can also arise when we know that some causal link exists between a hazard and the damage it causes, but are unable to say what it is. Or a person may not know exactly how a system behaves; or may have recognized some, but not all, of the possible causal relationships. In practice, uncertainty arises from a combination of some or all of these factors. Sometimes, uncertainty can be reduced by experimentation. At other times, it cannot.

In this book, "risk" and "uncertainty" are used interchangeably to mean an uncertain outcome that is also undesirable. In this sense "risky" means both "potentially dangerous" (since it applies to an event that should be dealt with carefully) and "precarious" (since it involves uncertainty or insecurity). One can thus talk about the risk of cancer caused by ingesting a certain product or the risk of unemployment when referring to the probability that a certain individual will lose a job or risk a loss in status.

When public policy issues are discussed, the term "private risk" refers to actions that affect individuals but not society. Private risks turn into social risks when the general public bears the costs of the negative outcomes associated with a particular action. Thus, an individual who constructs a house near a fault line may have to suffer the financial burden should the structure suffer damage from an earthquake. In this case, the risk is "private." If the federal government were to pay for all earthquake losses, the risks would become social. In the last few years, more and more risks have been socialized.

Decision Process under Risk

Risk is omnipresent. We read that obesity may cause heart attacks, excessive consumption of milk may cause cancer, and a variety of home appliances may cause injury; children may be caught inside refrigerators, harmed by badly designed toys, or poisoned by lead pencils or paints; shareholders may lose money because the stock market can fall; workers may lose their jobs because their employers can fire them; or they may lose their limbs in the machinery or be exposed to asbestos and lose their lungs to cancer; and owners of firms can go bankrupt because of some unpredictable change in demand or technology, or because the plant burns down. The interesting question to be explored is, what courses of action do people take when they face risk?

Obviously, since most people are not much moved by what goes on beyond themselves, their immediate families, and perhaps their friends and acquaintances, they worry little about the world at large. A statistic like that for road accidents (i.e., the risk of fatality is 1 in 5000) is a number that assumes a personal dimension only when the victim is, say, one's own child. A 6 or even 7 percent unemployment rate is frictional unemployment for the politician, but a major catastrophe for the unemployed. The risk of starvation in Bangladesh is many times higher than the risk of minor malnourishment for an American child, but many Americans worry more about whether their children have vitamins than they do about starvation in Bangladesh.

Even when there is a probability of hazard to an individual, some people may not know what the probability of the hazard is, simply because they ignore it or do not have the relevant information. Indeed, empirical studies show that people tend to ignore certain low-probability risks altogether, treating them as if they do not exist until their personal experience vividly demonstrates that a problem worthy of attention exists. As one example, in experimental laboratory tests on insurance it was found that people do not even reflect on the consequences of an event if its chances are sufficiently low.[2] These results are thought to explain the behavior of people toward the risk of natural hazards: most individuals in flood-prone areas do not voluntarily buy insurance against this risk even at the highly subsidized rates offered by the National Flood Insurance Program, and less than 5 percent of all homeowners in California purchase insurance against earthquake damage.[3] In fact, after tropical storm Agnes wreaked havoc on the northeastern United States in 1972, causing flood damage of more than $2 billion, only 1580 claims totaling $5 million were paid under the National Flood Insurance: the majority of the individuals eligible for the insurance did not purchase it.[4] In this case, as in many others, Congress did not allow the irresponsible individuals to suffer the consequences of their negligence; it responded to the plight of victims with liberal relief through the Small Business Administration Disaster Loan program. In fact, it seems safe to assume that Congress will respond with generous relief anytime a natural disaster occurs against which most individuals are not insured.

Even when the probable outcomes of a particular event are agreed upon and the probabilities for each outcome occurring are calculated, all people will not act the same. Some are risk-averters by nature and will always prepare for the worst. Others may be willing to act on the basis of expectations (i.e., rely on the averages). Still others like to gamble, and some will simply make their plans as flexible as possible so that none of the possible contingencies will catch them wholly unprepared. A distinction therefore has to be made between agreement on a likelihood and the proper response to it. People can disagree on the probable consequences of an event, or on their order of likelihood, or have different estimates of a situation or of the reliability of estimates made by others. But even if they agree on all these points, they can still differ on the action required to allow for the uncertainty involved.

People often disagree on the desirability of reducing uncertainty. Uncertainty can be decreased by searching for more information and collecting more data. For some, life is dull if too much is known about the future; they prefer surprises. For others, the prospects of a quiet life and long-range plans are preferable. The latter favor the comforts of a fixed rate of exchange or of governmentally determined prices; the former choose the impersonal and biased — but also unpredictable — market. The unknown causes anxiety, and many would rather not examine it too closely.

Finally, the same person can have different attitudes toward different kinds of risk. An individual may be willing to gamble in a casino, thereby accepting risks greater than the mathematical expected value, and then turn around and insure his or her house against fire — usually paying more than is warranted by the mathematical expected value. Behavior like this puzzled economists for a long time; for the purpose of our discussion here, there is no need to go into the so-called utility functions economists have since come up with to explain it.

For a variety of reasons, there are differences between the assessment of risk, known or unknown, and the willingness to bear the risk, as exemplified in daily behavior. Some may even behave as if the risk did not exist. Everyone knows that there is some probability of death from a heart attack, but most people do not let it alter their everyday lives. They are either not concerned with it or assign it a very low priority; or they accept it as something about which very little can be done. To be sure, heart attacks are correlated with certain behavior patterns — cigarette smoking, lack of exercise, and the intake of some kinds of food — and some people actually try to avoid these things. But most people don't, though at the same time they want protection against the consequences of their behavior. A person may have the same assessment of risk and even the same attitude toward risk, but willingness to bear the consequences may change, if, for example, that person's wealth changes: rich men (and nations) are sometimes willing to accept fewer risks than poor ones. Willingness to bear risks also can change when institutional arrangements are available that enable individuals to spread their risk-bearing through insurance.

Forms of Risk-Avoidance

It is important to be clear about the forms that risk-avoidance may take. For this, the earlier example of car accidents will serve. The surest way to avoid car accidents is to abolish cars. If there are no cars to drive, it follows that no one will be killed by them. Even the simplest risk/benefit analysis will convince people that such a course of action is not very desirable, not because it will be ineffective, but because the other costs (or losses to society) of such a system are considered too high to outweigh the risks involved.

The next possibility is to try to reduce the hazards of getting killed in an automobile accident. This is the rationale behind such acts as prohibiting drunk driving or requiring every driver to get a license proving his or her ability, when sober, to control a car. Then there is the further possibility of changing the environment to reduce the probability of accidents; well-lighted roads, gradual curves, and more traffic lights are introduced. This results in all sorts of costs, so someone then has to decide whether these costs should be incurred as well as how will they be paid and by whom.

Instead of, or in addition to, reducing the probability of an accident, we can also try to mitigate losses caused by accidents. Cars may be required to be equipped with better and stronger bumpers and airbags, or drivers may be required to wear safety belts. In these cases, the problem arises of how to reach some compromise between the costs of these safety devices and the probable benefits that result from their use.

Another way to mitigate the consequences of an accident is to purchase insurance. Human lives are precious and irreplaceable; and death brings hardship to those who survive, especially in the case of the loss of the breadwinner in a family. Even nonfatal accidents result in bodily injuries, the costs of medical attention, and time lost from work. Obviously, insurance schemes will not reduce the probability of accidents, but they will alter both the consequences of accidents and the attitude toward risking an accident.

Whether resources are used to reduce the probability of risk, or whether insurance is used to mitigate its consequences, cost is involved. To reduce the probability of risk, resources must be used; and these resources are not free goods. Strong bumpers, safety belts, better roads, and traffic lights all cost something. A decision to employ any one of these devices means resources diverted from other alternatives to cover the costs involved. If the probable benefits (e.g., the number of human lives saved by the installation of a traffic light at a certain intersection) can be calculated, the costs can be weighed against the probable benefits.[5]

When an insurance scheme is used, there is no immediate reason to assume additional costs; it simply shifts the incidence of the costs from certain unfortunate individuals to a larger group—or in the case of a compulsory statewide one—to all citizens. Such coverage may be direct, as in the case of social security contributions; or it may be invisible, as when risks are covered by all citizens as taxpayers. The government, acting as a huge insurance company, does not spell out, or even calculate, costs. It simply covers them from general, or through other more invisible, taxes such as inflation, or through changes in private property rights.

The statement that insurance schemes merely distribute the premium costs must be amended in two important ways. First, the administration of the insurance scheme is not without its own costs, and these must be reckoned with when insurance schemes are discussed. Second, the very existence of the insurance tends to increase the costs. Human nature being what it is, people tend to use more services when they do not pay for them directly. If a person is fully covered by medical insurance, his or her demand for medical services is apt to increase, and the same is true for every other insurance scheme.

Researchers have pointed out that when people are insured, they become more careless; a person insured against unemployment has much less incentive to keep his or her job, and a fire insurance policy weakens the incentives to protect against fire. This phenomenon is known in the insurance literature as the "moral hazard," and its existence affects the terms on which insurance is offered, often by selling less than 100 percent coverage.[6]

To sum up, in order to avoid or reduce risk, we can try to reduce the probability of a loss, reduce the size of the loss, insure ourselves against the hazard when it occurs, or ignore the hazard and continue to live as if it did not exist. Each method entails certain costs that must be evaluated against possible benefits. Any one method can be used voluntarily by individuals or enforced through governmental action.[7] The new social order has brought with it (1) an increased awareness of certain consequences and therefore a larger number of events perceived as risky; (2) intensified demands for protection against events previously considered unavoidable calamities; and (3) a greater sensitivity toward inequities of risk-bearing and probably also greater knowledge of how to prevent risk or use the various diversification techniques that insure against losses. Most important, all these changes were coupled with the growing ability of more and more people to put pressure on the government to change the distribution of risks. The willingness to bear private risk was reduced both by the spread of power among more people and by a national prosperity that allowed more resources to be used for risk-prevention. The demand for social (rather than market-determined) insurance and other means of shifting the risk-bearing has been intensified as more and more groups use their political clout to divest themselves of risk, hoping others will pay the costs. For this shift to have happened, people have not necessarily become more risk-averse than in the past. It may well be that individuals have simply learned to transfer costs associated with risk-bearing to others.

Intensified Demands for Protection

In many ways, individuals are less exposed to risks today than in the past. The conditions of work in the grim factory of the industrial revolution were far more dangerous than those of today; and the hazards to health, even a few decades ago, were many times greater. The probability of a deep depression fifty years ago was much greater than that of a smaller recession today; water pollution in some lakes at the beginning of the century was so high that no fish were left in the water, and pollution and sanitary conditions in the cities resulted in frequent epidemics. Pneumonia, influenza, and tuberculosis were among the many fatal diseases (with almost no doctors around) at the beginning of the century; and the majority of the population suffered from spoiled food, filthy streets, diphtheria, industrial accidents, and a vast array of other hazards that have almost vanished today.

Otto L. Bettmann, in a "modest attempt to redeem our times from the aspersions cast upon them by nostalgic comparisons,"[8] published some poignant items from his pictorial archives, portraying the hazards of life in New York City at the beginning of the century. This was a city with 150,000 horses in its streets; a noisy "El" roaring overhead; piles of kitchen slops, horse manure, coal dust, broken cobblestones, and dumped merchandise; and workers, including children, employed in sweatshops for 60-hour weeks at a dollar and a half a day. Hazards to health and life in the rural areas of the United States were scarcely fewer: "Unceasing vigilance was necessary in contending with the hazards of axles, mules, stinging insects, boiling laundry kettles, tetanus-inducing rusty implements and barbed wire, impure water, and spoiled food."[9]

Economic risks were also high. The post-World War II generation living in the developed world may find it hard even to comprehend the depth of desperation and the extent of human misery caused by a depression. The magnitude of the disaster may be captured by a few figures. In the period between 1929 and 1933 the GNP in the United States fell from $103.4 billion to $55.8 billion (or, in constant 1968 dollars, from $204 billion to $142 billion); unemployment zoomed from 1.5 million to 12.8 million, or 25 percent of the work force; wholesale farm prices fell by more than half; the value of building construction fell from $3 billion in 1929 to $500 million in 1933; and the Dow Jones dollar average per share of sixty-five stocks tumbled from $125 to $36.[10] In Europe, the situation was as bad and sometimes worse. Most historians will agree that the depth of the despair caused by the depression and the swelling number of unemployed were the major reasons for the rise to power of Hitler. The pervasiveness of business fluctuations in the Western economies and the human miseries caused by the recurring depression have often been cited as a major reason behind the increasing role of government in the economy.

Risks in the 1980s are much lower than they were sixty years ago. Infant mortality in the first year of life in the United States went down from 13 in 10,000 in 1900 to about 2 in 10,000 in 1975; the average life expectancy at birth went up from 54.1 in 1920 to 70.8 in 1970; the risk of unemployment has been materially reduced, and the consequences of unemployment have been mitigated by insurance, social security, and Medicare. Most major diseases have been conquered, and lethal epidemics are virtually unknown. Anxiety is now more apt to center on weight-loss diets or vitamin pills than on tuberculosis or typhoid; the marketplace is no longer ruled by *caveat emptor* (let the buyer beware); and workplaces are safer. The rate of fatal accidents in British coal mines went from nearly 4 per 1000 employees annually in the 1850s to less than 1 per 1000 in the 1970s; the average annual rate of fatal accidents per 100,000 employees in all British factories was 17.5 in the first decade of this century. It fell to 4.5 in the 1960s.[11]

While many risks of living in an affluent society are minuscule compared to what they once were, the calls for more publicly supplied protection and insurance intensify. Americans have traveled a long road since slaves were property and could not be freed because the Constitution guaranteed private property rights. The admiration for the rugged individual has given way to the preservation of societal values from concern for the exploitation of labor to attempts to maintain featherbedding; from management's rejection of fringe benefits as not a proper part of a collective bargaining agreement to agreements that preserve the right of employment in the same firm; from a belief in government as "night watchman" to a belief in government as watchdog round the clock, in the form of bureaus, offices, committees, and other organizations that constitute a modern government in Western society.

As people grow richer they also grow less willing to suffer hardship, whether the risks of unemployment, pollution, or inadequate health care. And as they grow more confident they become even more firmly convinced that these problems can be solved and risks can be avoided. Social fatalism has vanished. Allowing social events, technological progress, or economic processes to be determined by the blind interplay of market forces is seen as passive submission, and fewer and fewer groups in society are willing passively to submit. Instead, there have been demands for more citizens to participate, and critics of technological change are guaranteed a base of political power. Those who pay the price of progress challenge its desirability.

Hesiod, in the eighth century B.C., maintained in *Works and Days* that the peasant gained dignity by knowing his place, performing his duty, and doing his work.[12] Until the end of the nineteenth century, a poor man was considered a moral rather than an economic problem: he was poor because he was lazy, avaricious, or prodigal. Each individual was considered responsible for his or her own fate, and hard work represented the virtuous life. The community was not responsible for the fate of the individual. Unequal distribution of wealth was no more unjust than the law of gravity: "Is the law of gravitation unjust when a child accidentally falls out of a second story window and is injured for life?"[13] The poor were badly taught, badly fed, and often unemployed. When they worked, they labored in factories where conditions were unhealthy and occupational diseases and accidents routine; yet most of the workers saw these conditions as an integral part of the social order. They taught their children to fear God and the employer.

Some of the rich, of course, genuinely tried to alleviate a few of these conditions. When slavery was abolished after the Civil War, the Thirteenth Amendment represented to some extent the triumph of the wage-based economy of the industrialized North over the plantation economy of the agrarian South, though humane considerations, based on the declaration of human rights and the genuine belief that "all men are created equal" were involved as well. In Europe throughout the nineteenth century, socialist leaders preached the religion of public ownership as the only way to free the workers from their chains. The Paris Commune of 1871 was exalted by Marx as the first workers' government, and many dreamed of an international uprising of oppressed workers.

At the turn of the century, even if the established order was not always accepted as beneficial to all, in the United States those people excluded from bliss could at least believe that they would eventually achieve the American dream and find a better place for themselves or for their children with luck and hard work. In Europe, nation-states were in the process of welding their people into a purposeful unity to command each citizen's loyalty.

Marx predicted that workers, having nothing to lose but their chains, would revolt; in fact, most of them chose to use their power in the existing system. In time, the power of organized groups to withhold their labor or disrupt the social organization prevented even despotic governments from imposing their will. In democratic societies, old privileges died out and new ones were won. The belief in equal opportunity turned into a demand for equal results, and equal results often involved the right to receive insurance against a growing array of misfortunes.

Parallel with increasing democratization came the realization that benefits could be gained through political allocation over and above those that could be achieved through the market. Governments once would not protect people against certain risks either because they did not know how or because they did not think them worth protecting; today, universal suffrage and the consequent shift in political power have increased the number of those entitled to protection and changing social norms have increased the demand for protection. In addition, the more intensified were the demands of previously passive or unorganized groups, the stronger were the pressures of the old and established groups to protect *their* achievements.

Government has always been expected to protect its citizens against certain risks. Providing law and order or enforcing the law of contract is enormously important for reducing the uncertainty of transactions and the protection of property. With time, both the number of those demanding protection and insurance, using the political machinery, and the areas of such protection have severely increased. Initial demands for the supply of more services—from roads to education—expanded to calls for protection against a whole gamut of risks. Such a trend is understandable. The have-nots start with a demand for basic necessities such as food and lodging. With more affluence, and once these basic needs are satisfied, the demands are for more insurance and protection. Those once portrayed as having nothing to lose are now in a position where they can lose a lot. They therefore demand more coverage against risks and more protection of their status. These demands may harm those at the bottom of the ladder, who have even less. Indeed, at any point of time, demands for insurance come from those who may have something to lose, not from the very poor. Insurance of a minimum wage is called for by those who are employed, not by the unemployed. Protection against change in the mortgage rate is demanded by the homeowner, not by the small saver whose savings are wiped out by inflation partially because of the ceiling on interest rates saving banks are allowed to pay; and calls for protection against competition come from established firms faced with shrinking markets, not from their newly arriving rivals.

In the post-World War II period, no individual was allowed to suffer the consequences of almost all personal disaster; he or she was to be insured, not only against unemployment, but also against an ever growing array of untoward events. Consumers were insured against faulty products, victims against criminals, property owners against acts of nature, drug manufacturers against misconcocted serums, depositors against bank loss, lenders against mortgage defaults. About the only group that was not insured were the believers in governmental omnipotence.

Employers were not left to suffer the vicissitudes of changing conditions and the uncertainty of a market economy. Beginning in the 1950s and '60s, governments were expected to achieve a high rate of economic growth; they became the major suppliers of funds for research and development ventures, thus shifting the risk and uncertainty of these ventures from the private firm to the taxpayers. In Western Europe, governments promoted and aided mergers and subsidized their activities, hoping in this way to create national champions that would assure additional economic growth and technological change. The national champion was expected to abide by governmental directives and increase its output. In return, it was guaranteed the quiet life of a monopoly, shielded alike from foreign and domestic competition. In most countries, programs guaranteed farmers against loss of income from bad weather and, often, even from the inefficiencies of their own production. Major bankruptcies were virtually eliminated. Firms demanded and received government guarantees of a minimum rate of return on investment, shifting the risk, even the risk of bad management, to the taxpayers. In the United States, defense contractors were often granted "cost-plus" contracts, guaranteeing them reimbursement for all costs. In addition, farm prices were insured; steel, textiles, shoes, and other products were shielded against foreign competition; licensing arrangements and route structure protected existing trucking firms or airlines against new entrants; and so on. Government has also been assaulted by demands to reduce risk to health by cracking down on any remote possibility of exposure to carcinogens and banning potentially hazardous products with total disregard to possible benefits.

Risk-Reduction by Government Decree

One way to reduce risk is to abolish, eliminate, or at least reduce its cause. If saccharin causes cancer, prohibit the use of saccharin. If DDT poisons the environment, ban DDT, or restrict it to the point where it is no longer a threat. If power mowers cause injuries, declare them illegal; if refrigerators are death traps for children, make it against the law to produce and sell refrigerators that cannot be opened from the inside.

The government of the United States has prohibted, regulated, or closely monitored certain risks in attempts either to eliminate or reduce them. Safety standards have been tightened in a number of areas. The Food and Drug Administration has intervened to the point where almost every commercially available food and drink is expected to conform to its standards. Federal regulations have been concerned with safety standards on most products, from children's toys to jet airplanes. Goods that do not meet these standards are removed from the market. The Environmental Protection Agency is charged with eliminating, or at least closely regulating, major threats to the environment, and most regulatory agencies protect firms against competition.

New regulations have brought many benefits but have also accelerated the trend to protect people whether or not they want protection. If individuals are assumed to be responsible actors, knowing their own interests best, they need to be informed of a variety of dangers so that they can decide the appropriate risk level they are willing to introduce into their lives. In the new social order it has become social policy to force people to be protected. Workers cannot decide for themselves whether they need helmets or safety goggles; they are required by law to use them.

It is argued that the reason behind the enforcement of these regulations is to avoid the damage suits that might otherwise result if workers are injured or otherwise suffer on the job. This argument assumes the employer is responsible for worker safety even if the worker is negligent. A possible alternative is to require employers to supply safety devices by law. If a worker suffers an injury through neglecting the use of a helmet, goggles, or other legally required safety devices, he or she cannot receive indemnity because of contributory negligence. By the same token, each individual could be allowed to decide whether to purchase safety belts or install airbags in the car. Those who chose to purchase safety devices could be charged lower insurance premiums.

Changes in the responsibilities for work-related accidents and occupational diseases took place much before other shifts of risk from the individual to the society. In the mid-nineteenth century, an employee had to sue his employer to collect damages resulting from industrial accidents, and because of his financial plight, he was at a disadvantage in doing so. In addition, if the employee knew about the dangers in the job, that knowledge might defeat his claim, since it was assumed that he agreed to take the occupational risk.[14] Workers' compensation statutes started in Germany under Bismarck, were copied to England, and by 1911 a number of states in the United States had passed similar laws. In all these statutes, the notion of negligence and fault was abolished. Instead, any employee involved in a work accident was entitled to compensation of a percent of wages lost (rather than damages or payments for pain or suffering). The employer's liability is secured by private insurance in most states, by either private or state insurance in twelve states, and exclusively by state insurance in six more states. Since it was felt that the employer was able to reduce the number and severity of accidents by investing in safety devices, the insurance premium was based on experience rating, thus giving incentives to the employer to invest in safety. Unfortunately, the maximum wage limits in the laws did not always keep up with the changes in real wages; thus the requirement in many laws that compensation should be two-thirds of weekly wages was not always met.

Basically, however, the system of compensation insurance protected the worker against a major abuse and required minimum safety standards but left the decision on the amount of safety devices to be installed to each firm, based on its calculations of the risk of paying compensation and the costs of the safety technology. This approach has been criticized by the Industrial Union Department of the AFL-CIO: "Since it is generally cheaper to let easily replaceable workers die than to reduce risk below unnecessary levels, when methods of cost-benefit analysis are used, the worker's life is sacrificed."[15] Indeed, it is increasingly argued that the hazards of industrial production should be minimized through government improved standards and that the community should be responsible for comprehensive insurance against such hazards.

In the United States the long-held belief has been that market forces should function in the work environment—allowing the *employer* to choose the level of safety. Recently, however, the Occupational Safety and Health Administration was created to ensure employees a workplace "free from recognized hazards that are causing or likely to cause death or serious harm."[16] Based on this mandate, OSHA issued many safety standards, but was often criticized for being too stringent or too lenient—depending on the source of criticism. It is generally agreed, however, that the standards are often too rigid, and they are certainly controversial and expensive to enforce.

In many cases, the law could require the risk-taker to suffer the consequences and the risk-avoider to be allowed a reduced insurance premium. Yet governments often legislate rules forcing all individuals to protect themselves; insurance is not limited to the timid and the doubtful. Governments often forbid the confident and venturesome from taking risks as well.

The more government protects the individuals against risks, the more it feels entitled to restrict individual choice. Societal assumption of risk means not only the coverage of benefits but also concern to reduce the size of payments through added safety. An individual who suffers injury through neglecting the use of a safety device should not be allowed to receive indemnity, or his insurance costs should be increased. But if that individual is eligible for health or disability insurance, many would claim that he still should be compelled to be cautious, since it is society that covers the cost of hospitalization, of incapacity, or of burial. In this way, expanded social insurance reduces freedom. It also reduces the incentive to be cautious.

Often, demands for reduced risks seem to totally ignore the costs involved or to compare the risk to the costs. The government is expected to drive all carcinogenic materials from the marketplace and from the environment, whatever the cost and however small the risk.[17] The government also is expected to eliminate all pollutants from the water by 1985, again ignoring costs and benefits.

Unknown Events

In some cases, the reason for the demands for risk-avoidance is that the facts are unknown and the usual tools of prediction are useless. All future events have their unknown quantity; we can never know whether a certain act, or a certain product, will cause some unforeseen and undesirable result. Ignorance, or insufficient information, increases uncertainty and encourages caution or the prohibition of products or processes that might involve unknown risks, however small. Greater risks are tolerated if the risk is voluntary, familiar, controllable, and previously known.[18]

Many times, experimentations to determine future consequences are sharply limited, and attempts to calculate the possible risks of a catastrophe must be based on judgment, guesses, and intuition. In a world in which hardships and catastrophe are no longer fatalistically accepted as unavoidable phenomena over which humanity has no control, in a world of declining public confidence and trust in authority or in science, many unknown events are interpreted as intolerable risks.

Consider nuclear reactors. The use of reactors may cause an accident, and an accident may cause deaths from radiation. The magnitude of this risk is extremely difficult to calculate, despite many scientific studies on the subject. The U.S. Atomic Energy Commission released in October 1975 the report of a committee chaired by Norman C. Rasmussen. According to this report, the risk of accidents in nuclear plants is smaller than that from many nonnuclear accidents with serious consequences. Nonnuclear accidents examined in this study, including fires, explosions, toxic-chemical releases, dam failures, airplane crashes, earthquakes, hurricanes, and tornadoes, were found to be more likely to occur and to have consequences comparable to, or worse than, nuclear accidents. According to this study, the chance of a coremelt is 1 in every 25 centuries per 100 plants, and for accidents involving 1000 or more fatalities, the probability is once in a million years.[19] The probable costs of such a meltdown were estimated to be about 3300 "early" deaths, 45,000 "early" injuries, and $14 billion in property damage. "Delayed" fatalities were estimated at 45,000, and "long-term" injuries at 128,000.

This assessment of risk factor in such an exceedingly complex technological field was not left unchallenged, and the Union of Concerned Scientists claims that the risks of radiation are much higher and the harms projected in the report are too low. A layperson with no knowledge of nuclear physics cannot even attempt to evaluate these various studies. The point here is simply that, faced with the unknown, people are inclined to prohibit the new technology rather than accept the unknown results of a malfunction.[20]

At the same time, as long as energy production is necessary, some alternative to nuclear reactors must be found. One possible alternative is to use more coal, but that solution could involve an alarmingly high loss of life in mine accidents and in the incidence of cancer. For example, according to a congressional estimate made public in June 1979, the number of deaths attributable to pollutants from coal combustion, using 1975 as a base, is 48,120 a year. Should the use of coal rise dramatically over the next decade (as expected), the estimate continued, that number was calculated to rise to 55,835. A New York Times article of July 1, 1979 commented that "it could be that the economics of the health and environmental problems posed by expanded use of coal might make nuclear power the cheaper alternative in the future, even considering increases in costs as more safety equipment is added to nuclear plants."

Of course, conservation and solar energy, if heavily promoted and encouraged, will help reduce the need for other energy sources. Even according to the most optimistic estimate of U.S. energy supply, however, conservation and solar energy cannot provide more than two-thirds of the additional energy needs and will not reduce dependence on imported oil.[21] The alternative of increasing oil imports entails the obvious risk of a supply interruption. Another risk is a constant increase in real oil prices. A hike in oil prices, in turn, would cause a reduction in national income, would force the U.S. government to adopt deflationary policies, and would result in an economic slowdown. In addition, it would result in increased tension among oil-importing nations.

Thus, even if one assumes that oil resources will not be exhausted, an oil alternative entails greater political as well as economic dependence on the oil-producing countries and many problems in the international distribution of wealth. Any one of these alternatives might be riskier than nuclear reactor accidents, but the exact risks cannot be weighed correctly if people simply continue to remain ignorant about them. When the risks of using nuclear technology are unknown, and experts disagree on its magnitude, its use is opposed. An additional problem is, of course, that a risk, however slight, of nuclear malfunction in the neighborhood is perceived as much worse than nuclear malfunction somewhere else or what may be the larger risk of dependence on some remote oil country.

This is precisely the problem with ignorance: there is no way to know the risks involved. Thalidomide was developed, tested, and found safe, efficacious, and relatively inexpensive as a sleeping pill. It was on the market for several years before the first case of infant deformity caused by thalidomide was reported.[22] DDT was in widespread use for several decades before the first suspicions about its devastating effects on the environment were raised. Until then, the wonder of DDT as a general insecticide and as a potent fighter against typhus epidemics was widely celebrated, and both the U.S. and the British armies used it extensively. Its toxicity was judged manageable if it was properly used, and the scope of "proper uses" increased at a fantastic rate. DDT was discovered in 1942 and was used extensively almost immediately; the first mild warning did not appear until March 1945. ("Too little is yet known about the harm that DDT may do to beneficial insects, plants, soil, livestock, wildlife or to consumers of fruit and vegetables containing DDT residues.") And it was not until the late 1950s, after millions of pounds of DDT had already been sprayed on the planet earth, that the poisonous properties of DDT began to reveal themselves. The publication of Rachel Carson's *Silent Spring* in 1962 was the first news that most people had of the alarmingly widespread use of DDT on earth and its contaminating effects.[23] The use of DDT was not banned until 1972, and even this ban has been lifted in some cases.

There are often long latency periods before a work-related disease is discovered. The debilitating effects of working with asbestos or lead were not known for a long time. Now it is known that certain industrial carcinogens may not manifest themselves until more than ten years after initial exposure. By then a worker may have changed his or her place of work several times. Given these long latency periods and the uncertainty regarding the long-term effects of working with many toxic substances, some government-imposed safety rules are needed.

The disturbing problem is that in each of these cases, the risk cannot be measured in terms of known probabilities of damage. Rather, the real question is what might happen in the distant future. The relevant question about nuclear accidents is not whether an accident occurred in the past. It is not even whether any substantial damage resulted from a nuclear accident such as the one that took place at Three Mile Island in Pennsylvania, but whether a potential—however slight—exists for an accident of truly catastrophic magnitude. The very thought that such a possibility exists makes many people edgy and unwilling to allow any continuation of any nuclear energy. Public distrust has been intensified "by a series of disclosures of secrecy and deception on the part of the Federal officials, up to and including President Eisenhower, who sought to mute the hazards of fallouts from atomic weapons tests."[24] This kind of mistrust is summarized in a *New Yorker* article: "Just as one cannot remove

the ozone layer in order to find out how important it is to the earth's environment, one cannot release large amounts of radiation into the atmosphere in
order to discover its effects on human society. Lacking these experiments, the
earth itself becomes the laboratory: it is on the earth that the effects of a particular one-time catastrophe must originally become known. Twenty years
later, we find out how many cancer deaths may have been caused. In the last
analysis, therefore, the limit that restrains our nuclear pioneering is the
singularity of the earth. Because there is only one earth, and one mankind living on it, all our experiments with nuclear devices and other lethal substances
and machines are at the same time actions taken in real life. Of course, science
is capable of many wonders, including, for example, the cloning of a frog.
Maybe one day, in some other solar system, our scientists will succeed in cloning the earth itself. Once the human population has been removed, this ter-
restrial doppelgänger could be turned into a laboratory—a sort of practice-
earth—on which the nuclear advocates, the pesticide manufacturers, the
doomsday scenarists (who also could use a spare planet or two to test their
theories and all the other enthusiasts and practitioners of the new life-as-risk
philosophy) could try out their ideas to their hearts' content. Until then,
though, they would do well to leave our present earth—the parent of us all and
our only home—alone."[25]

Yet, as far as we know (and this qualification must always be added), although scientists have been unable to resolve some basic questions surrounding the hazards of radiation, they all agree that even with a complete meltdown, the magnitude of the catastrophe, although enormously high, would
not wipe out the whole earth. This raises an interesting question: Why do we
tolerate the certainty of almost 50,000 deaths from car accidents annually and
do not suggest that cars be abolished, while we are less willing to tolerate the
slightest chance (if at all) of 50,000 deaths in a complete meltdown? In the
former case, we seem to allow individuals to take risks in exchange for some
benefits, while in the latter, benefits are totally ignored. It seems that most
people are alarmed by even a slight chance of a disaster of large magnitude
while they tolerate much higher levels of risk when deaths occur one at a time.
Yet people continue to build their houses in flood-prone areas, and nations
continue to fight wars with a large number of casualties!

Whatever the exact explanation, the fact is that while some are alarmed
by the possibility that Spaceship Earth will always founder in ignorance, and
thus danger, numerous others view scientific knowledge as the greater danger
and ferociously defend their right to be protected against it. In the 1970s, debates on the question whether scientific explorations in biology in general, and
genetics in particular, should be continued brought this issue to the fore. In

1976 Har Gobind Khorana, of the Massachusetts Institute of Technology, announced that he had successfully synthesized the first fully functional gene from off-the-shelf chemicals, the latest in a series of stunning scientific discoveries that made people wonder whether scientific work along these lines should continue unfettered. An increasing number of people have become alarmed at the potential of untold and unknown perils to earth and human civilization and have called for a pause, if not a halt, to biological research, at least until some moral and ethical problems and the risks of this research have been explored more fully.

The revolutionary breakthroughs in biology have been hotly debated and controversial topics in certain circles. The debate has involved complex scientific and ethical questions and has revolved around the question whether to continue research on DNA. In this case, as in many others, government has been called upon to protect people from what some consider to be the irresponsible behavior of its elite members. The National Institutes of Health, faced with the growing furor over genetic manipulation, published guidelines intended to regulate this research, guidelines that some felt were inadequate because they allowed continued experimentation with so-called crippled forms of *E. Coli* that others felt were unnecessary. But if government simply cut off funds to these biologists, industry might begin to supply them to reap commercial benefits; so instead, even more comprehensive controls were demanded, prohibiting further research altogether. It was asserted time and again that knowledge and the means of acquiring it are not always beneficial, and that the forces scientists now wield might drive the human race toward an unforeseen doom.

A by-product of the release of nuclear energy is different types of waste: high-level waste, transuranic water, and low-level waste are contaminated with plutonium (TRU) or with different levels of radioactivity. In the past thirty-five years, the nuclear industry has produced millions of gallons of liquid and solid wastes. These wastes can contaminate food and the air we breathe, raising risks of cancer, genetic damage, and other calamitous effects. It was expected that these wastes would be reprocessed as soon as enough reactors were in operation to make reprocessing economical. However, fear of nuclear weapons proliferation and the possibility that reprocessing of light water-reactor fuel could be used to make atomic bombs caused a change of heart.

In 1977 the Carter administration prohibited reprocessing for an indefinite period. As a result, the problem of spent fuel became acute. In the meantime, the spent fuel was stored at storage pools near the plants. Since the pools would be filled by 1985, another solution was necessary. One suggestion was to build "away from reactor" (AFRS) pools that could safely store spent fuel for many years. However, state legislatures imposed various prohibitions on the construction and expansion of nuclear waste storage facilities or the transport of radioactive waste through the state. No one wanted to be the nation's dumping ground for high-level nuclear waste. A 1976 California statute prohibited future construction of nuclear power plants until "a demonstrated technology or means for the disposal of high-level nuclear waste" was developed and approved.

In early 1978, the government designed a program called "Waste Isolation Pilot Plant" (WIPP) to bury these wastes in the saltbeds in New Mexico. Such a scheme means that these wastes have to be transported, thus exposing the waste to the risk of a rail or highway accident. The Department of Energy felt that such a scheme is safe. But no one knows enough about the problem to say with complete assurance that there is no risk—however minuscule—of an earthquake in New Mexico or some other cause of change in the salt formation. No one can say without any doubt that the salt formations are totally safe for housing the waste, and no one can guarantee that an accident involving a truck carrying the waste on the road will never occur. The controversy over the technical adequacy of WIPP forced the Carter administration to promise New Mexico's governor a veto power on a decision to begin construction.[26]

Scientific research is often contradictory and adds to the uncertainties surrounding nuclear waste disposal. Today, 75 million gallons of high-level radioactive waste materials exist, and 2 million more gallons are added every year. A growing number of citizens have been organized into protest groups against this hazard. In some cases, these groups have been able to stop traffic of the waste. The Natural Resources Defense Council went to the Supreme Court, claiming the government did not adequately consider the problem of disposing of atomic wastes; the council lost the case. It is almost certain, however, that the question of whether the federal government or the states have the ultimate authority in deciding where nuclear waste is to be stored, and which routes it can be moved over, will be appealed to the Supreme Court.[27] In the 1980s, nuclear power plants will not solve energy problems in the United States. A wide range of individuals argue that nuclear power plants are unsafe and the disposal of radioactive waste material is hazardous. Debates have already caused delays and have paralyzed the nuclear industry. Since 1975, only a few nuclear reactors have been purchased, and many earlier orders have been canceled. Since 1974, cancellations have exceeded orders by four to one (53 to 13).[28] If all plants under construction and ordered are built on schedule, the nuclear capacity of the United States in the 1980s will be only half that officially projected in 1974. Moreover, unless an agreement is reached on waste disposal, many nuclear plants will run out of spent fuel storage within four years.

Ignorance has always been a cause of uncertainty and therefore fear. Primitive man was afraid of thunder and worshiped many natural phenomena as gods that had to be appeased. Galileo created havoc by proposing that the earth was not the center of the universe, and was punished for his thoughts. People in Salem, Massachusetts, believed that certain women were witches, and hanged twenty of them. I do not mean to imply here that nuclear physicists or biological researchers are necessarily the innocent victims of mass hysteria. Nuclear physicists brought upon us the classical Faustian choice by developing nuclear and hydrogen bombs, and many of them felt—and still feel—this discovery should never have been made.

The problems of control over scientific inquiry are certainly extremely important and excessively complex. It is not only unclear how control can be achieved but also who the controllers should be and how they should administer the controls decided on. Opinions on these and many other questions differ widely. Some declare that the frontiers of knowledge should be challenged, while others proclaim that in some cases ignorance is bliss.

Three things seem clear. First, continuous scientific discovery and technological growth entail many perils. They may not only despoil nature but also may allow the vile and brutish to have at their disposal dangerous devices that can wipe out the whole world. Second, the achievements of science have outpaced human ability to cope with them. Scientists promise us a world in which death can be deferred through organ transplants; where artificial organs can replace natural ones; where the sex of a baby can be decided in advance, behavior conditioned by drugs or electrodes, and surveillance become widespread.

At this stage, we do not really know how to cope with the many ethical, legal, and distributional problems these developments have engendered. Human beings have always been afraid of the unknown and the unpredictable, and their rule of thumb is apt to be "when in doubt, don't." Government is called upon to control scientists and check their research, or, since it is unclear how a government can control scientific discovery, to stop it altogether, at least until some solutions to the moral and social problems it creates are on the horizon. In some cases, the lack of a solution has already resulted in curtailment. The National Institute of Health has stopped work on the development of an artificial heart largely because government is reluctant to face the unsolved problem of how they will distribute this expensive invention when it is made. A group called Responsible Genetic Research has also petitioned Congress to extend and tighten federal guidelines for research on recombinant DNA.

Third, fear of total annihilation in a nuclear war is so overwhelming that no one dares take a chance on missing some new military advance that can come out of scientific work. Paradoxically, it is often easier to stop scientific advances in areas designed for bettering the lot of mankind than to use the same restraint in research on new and more efficient weaponry.

Whatever the ultimate solution to these difficult and complex problems, it is clear that the responsibility for protecting the human race from unknown dangers that might drive us to catastrophe has been shouldered on the government. It is also clear that in many of these cases, people are not willing to compare the risks and the benefits. They would rather not have the risks! It is increasingly believed that we have reached a high enough level of affluence that we do not have to take chances anymore.[29] It is precisely this attitude that has reduced competition and increased inflation.

A similar attitude is manifested in the area of pollution abatement and safety. Demands for reduction of environmental pollutants or the installation of safety devices are justified by the need to reduce the risks of disease and morbidity. Since there is no way to charge citizens directly for the costs of safety or clean air, the additional costs of risk-reduction are borne by consumers in the form of higher prices.

An alternative method for pollution abatement might be auctioning off the rights to pollute: any polluting firm would bid for an effluent price to be paid to the government for any marginal amount of pollution. If all the information is correct, and in the absence of transaction costs, the price of a pollution right would equal the capitalized marginal value of treating the marginal pollution. Since each bid would represent the best interests of the polluter and since the additional costs would be passed on to the consumers, the pollution price would also reflect the amount consumers were willing to pay for the reduction of pollution. As Ackerman rightly points out, however, "the use of the effluent charge device carries with it the symbolic implication that public authorities do not consider all pollution an unambiguous evil, but instead believe that the costs of totally eliminating manmade pollution everywhere exceed the benefits generated by a return to an (urbanized) state of nature."[30]

To the environmentalist, conservation, like morality, is priceless. Based on the environmentalist's perception that pollution is priceless, the U.S. Federal Water Pollution Control Act of 1972 declared as a national goal "that the discharge of pollutants into the navigable waters be eliminated by 1985."[31] One estimate of the costs involved in removing all pollutants from waterborne wastes in the United States was $317 billion.[32] And if it is not a feasible alternative, the law will simply be flouted, since no one seriously thinks that it will ever be implemented.

One result of risk-reduction is an enormous increase in the cost of systems. Many systems are designed today to avoid even as low as a one-tenth of one percent probability of malfunctioning. The many backup devices involved tremendously increase the cost of developing these devices.

The major costs of risk-reduction systems, however, are the increasing costs to the private sector; most costs are not shown in the government's budget. Instead, they are borne by consumers in the form of higher prices. (This phenomenon of the "invisible government" is discussed in a later chapter.)

The number of regulations designed to reduce the causes of risk has mushroomed. They cover such obvious areas as radiation, safety at the workplace, safety at home, and disease. Some are designed to eliminate the causes of risks, including the risk of reduced income. The Securities and Exchange Commission is entrusted with ensuring that prospective and actual security holders receive the fullest possible disclosure to reduce the risk of losses owing to fraud or calamity.

To be sure, government has been inconsistent in its efforts to legislate risk-reduction rules. In some areas, government regulations are both detailed and broad. In others, government is satisfied with disclosure of information; the best-known example of this variety being cigarettes. Despite many research findings that connect cigarette smoking to cancer, heart ailments, and respiratory diseases, cigarette smoking is neither regulated nor banned. In this case the government agreed to a compromise: cigarette advertising is banned on television, but not in newspapers, and each pack of cigarettes (as well as each cigarette advertisement) must contain a warning stating that the surgeon general has determined that cigarette smoking is dangerous to health. Political pressures on government, rather than any considerations of the public interest, are behind this inconsistent behavior. It might be noted, too, that the warning is omitted on cigarettes sold outside the United States. Since the degree to which risk is eliminated is thus constrained by politics, it stands to reason that the cost of the risk-elimination affects small businesses more than it does large ones.

Shifting Responsibility for Risks

Increased participation in democratic politics has meant concerted efforts of hitherto unorganized groups to get rewards and privileges and shift the responsibilities for risks. One result has been a shift of responsibility from the individual to society. Another has been a shift of responsibility from the individual buyer to the producer and from the individual employee to the firm.

Take the question of consumer protection. In a contract between a buyer and a seller, who is to be held responsible if a product turns out to be faulty? Before the industrial revolution, most business transactions were closely regulated by the government, and both the quality of food sold and its weight were closely watched and controlled. Cheating was heavily penalized both by municipal authorities and by the guilds.[33]

By the nineteenth century the legal view had changed, and judges began to accept the view that the buyers should beware when they buy products: *caveat emptor,* "let the buyer beware." The rationale was that the buyer had as much knowledge of what he or she wanted as the seller of the product; in any event, the market would punish an unreliable seller. Individuals were assumed to be rational maximizers of their own self-interest, whatever this self-interest might be, and the law (and the courts) did not see any reason to intervene in a contract freely drawn up between two rational, responsible adults. Perhaps the law (and the courts) also preferred to protect manufacturers rather than consumers.

In the twentieth century, *caveat emptor* has gradually lost its rationale because manufactured goods are often impossible for the consumer to control. The producer is now held responsible for any product he places on the market. Any defect in any product that causes injury—whether to the buyer or anyone else—is assumed to be the liability of the producer. The injured party can claim redress not only from the seller of the product but also from its manufacturer.

Until the 1960s, product-liability cases were rare. Winning damages in a product-liability case was a long, convoluted, and difficult process. To win, there were several possible routes. One was to prove "negligence" under the tort law. However, many consumers could not provide proof, nor could they prove that the user's negligence contributed to the product's failure. The other approach was to claim a breach of warranty under the contract law. But the doctrine of *privity of contracts* limited these suits to claims against the immediate seller (namely the retailer). To be sure, the privity of contract was more widely interpreted in 1916 in *MacPherson* v. *Buick Motor Company.* Here, Judge Cardozo ruled that whenever "inherently dangerous products" are concerned and the producer knows "that the thing will be used by persons other than the purchaser and used without new tests" then "the manufacturer . . . is under a duty to make it carefully."[34]

In 1960, however, a New Jersey court ruled "implied warranty" in *Hennigsen* v. *Bloomfield Motors, Inc.*[35] The court allowed the purchaser of a defective car to sue both the dealer and the manufacturer without showing either privity or negligence. In 1963 a California court held a manufacturer "strictly liable" in torts if the product sold had a defect causing an injury.[36] In 1965, a Restatement of Torts[37] guided the courts to hold the seller strictly liable for any product "in a defective condition unreasonably dangerous to the user or the consumer, or to his property" even though the consumer "has not bought the product from the seller" and even though "the seller has exercised all possible care in the preparation and sale of his product." Following these and other decisions, product-liability cases escalated. While before 1960 such cases were rare, there were nearly 50,000 of them in 1963, and in 1966 the number was more than 100,000. In the 1970s, both the number of claims and the size of settlement awards zoomed. A California jury recently awarded more than $125 million in punitive damages after one person was killed and another badly burned when a Ford Pinto was hit from behind.[38] The enactment of the Occupational Safety and Health Act (1970) and the Consumer Product Safety Act (1972) also stimulated liability claims and lawsuits.[39]

The escalation of the frequency and the severity of product-liability claims and lawsuits caused a sharp increase in liability insurance premiums. The cost of additional quality control and that of litigation insurance are shifted by the large firms in one way or another to all consumers. As a result, the risk of purchasing a defective product has been shifted from the few unlucky buyers to everyone. Small firms were less able to shift the additional costs to the consumers, and these problems contributed to the failure of some firms. In addition, at least some new product development has been retarded.[40] When President Ford nominated a task force to look at the problem, the task force recommended a new model code.[41] At least some states limited the wide-open product liability the court decisions had tended to establish.

Changing attitudes toward risk-bearing is apparent in many other fields. Consider malpractice suits. One study, called for by President Nixon in February 1971, stated: "During the nineteenth century and the first two or three decades of the twentieth . . . sickness was accepted as a usual and expected thing . . . medicine itself was comparatively limited and adverse results were either regarded as the natural outcome of the disease or attributed to the 'will of God.' "[42] There is no evidence that medical doctors are more negligent today than they were at the beginning of this century. Yet the number of malpractice suits has mushroomed. As with product liability, one gets the impression that jurors do not consider "whether or not culpable negligence was present but, rather, who is better able to bear the burden of loss?"[43] The burden of proof has been shifted from the plaintiff having to show negligence to the defender having to prove its absence. The result was an increase of up to 100 percent annually in professional liability insurance premiums during the 1970s and the withdrawal of a growing number of private insurers from the market. It is estimated that 70 to 90 percent of the cost of insurance is ultimately passed on to consumers.[44] Again, the risk has been shifted from the unlucky patient to society at large. Costs are also said to be increasing because of unnecessary tests designed to build a defense against a possible malpractice claim.

The above examples should not be interpreted as a plea for reduced liability in cases of negligence. The manufacturer whose products are faulty and who continues to sell them, or the doctor who fails to exercise reasonable and ordinary diligence, should certainly suffer the consequences of their negligence. The point is simply that there has been an increasing trend toward shifting the consequences of risky events from the individual to larger groups. To be sure, Americans seem to have become the most litigious people in the world, and the pendulum seems to have swung too far from almost total responsibility of the individual to an almost total shift of the responsibility to society.

The eagerness to find culprits for every mishap can reach ridiculous dimensions. A *Time* essay of August 28, 1978, told of skiers who held slope owners liable for injury; a pending suit against the National Park Service demanded six-digit compensation for negligence because park employees didn't warn visitors of the possibility of being struck by lightning; a camper who received leg wounds from bears while camping in the vicinity of Yellowstone National Park argued that the Park Service was negligent in not warning more sternly against the risks of bears (he lost the case); and a woman sued San Francisco on the grounds that her fall against a pole in a runaway cable car transformed her into a nymphomaniac (she collected $50,000 damages). A pedestrian who suffered a broken jaw when the wind toppled her against a guardrail claimed the structural design of the nearby building increased wind velocity and that the building's management was negligent in failing to prohibit her from crossing the plaza. The new attitude toward risk is manifested not only in such isolated cases but also in the epidemic of malpractice and product-liability suits. Reduction and avoidance of risk are demanded in all walks of life.

Some of the extreme and irreversible consequences of this increasing trend for risk-avoidance and risk-shifting may be corrected by certain changes in the law. Thus it has been suggested that a statute of limitations defense be allowed for product liability; that the fact that a method of manufacturing a product conformed with the state of the art at the time of manufacturing or with government standards be considered a defense against considering the product defective today; and that misuse by the consumer consist of a complete defense to a product-liability claim. Some also suggest that a limitation should be enacted to the prevailing attorneys' practice of taking cases under a contingency fee, claiming that the existing system encourages lawyers to suggest bringing suits of product liability, malpractice, and workers' compensation. Others suggest limitations on the damages to be granted, or the payment of such damages in installments. None of these is a panacea, and none will be discussed in detail because they are not very relevant to the main theme of this work. What should be noted is the changing attitude toward risk and its bearing. In fact, while the federal government suggests a new model code, two recent court decisions[45] require the manufacturer to show that the utility of his product outweighs the risk of its design—another sharp change in the burden of proof.

The burden of other risks has been shifted from the employee to the employer. Health-care benefits have increasingly been provided as an employee fringe benefit. In 1956 Congress enacted the Federal Employees Health Benefits Program, adding the 8.5 million federal employees to the many who receive health benefits as a fringe benefit. In fiscal year 1977, 94 percent of all hospital bills and 70 percent of total health costs in the United States were paid by a third party. The 70 percent has been made up of 40 percent paid by the government and 30 percent paid from private health insurance.[46]

The Increasing Umbrella of Insurance

Government cannot abolish or even reduce all risks. Natural disasters and accidents are bound to happen. The causes of some risks are either not well understood or completely unknown; their elimination, therefore, is impossible. People are sometimes careless, and despite all precautions, accidents occur. To protect himself or herself, any individual can combine his or her resources with those of other individuals, paying premiums that will provide aid should mishaps occur. Each individual can pay a certain amount of money so that in case of accidental death, his or her heirs will receive a cash benefit. An individual can purchase insurance against earthquakes, typhoons, ill health, or any variety of disasters. In all these instances, individuals voluntarily enter into a contract according to which they pay certain premiums and get a certain amount of insurance. This voluntary agreement can be made either by a group or by specialized insurance companies. When government insures individuals, these schemes are generally mandatory rather than voluntary, and the premium may or may not be paid by the same group that is entitled to the benefit.

Demands for risk-shifting have been especially loud when they are in the form of insurance against unemployment. Government is expected to provide a world in which every worker is effectively insured against unemployment and, in many cases, even against a change in jobs. Governments and international institutions made the achievement and maintenance of full employment not only one of their major aims but an almost absolute right, equal to life, liberty, and the pursuit of happiness.[47]

Employment insurance was then broadened to include the right to "meaningful" work. Differences exist among countries as to what these rights consist of: in some places, it is the right to have some job; in others, it is the right to have a job commensurate with skills and status; and in still others, it is an absolute right to continue in the same job until retirement, even if the government has to keep the firm solvent. In some countries and in some industries, workers are protected against any change in job, whether or not the job is socially useful and whether or not the worker is competent. In other places, the right to work is broadened to include grounds of religion, sex, color, or age group.

From the middle of the eighteenth to the end of the nineteenth century, the employer had an inalienable right to hire workers and dismiss them as he pleased. The relationship between employee and employer was held to be a voluntary agreement between two responsible and free persons, each of which could enter into a contract of work or leave it as he wished. This voluntary contract was considered a huge leap forward compared to the days when men were confined by regulations to a hierarchy that controlled their movements in a trade and from one place to another. Yet the new system, in which labor essentially became a commodity traded in the market, meant that free men could starve while looking for one of those "voluntary" contracts. It was Anatole France who commented that "the law in its majestic equality forbids the rich as well as the poor to sleep under bridges, to beg in the streets and to steal bread."

In rural society, unemployment was largely disguised; everybody worked on the land, but they could work and still suffer from famine if the weather were poor or wars or pests devastated the countryside. Yet, to a large extent, rural society was self-sufficient. Once workers migrated to the cities, they became entirely dependent on their wages. Getting work was essential, and the right to earn decent wages was demanded. Workers organized into labor unions, using their collective power to win better wages, better working conditions, and, later, to insure themselves against the probability of dismissal and unemployment.

As in all cases discussed in this book, the risk of unemployment can be reduced or its consequences avoided through an explicit insurance program. Governments were expected to manage the economy in a way that would ward off the risk of unemployment. Full-employment policies were maintained even at the price of increasing inflation, or at the cost of rescuing large firms which, because of bad luck or mismanagement, or a combination of the two, were faced with laying off workers. The costs of these policies — inflation and increasing public debts — were shifted to the taxpayers in general.

Governments were also expected to provide labor-market information, manpower development and training programs, and public employment. Governments were to alleviate the economic consequences of actual unemployment. This was achieved mainly through a compulsory unemployment compensation insurance. The insurance premiums are paid by some combination of contributions from employers, employees, and taxpayers.

In practice, of course, the line of demarcation between risk-reduction and insurance against its consequences has been subtle. Thus, governments sometimes have alleviated the hardships of unemployment by effectively insuring workers against dismissal: subsidies have been paid to private firms, or (in Europe) firms have been nationalized to avoid a reduction in employment level, whether or not this employment was useful or necessary. According to a UNIDO study, "In those countries which have a sizeable nationalized industry sector the emphasis shifted towards employment maintenance and seems to have led to labour hoarding."[48] In many cases, governments safeguarded jobs by providing credit and interest subsidies, by tariff and nontariff barriers to imports, and by selective intervention to help declining industries. (These trends are discussed in chapter 6.) In other cases, public employment programs have been carried out in conjunction with public assistance programs. Thus, under the Work Incentive Program, established in 1967 and strengthened in 1971, subsidies are granted to encourage public service employers to provide jobs to recipients of Aid to Families with Dependent Children.

Compulsory public insurance programs for the unemployed started in the United States only in 1935. To be sure, there were some sporadic attempts to introduce such bills in several states, especially during the 1920-21 depression, but none of them passed. Prior to the enactment of the Social Security Act of 1935, only five states had passed unemployment compensation laws and only two of them (New York and Wisconsin) had become effective. The Social Security Act of 1935 levied a 3 percent payroll tax on employers to provide money for state-operated unemployment compensation programs. Employers were allowed to deduct 90 percent of this tax to pay state unemployment tax. Given this incentive, all states enacted unemployment compensation programs. Today, the federal payroll tax is 3.4 percent on the first $6,000; state taxes are still limited to 2.7 percent. The funds collected by the states are deposited in a special federal unemployment trust fund. Since the Employment Security Amendment of 1970, almost all workers including the self-employed are covered by unemployment insurance. Unemployment insurance, however, is limited to those who previously belonged to the workforce and lost their jobs. Those who are unsuccessfully seeking their first jobs do not qualify for insurance compensation. As a result, the unemployment rate is higher than the insured unemployment rate. In 1980, for example, the unemployment rate was 8.0 percent, but less than half of these persons were entitled to unemployment benefits.[49]

As in most compulsory insurance programs, some claim the program is too generous while others feel more benefits should be enacted. Martin Feldstein represents the first point of view. He maintains the system is overgenerous for most workers and creates incentives for employees and employers that cause higher unemployment.[50] William Papier, on the other hand, feels the maximum weekly benefits should be raised and disqualification penalties reduced.[51]

Certainly employees today have much better protection against unemployment than employees in earlier years. This protection is achieved both through the reduction of risk of unemployment and by protection against some of the consequences of being unemployed. Like other insurance schemes, both visible and invisible, unemployment insurance gives benefits to some that have to be paid by others. The exact distribution of costs or the incidence of benefits is often not calculated at all.

The right to work is sometimes interpreted as the right to work at the same job, whether or not the job is necessary. "Featherbedding" is one of the practices designed for that purpose. U.S. railroads continued to employ two persons in each locomotive long after only one was needed; hundreds of ticket clerks in British Airways struck when the company proposed to start a shuttle service in which tickets would be sold on the plane; French workers in the Lip factory seized the factory when told that they would have to be laid off since the factory could not sell its products (watches) because of foreign competition.[52] The workers refused a proposed settlement guaranteeing them employment in a different place, claiming that they had the right to work where their grandfathers were buried. Dozens of business firms in Europe have been nationalized and state-owned firms prevented from closing down obsolete plants, with the taxpayer footing the bill for maintaining redundant employment.

In these cases, and in hundreds of others, workers do not mean to sabotage the system. They are all probably God-fearing, moral individuals and lovers of their country. They do feel that the right to work in the same place and at the same job is a basic right to which they are entitled, and many have no other skills. Having given loyal service to their employers, they feel it is unfair not to allow them to continue supplying the same loyal service — even if this service, for reasons beyond their control, ceases to be needed. So they shift the results of change to society at large.

An additional insurance is the requirement to pay severance pay (or, to use the British terminology, "redundancy pay") according to length of service and last wage level. This payment can increase the cost of dismissal to the point where it sometimes pays to continue the unneeded services rather than dismiss the employee. Employers, too, look for additional protection from the state that will allow them to continue the same level of employment even when, because of changing demand or foreign competition, the firms cannot profitably maintain their workforce.

Governmental protection does not stop at insuring individuals against major catastrophic events, protecting people against unemployment, or allowing them to avoid the perils of a change. Protection is now available and insurance is mandatory in a wide variety of areas including not only disability, major illness, or reliability of products but extending to safety, guarantee of income, and even guarantees of status, dignity, and position.

Inflation

The recent proliferation of insurance schemes, risk-reductions, risk-shifting, and damage suits involves major costs in terms of resource use and reduces the ability of the economy to make adjustments. One result of both costs and the lack of flexibility is two-digit inflation. Inflation is nothing more than a disguised tax, and one that bears most heavily on those whose incomes are fixed. Government deficits and higher costs in private firms are caused in part by competing promises to achieve a no-risk society; they produce continuing inflationary pressures, which only serve to call forth renewed pressure for protection against this new risk.

At the beginning of the inflationary period, most people seemed to accept, or at least be resigned to, the fact that inflation would reduce the value of their income and savings. In time, however, demands were heard for protection against future inflation and its attendant risks. In one country after another (and in the United States mainly since 1974), cost-of-living escalation clauses were added to price and wage contracts. In some countries (Brazil and Israel are the best examples), almost all long-range contracts are linked to the cost-of-living index. In Israel, where the rate of inflation in 1980 hit an all-time high of more than 130 percent, escalation clauses are found in life insurance policies, debt contracts, collective bargaining agreements, social security and welfare payments, and income tax rates. In the United Kingdom, such clauses are part of savings schemes. In the United States, at this stage at least, they have not yet become popular in financial instruments, but they have been used in labor contracts and price agreements and in the calculation of social security benefits.

Indexation schemes are risk-reduction devices *par excellence*. When two parties enter into a long-term contract, both of them, if they behave rationally, attempt to forecast the future rate of inflation so that they can estimate the real rate of interest paid or received, or the rate of increase in real wages. Since making such estimates is exceedingly difficult, both sides can reduce the uncertainty by putting cost-of-living escalators into their contracts. Instead of having to estimate the rate of inflation, the indexation clause prevents those signing contracts from being hurt by unanticipated changes in the rate of inflation. Cost-of-living escalation clauses are a perfectly rational response to inflation. But we do not see a more widespread use of this device, in particular in the bond market, because individuals cannot bear the risk involved in indexation schemes. Almost all linked issues in the United Kingdom, Brazil, and Israel (and in other countries in other times) were either issued by the government or guaranteed by it. One might erroneously believe that the government really has found the way to Utopia through the issuance of these indexed bonds. Why should one care about inflation? All one has to do is index all contracts in the economy, and the ugly risk of inflation will disappear.

The reason this cannot be done, in the simplest possible terms, is this: If the government borrows with linked debentures and lends the money in an unlinked form, it simply increases its debt to the public. This debt has to be paid, and the payment of the debt will necessitate increasing the taxes levied on the public. Therefore, it will be the taxpayers who pay for the indexation scheme. Again, as in all government insurance operations, the intervention of the government redistributes the costs of the insurance scheme, but it does not, nor is it able to, create free goods.[53]

The Impossible Dream

Risk pervades all aspects of life. A major role of government has always been to confine or set limits to the risks individuals have to face. Without government enforcement of law and order, the risks of being mugged, raped, or murdered are generally agreed to be excessive. Governments also attempt to increase the ability of economic agents to form reasonable expectations so that the national economy can run smoothly and efficiently. The laws and regulations governing commercial activities, such as contract law, bankruptcy procedures, procedures for dispute settlements and protection of private property, allow a tremendous reduction of uncertainty in day-to-day business life. In the case of international economic transactions, uncertainty is generally greater than in the domestic market, but enforced and enforceable international rules help alleviate some of that uncertainty.

Sometimes it can be shown that government should protect a certain group of individuals against a certain specified risk. Governments protect inventors against infringement of patents in the hope of increasing the probability of scientific investigations and investments. In the wake of the oil crisis of 1974, then Secretary of State Henry Kissinger proposed that governments should guarantee a certain minimum price per barrel of oil in order to increase private investments in the search for oil and encourage research on alternative energy sources. From the private investor's point of view, that research was not seen as profitable as soon as the risk of a breakdown in OPEC and its oil prices were taken into account. A high level of uncertainty can cause sluggishness in investments. High-risk premiums depress the level of investments, especially longer-term investments. The bottlenecks that result can cause idle capacity and unemployment. Government can then decide to reduce risk or increase the expected return on the investment. The risk of exposure to possible embargos leads some governments to protect a local industry to ensure supplies in wartime. This is said to be the reason for the protection of agricultural production in Switzerland. Governments also have been giving guarantees to diminish the risks involved in foreign trade, as well as guarantees to reduce the risks of direct foreign investments. These insurance schemes are voluntary, and the premium costs are generally paid for by international traders and investors.

Some voluntary insurance schemes have become enormously important. Adam Smith was very much against the joint stock company, but in the modern form of the corporation it turned out to be a most significant way to mobilize savings. It unleashed an enormous and unprecedented revolution that brought increased material production and allowed the working laborer to rise above a subsistence level for the first time in history. Nevertheless, limited liability is only one possible institutional arrangement; it is not forced on all individuals, but is offered as a possible device. Entrepreneurs can continue to do business without incorporating.

In some cases, the very size of a certain system or the magnitude of the possible damage may be a sufficient reason for avoiding risk. The risk of a power failure when the whole of the United States is connected to one grid is so large that such connection was stopped after the 1965 New York power debacle. The risk of a nuclear holocaust is so gigantic that meticulous precautions need to be taken. In a technologically interdependent world, certain risks have been increased and more precautions are needed. Certain catastrophes cause so much harm that insuring against them is prudent—for example, loss of life, limb, or income.

Nonetheless, there are still costs involved. The avoidance of one risk means the acceptance of another, and the creation of insurance means paying the premium. When insurance is widespread, the costs of its administration and of the "moral hazard" both grow.

But while more and more people demand protection, people are less and less willing to bear the costs. There are, therefore, two major reasons why a no-risk society is impossible. First, the total demand for insurance imposed and administered by the state far exceeds the willingness to pay, and attempts to control the "moral hazard" result in severe constraints on individual freedom. Second, avoidance of one risk often leads to increased exposure to others.

NOTES

1. For a technical treatment, see Kenneth J. Arrow, *Essays in the Theory of Risk Bearing* (Amsterdam: North Holland Publishing, 1970), esp. essay 1.
2. See Paul Slovic et al., "Preference for Insuring against Probable Small Loss: Implications for Theory and Practice of Insurance," *Journal of Risk and Insurance* 44 (1977): 237-58. For a theoretical discussion of the psychological theory, see Amos Tversky and Daniel Kahenman, "Availability: A Heuristic for Judging Frequency and Probability," *Cognitive Psychology* 5 (1973): 207-32.
3. Howard Kunreuther, "The Changing Social Consequences of Risks from Natural Hazards," *Annals of the AAPSS* 443 (May 1979): 108.
4. Ibid., p. 105.
5. See W. D. Rowe, *An Anatomy of Risk* (New York: Wiley, 1977); C. Starr, "Social Benefit versus Technological Risk," *Science* 165 (1969): 1232-38; and C. Starr, R. Rudman, and C. Whipple, "Philosophical Basis for Risk Analysis," *Annual Review of Energy* 1 (1976): 629-62.
6. Technically, the very act of purchasing insurance has the effect of increasing the probability of the events insured against. For a discussion, see Kenneth Arrow, "Uncertainty and the Welfare Economics of Medical Care," *American Economic Review* 3 (December 1963): 941.
7. The reduction in the probability of a loss is referred to in the technical literature as "self-protection" or "loss prevention." The reduction in the size of the loss is known as "self-insurance" or "loss protection." For a formal analysis of these problems, see Isaac Ehrlich and Gary S. Becker, "Market Insurance, Self-Insurance, and Self-Protection," *Journal of Political Economy* 80 (July/August 1972): 623-48.
8. Otto L. Bettmann, *The Good Old Days—They Were Terrible!* (New York: Random House, 1974), as quoted in William W. Lowrance, *Of Acceptable Risk: Science in the Determination of Safety* (Los Altos, Calif.: William Kaufmann, 1976).

9. Ibid., p. 5.
10. Broadus Mitchell, *Depression Decade: From New Era Through New Deal, 1929–1941* (New York: Rhinehart, 1947).
11. *Safety and Health at Work, Report of the Committee,* Chairman Lord Rubens (London: HMSO, 1972), p. 3.
12. George Cabot Lodge, *The New American Ideology* (New York: Knopf, 1975), p. 48.
13. Quoted from Edward Chase Kirkland, *Dream and Thought in the Business Community, 1860–1900* (Ithaca: Cornell University Press), 1956, p. 23.
14. Harry Weiss, "Employers' Liability and Workmen's Compensation, " in John R. Commons, *History of Labor in the United States 1896–1932* (New York: Macmillan, 1935), 3:565-66.
15. *IUD Spotlight on Health and Safety* 7, no. 2 (Fourth quarter 1978): 2.
16. The Occupational Safety and Health Act of 1970.
17. For an extensive cataloging of chemical and environmental substances that induce or are related to cancer in humans and a strong plea for their removal, see Samuel S. Epstein, *The Politics of Cancer* (San Francisco: Sierra Club Books, 1978). See also Environmental Defense Fund and Robert H. Boyle, *Malignant Neglect* (New York: Knopf, 1979).
18. Baruch Fishhoff, Paul Slovic, Sarah Lichtenstein, Stephen Read, and Barbara Combs, "How Safe Is Safe Enough? A Psychometric Study of Attitudes Toward Technological Risks and Benefits," *Policy Science* (April 1978): 127-52.
19. Interestingly, as was pointed out in the report, this was approximately the same risk as that associated with a meteor strike (in the United States) with a fatality rate of 1000 persons.
20. The Nuclear Regulatory Commission officially disavowed the risk estimates of the Rasmussen report in January 1978. See Ronnie D. Lipschutz, "How Safe the Nuke? Nobody Knows," *Business and Society Review* (Winter 1978-79): 45-49. For strong views against nuclear energy, see Dr. Helen Caldicott, *Nuclear Madness: What Can You Do?* (Brookline, Mass.: Autumn Press, 1978); and *Shut Down* (Summertown, Tenn.: Book Publishing Company, 1979).
21. See Robert Stobough and Daniel Yergin, eds., *Energy Future: Report of the Energy Project at the Harvard Business School* (New York: Random House, 1979), p. 232.
22. H. Sjöström, *Thalidomide and the Power of the Drug Companies* (Harmondsworth, England: Penguin, 1972).
23. Rachel Carson, *Silent Spring* (Boston: Houghton Mifflin, 1962).
24. *New York Times,* 1 July 1979, p. 28. For a catalog of seeming concealment and distortion by the government, see *The Risks of Nuclear Power Reactors: A Review of the Nuclear Regulatory Commission's Reactor Safety Study* (Cambridge, Mass.: Union of Concerned Scientists, August 1977).
25. *The New Yorker,* 25 June 1979, pp. 21-22.
26. *New York Times,* 1 July 1979, p. E7.
27. I.C. Bupp, "The Nuclear Stalemate," in Robert Stobough and Daniel Yergin, eds., *Energy Future* (New York: Random House, 1979). p. 130.

28. William Walker, "Prospects for Nuclear Power in the 1980s" (paper presented at the International Symposium on Industrial Policies for the 1980s, Madrid, 5-9 May 1980), p. 4.
29. See Marshall S. Shapo, *A Nation of Guinea Pigs: The Unknown Risks of Chemical Technology* (New York: Free Press, 1979).
30. Bruce A. Ackerman, Susan Rose-Ackerman, James W. Sawyer, and Dale W. Henderson, *The Uncertain Search for Environmental Quality* (New York: Free Press, 1974), p. 276.
31. Ibid., p. 219.
32. Allen V. Kneese and Charles L. Schultze, *Pollution, Prices and Public Policy* (Washington, D.C.: Brookings Institution, 1975).
33. See, for example, Reed Dickerson, *Products Liability and the Food Consumer* (1952; reprint ed., Westport, Conn.: Greenwood Press, 1972), p. 20; and Henri Pirenne, "Urban Economy and the Regulation of Industry," in *Economic and Social History of Medieval Europe* (New York: Harcourt, Brace, 1933).
34. 217 N.Y. 382, 111 N.E. 1050 (1916).
35. 32 N.J. 358, 161 A.2d 69 (1960).
36. *Greenman* v. *Yuba Power Products, Inc.*
37. Restatement of Torts (second), 1965, Sect. 402a. See William L. Prosser, *Law of Torts* (4th ed.; Minneapolis: West, 1970), p. 656.
38. David F. Pike, "Why Everybody Is Suing Everybody," *U.S. News & World Report,* 4 December 1978, pp. 50-54. On the other hand, in 1979, a Winamac, Indiana, court decided in favor of Ford in a case of criminal charges of reckless homicide involving a 1973 Pinto accident in which the fuel tank of the car ruptured. See *Time,* 24 March 1980, p. 20.
39. R. M. Bieber, "Product Liability Loss and Its Control," in *Products Liability: An Area of Growing Concern* (Malvern, Penn.: Society of Chartered Property and Casualty Underwriters, 1976), p. 43; and *Federal Register* 43, no. 67 (16 April 1978): 14612.
40. S. J. Paris, "Analysis of the Consumer Product Safety Act of 1972 and Its Effects on Product Liability Litigation," in *Products Liability,* pp. 111-12.
41. *Interagency Task Force on Product Liability, Final Report* (Washington, D.C.: Department of Commerce, 1977). The task force study was initiated in June 1976 apparently as a result of business pressures to solve the "product liability crisis."
42. U. S. Department of Health, Education, and Welfare, *Report of the Secretary's Commission on Medical Malpractice* (Washington, D.C.: HEW, 1963), pp. 2-3. See also Sylvia Law and Steve Polan, *Pain and Profit: The Politics of Malpractice* (New York: Harper & Row, 1978).
43. Charles P. Hall, Jr., "Medical Malpractice Problem," *Annals of the AAPSS* 443 (May 1979): 86.
44. Ibid., p. 92.
45. *Barker* v. *Lull Engineering Co.* (Calif., 1978); and *Turner* v. *General Motors, Inc.* (Texas, 1979).
46. U. S. Department of HEW, *Social Security Bulletin,* July 1978, p. 7. The lowest rates of third-party payments were for dentists' services (20.5 percent), eyeglasses (8.1 percent), and drugs (16.9 percent).

47. Promotion or guarantee of full employment was incorporated into the UN Charter (art. 55 and 56). The Universal Declaration of Human Rights, adopted by the UN General Assembly on 10 December 1948 proclaims "the right to work, to free choice of employment, to just and favorable conditions of work and to protection against unemployment." The United States did not guarantee full employment in its Employment Act of 1946, but came very close to such a declaration; and the British Employment White Paper of 1944 officially initiated a policy of eliminating the business cycle to achieve full employment. Other governments followed similar policies.

48. United Nations Industrial Development Organization, *Structural Changes in Industry* (Vienna: UNIDO, December 1979), p. 143.

49. Unemployment rates from U.S. Bureau of Labor Statistics, *Employment and Earnings*. Figures on unemployment compensation from the explanations to the 1981 budget.

50. Martin S. Feldstein, "Unemployment Insurance: Time for Reform," *Harvard Business Review* 53 (March-April 1975): 51-61.

51. William Papier, "Standards for Improving Maximum Unemployment Insurance Benefits," *Industrial and Labor Relations Review* 27, no. 3 (April 1974): 376-90.

52. For details, see *L'Affaire Lip,* Harvard Business School Case No. 9-375-024.

53. For a technical economic discussion, see Nissan Liviatan and David Levhari, "Risk and the Theory of Indexed Bonds," *American Economic Review* 67, no. 3 (June 1977): 365-75.

4. The Insurance State

The first and most obvious result of the pressures for increased government-supplied risk-reduction and insurance is an increase in the scope and size of insurance programs operated by the government and registered as such. Mainly, these are programs in which premiums are paid to a special fund. Many government operations designed to reduce risk or insure against its consequences are organized in a different form: in some cases they are financed from general taxation funds and not shown as a separate insurance program. This is true of most regulatory agencies, all of which carry out some risk-reduction and insurance programs, either against changes in the market share of the existing firms or against occupational hazards, consumer fraud, and so forth. The direct costs of these activities will be shown by an increase in the size of general governmental expenditures. However, government often increases its risk-reduction insurance activities by invisible methods—where the costs of the programs are shown in the books of private firms or not shown at all. Thus, most of the increased costs of safety regulations are not shown in the government budget. Instead, they result in an increase in cost to the private sector. They, in turn, attempt to shift the cost to consumers. Other risk-reduction costs are not registered at all.

In some cases, the premiums of the insurance program are paid by the same group that is entitled to the benefit. The operations of the Federal Deposit Insurance Corporation (FDIC) can serve as an example. The history of the United States is replete with bank failures, and in each of them depositors were usually innocent victims losing their money, sometimes the accumulated savings of many years. Under the New Deal a new scheme was devised: all depositors were to be insured by a special federal agency so that the failure of a bank would not cause undue and, one might add, unfair hardship. This scheme protected the small saver against loss, recognizing that the depositor cannot influence the way a bank is managed and that many bank failures result from mismanagement. It was believed that this insurance scheme was necessary to maintain the confidence of depositors in the banking system. The insurance was limited to a certain sum of money and was designed to protect the small investor.

FDIC insurance is mandatory. The cost of the insurance is paid to a large extent by depositors. The insurance premium is technically paid by the insured banks, but this premium increases their costs, which are generally passed on to the depositors.[1] Inasmuch as the shareholders of the bank can be said to be paying part of the insurance, this seems to be justified since they, too, receive the benefit of additional depositors' confidence and the avoidance of suits against the bank.

Usually, though, the insurance cost is not paid for by those directly benefiting from it. An opposite case is found in protection of domestic producers against foreign competition by using quotas or other barriers. This protection is at least partially an insurance scheme, only this time workers and owners of protected products are insured against unemployment or loss of income. The cost of this insurance is borne, not by this particular group, but by the consumers (in the form of higher prices for the product), and by citizens of other countries (whose exports to the country are restricted), in the form of reduced opportunity for income. If the United States imposes quotas on the import of shoes, the cost is borne by consumers, who pay higher prices for shoes, and by producers and workers in the shoe industry abroad, who cannot sell in the U.S. market. The beneficiaries, however, are workers in the American shoe-manufacturing business and those whose income and employment are dependent on these persons; they are insured against unemployment and against loss of income. It might be argued that protection against foreign competitors increases benefits or income rather than reduces risks. Yet, generally, protection is demanded and approved in order to guarantee employment. In the United States the 1974 Trade Act empowers the International Trade Commission to recommend relief to domestic industries if employment is threatened by imports.

Let us look first at the growth of the visible part of the government, starting with programs officially designated as insurance programs. Not surprisingly, both federal and state governments have steadily enlarged their insurance operations. In 1960 the federal government alone collected about a quarter of the total insurance premiums in the United States; this share grew to 39 percent in 1965, 42 percent in 1971, 44 percent in 1974,[2] and 46 percent in 1977.[3] According to one expert's estimate in 1976, total insurance premiums collected by the federal government will surpass those of the entire private sector by 1980.[4] These figures do not include state insurance funds, for which no aggregate data are available. Yet it is known that state governments establish unemployment insurance programs; workers' compensation insurance also operates at the state level. Many states allow private insurance firms to administer the funds, but employers are required by law to have the insurance. In twelve states, state funds compete with private insurers in the insurance and administration of the workers' compensation laws, while in six states the state is the exclusive agent for these insurance operations.[5] State governments also operate life insurance (Wisconsin), automobile insurance (Maryland), funds for drivers unable to collect from uninsured drivers (Maryland, New Jersey, North Dakota), hail insurance (North Dakota, Montana, Colorado), and land-title insurance (Massachusetts, Ohio, California, North Carolina); and most states operate state-owned pension funds and self-insurance of their own properties.[6] Note that some compulsory insurance, such as workers' compensation or third-party liability for car drivers, is administered by private insurance firms, but their magnitude is determined by compulsory laws of the state.

Compulsory automobile liability ($18,870 million) and workers' compensation insurance ($9,919 million) were 41.4 percent of all total privately collected property and liability insurance. Workers' compensation premiums zoomed from $3,492 million in 1970 to $9,919 million in 1977 — an increase of 284 percent.

On the federal level, the budget of the United States shows twenty-nine insurance agencies operated within the budget of the federal government. They include fifteen insured loan agencies, six property insurance agencies, six life insurance agencies, the unemployment trust fund, and the Social Security Administration. In addition, the federal government operates a number of funds to guarantee loans. (See Appendix.)

The Social Security System

The largest federally operated insurance program covers the risks of old age and premature death. This insurance, old age and survivors' (OASI), is part of a system of old age, survivors', disability, and health insurance (OASDHI) established in accordance with the Social Security Act. Programs established under this act have undergone major changes since the act was passed in 1935. These changes expanded both benefits covered under the system and number of people covered. Today, social security programs cover over 90 percent of the working population of the United States and are estimated to have paid more than $135 billion in retirement and disability insurance in FY 1981. Over the 1971-76 period, all benefits paid by the program increased in real terms by 50 percent, while real gross national product increased by 13 percent.[7] In 1977 old age and survivors' benefits payments were $71.3 billion, and disability payments were $11.1 billion. In 1978 they grew to $78.5 billion and $12.2 billion respectively; in 1979 to $87.6 billion and $13.4 billion; 1980 estimates are

$101.3 billion and $14.8 billion; and 1981 estimates, $118.3 billion and $16.9 billion.[8]

In terms of resources available to survivors and retirees, the Social Security System today provides about two-thirds of all benefits; 21 additional percent is provided by industry; and only 13 percent is represented by private individual purchases of life insurance.

Of course this is not the total picture; individuals provide for their old age and for their survivors through the accumulation of savings ranging from stocks and bonds to the increased value of their property. If all individual savings are included, the percentage of funds provided by social security is much lower. Still, the Social Security System is a growing source of provision for old age and premature death. Using the same definition as above (i.e., ignoring personal savings), the growth in importance of the Social Security System can be vividly demonstrated. In 1950 individual investment in life insurance consisted of 50 percent of the total resources in terms of current dollars available to survivors and retirees. This percentage declined to 25 percent in 1960, 20 percent in 1970, 14 percent in 1974, and 13 percent in 1976. By contrast, the Social Security System made up 18 percent of the total resources in 1950; its share swelled to 49 percent in 1960, 58 percent in 1970, 64 percent in 1974, and 66 percent in 1976. Industry (private pensions and group life insurance) shares were 32, 27, 22, 21, and 21 percent respectively.[9]

A majority of Americans believe that the individual is and should be responsible for his or her own financial support. Individualism is equated with freedom, and allowing freedom to flourish is assumed to necessitate minimum governmental intervention. Attempts to plan the economy, control the use of certain resources, or guide social evolution are scorned; suspicion of political power is deeply embedded. Yet, government has become the major insurer against the risk of old age and premature death. At the same time, a Louis Harris poll reported in early 1979 that 42 percent of all current employees and more than 50 percent of employees under age thirty-five have "hardly any" confidence that social security will pay them the benefits promised when they retire.[10]

When the Social Security System was started in 1935, it bore a much stronger resemblance to private insurance than it does today. It was designed to supply retirement benefits to workers on the basis of individual equity. In other words, each worker was expected to receive at least as many benefits as he or she had contributed. At that time the act covered only workers in commerce and industry. Since 1939, the system has been based on a social adequacy principle, universal and compulsory protection has become the goal, and benefits have been measured against a minimum standard of living rather than on the basis of contribution. The 1939 amendments eliminated the 1935 guarantee of a fair rate of return and replaced it by benefits based on average earnings during a shorter period of coverage. In addition, benefits for dependents and survivors of retired workers were introduced. In short, the Social Security System has become a compulsory saving mechanism expected to ensure retirement funds to those who (unwisely) did not save enough during their working years.

The simple wage-replacement role of the insurance has been supplemented by welfare considerations to allow minimum benefits for the needy and a progressive benefit formula. In 1956, disability benefits were added. Benefits for dependents and survivors of disabled workers were introduced in 1958. Health insurance for persons sixty-five and older were added in 1965, and supplemental income benefits for the aged began in 1972. The size of the benefits has been increased several times, and so has the level of earnings allowed after retirement without a reduction in benefits. In addition, automatic price adjustments were introduced in 1972. These adjustments not only compensated workers for inflation but also increased the maximum amounts of earnings creditable for benefit purposes on the basis of changes in average covered wages — not on changes in the consumer price index. Future retirees would enjoy double adjustment for inflation: from the adjustment of the benefit formula and from the higher taxable wage base owing to higher earnings. This compensation obviously increased the future cost of the system, and most experts felt the overindexation was an error that should be corrected.[11] The Social Security Amendments of 1977 (PL 95-216) revised the faulty benefits formula. The new formula ties retired workers' benefits to changes in the consumer price index, and those of future retirees to changes in wages. Yet indexation added to the financial burden of the Social Security System. For example, old age benefits payments were increased 6.5 percent in June 1978, 9.9 percent in June 1979, and 14.3 percent in June 1980.

These and other financial problems caused fears of "crisis" and even feelings that the Social Security System was bankrupt. In the mid-1970s heated discussion emerged on various facets of the system; some felt it should be contracted, others called for its expansion through increased benefits. One major point in the debate concerned the way in which the system is financed. Some felt it better to finance the system, as today, from the payroll tax. Others would finance it from general government revenues (or, recently, from a windfall profits tax on oil companies).

These controversies among the experts are actually based on a fundamental divergence of opinion and beliefs regarding the role of the individual and the state, and therefore on the role of the Social Security System. Some feel the program should be divested of any welfare considerations and be based on individual equity. They argue for payroll-tax financing and for benefits based on individual contributions to the program. They fear that general revenue financing would undermine the earned-right aspect of the program. Others stress the responsibility of society toward the poor, and would like to regard the system as a tax-transfer system to redistribute income. They call for increased use of general taxes, pointing out the regressive character of the payroll tax. By the same token, some feel that the government should not administer a program beyond the need for a guaranteed minimum level of retirement income. They would opt for a system that will not increase coverage beyond a base level, assuring a minimum income. Others argue in favor of the expansion of the system and increasing the wage-base level; they do not see private pensions as better than publicly supplied social security.[12]

In fact, the Social Security System today is a compromise composed of both need-related programs for poor retirees and compulsory earnings-related social insurance. Part of the need-related program is financed from general revenues and is based on a needs test; this is the Supplemental Security Income (SSI) legislated in 1972. The compulsory earnings part started with the idea of an individual contribution for insurance and was thus financed by a payroll tax. The initial payroll tax, which went into effect in 1937, was 1 percent paid by both employees and employers on the first $3,000 of wages. This initial tax was scheduled to rise in steps until it reached 3 percent by 1949. In fact, mainly as the result of a booming economy, the actual rate in 1950 was still 1.5 percent and was scheduled to increase to 3.25 percent by 1970. Because of an interim increase in benefits (mainly disability and Medicare), the actual rate in 1970 was 4.8 percent and was scheduled to rise to 5.9 percent in 1987. Today, the rate is 6.65 percent. For reasons explained below, it is most likely to rise to a much higher level unless benefits are reduced. In addition, there has been a continuous increase in the "wage base," the amount of taxable earnings on which the tax is imposed. The wage base was $3,000 in 1937; in 1953 it was $3,600; in 1973, $10,800. It was increased to $16,500 in 1977, $22,900 in 1979, $25,900 in 1980, and $29,700 in 1981. More important, despite the increases in absolute terms, the wage base remained constant as a percent of total earnings of covered employments until 1974. Then it started rising.

When the social security program started, it was inevitably small; the ratio of taxpayers to beneficiaries was very high. Over time, of course, the program matured; more persons retired from work after establishing eligibility. In 1950 there were fourteen taxpayers for each beneficiary; the ratio declined to four in 1970. Unfortunately, in the first years of its existence, the program did not charge the full future costs of the insurance; it was (and still is) based on a pay-as-you-go policy with tax rates big enough to pay the *current* program plus a moderate trust fund. Thus the increase in the payroll tax was built into the system and could be predicted. In addition, at the outset, marginal costs of any additional benefits were also artificially low. Finally, the program began small in terms of the coverage. With time, there was a gradual increase in the program's coverage.

Today, social security covers 90 percent of the workforce, including the self-employed. Exceptions are civilian employees of the federal government (covered by the Civil Service Retirement Act rather than by the Social Security System[13]) and a fraction of state and local government employees. Since 1951, most of these employees have been covered by OASDI; and since 1974, railroad retirement has been coordinated with the Social Security System. With each extension of coverage the period of the artificially low tax rate was prolonged: these extensions brought a fresh infusion of revenue while benefit obligations were deferred.

During its first three decades of operation, the Social Security System was unanimously acclaimed by the population. Benefits were many times as large as those actuarially purchasable from contributions paid, and payment was efficient and prompt. The situation changed considerably in the 1970s.

Today the Social Security System is suffering from some geriatric diseases. It has certainly reached maturity, paying benefits to 93 percent of the population over 65 years of age (21.8 million people), as well as to 12 million others qualified as survivors, dependents, disabled, or retiring from work at age 62. The ratio of taxpayers to beneficiaries is lower than ever, and will continue to decline as falling birthrates and higher expectations of life change the demography of the country. By the end of 1979, the ratio of workers to beneficiaries was about 3. It is expected to decline to 2.5 by 2015 and to 2 in 2030, when the post-World War II babies will retire. In addition, inflation has caused benefits to increase faster than expected.

The faulty benefits formula enacted in 1972 has worsened the deficit. And since approximately 90 percent of the workforce is covered, there is not much scope for increasing revenues by extending coverage. Those not covered by the program, mainly federal government employees, exert strong pressures against being included because they enjoy the benefits of the civil service retirement system.

In addition, since 1972 the benefits have been indexed. As a result, a severe and sudden deficit developed in the program, and Congress was forced to raise both payroll tax and wage base, with future rises certain to come. Since 1974, the wage base has risen faster than wages; it is expected to reach 91 percent of covered earnings, as opposed to 81 percent in the 1950s and '60s. A worker who entered the system in 1937 and paid the maximum tax for thirty years before retirement would have paid a very small fraction of the benefits received. Today, high-income workers may pay far more than they will receive in benefits.

The 1977 social security amendments increased the tax rates to make the system financially viable. However, these amendments turned out to be inadequate: the social security trustees failed to predict the high rate of inflation. The increase in the consumer price index since 1977 was almost double the 1977 forecast while the sole determinant of the income for social security—covered wages—increased slightly faster than projected but much less than the CPI. Further, unemployment was higher than predicted. The decrease in real wages and higher unemployment reduced revenues while the higher CPI increased expenditures, causing a dip in the social security fund. Just before the 1980 elections, Congress provided a temporary rescue by reallocating some disability insurance contributions for 1980 and 1981 to OASI. However, the Social Security System still suffers short term cash shortage as well as the long-run demographic problem caused by the decline of the ratio of covered workers to beneficiaries.

The Social Security System has thus been evolving into a national pension system rather than a basic floor of protection against unanticipated needs. The cost of the system has been growing, and is sure to grow more in the future.

Although the payroll tax is paid by employee and employer, there are strong theoretical arguments for the belief that the entire tax is borne by the employee. Employers who hire workers know they have to pay the payroll tax and adjust the wages they offer to take account of this fact. In other words, employers tend to reduce the wages by the amount necessary to pay the payroll tax.[14] Of course, strong labor unions may attempt to change the incidence of the tax. When this happens, it is plausible that large firms would shift the incidence of the tax to the consumers through higher prices. Some empirical work appears to suggest that the full burden of the payroll tax is borne by workers.[15]

A program may have costs other than those registered in its books. In the Social Security System, there are mainly two such costs: (1) its impact on retirement patterns, and (2) its influence on savings habits.

From 1950 to 1975, participation in the labor force of men 65 years of age and over declined from 45.8 percent to 21.7 percent. During the same period, the percentage of the same age group receiving social security benefits increased from 59 percent to 94 percent. Several empirical studies attempted to find out whether this dramatic reduction in labor force participation was

caused by the increased availability of social security.[16] There were some indi-
cations that the Social Security System indeed contributed to the decline. In
addition, provisions of the Social Security Act discourage persons 62 and over
from continuing to work.

A much more serious problem is the growing suspicion that the Social
Security System reduces the volume of savings in the economy. Remember
that the Social Security System is not based on an accumulation of a fund.
Rather, it is financed on a "pay-as-you-go" transfer system: social security
contributions are immediately paid out as benefits. If persons reduce their savings because of the availability of social security, the result is a net reduction in
savings that may lead to a severe capital shortage for investments. Some
studies on the impact of the Social Security System indeed conclude that aggregate private savings have been declining. One study even claims that savings in
1969 would have been more than double their actual amount in the absence of
social security.[17] Although there is no agreement on the magnitude of the
effect, it is clear that social security has had some negative effect on private
savings.

Of course, it is possible to solve the problem of reduced savings by financing the Social Security System through a trust fund, thus in effect replacing reduced private savings by increased public savings. There is little support for
such a program in the United States because the trust fund would have to be
invested by the federal government in private firms. Should such a fund be restricted to investments in government bonds, the amounts outstanding would
not be sufficient. In addition, the Federal Reserve System's open-market operations, today an important monetary policy tool, would have to cease. Finally, a rise in payroll tax to boost the national saving rates would increase the re-
gressiveness of the tax system.

It is not my intention to discuss all the ramifications of the problem. Several points are important for the discussion in this book. First, the Social
Security System has gradually evolved into a much more complex and much
more comprehensive insurance system than the simple retirement income program initiated in 1935. Today it covers 90 percent of the working population
and dispenses benefits to the tune of more than $100 billion annually. In FY
1981, the social security payroll tax accounted for more than 31 percent of
total federal revenues. Second, social security is an enormous program, with
many benefits, and also with a growing impact on all parts of the economy.
During the next ten years, the program will pay benefits, and require tax col-
lections, of over $2 trillion! The promise of old age benefits could influence in-
dividuals to trim their savings, and as a result, reduce the nation's rate of savings. A reduction in the rate of savings, in turn, would cause a shortage of
capital for investments. Third, individual Americans will have to get accus-

tomed to paying higher taxes to cover the costs of social security. The nation's World War II baby boom will one day reach age 65, producing a higher percentage of older persons, and if the nation experiences sustained inflation at high levels, indexed benefits will cost more. In addition, newly entitled beneficiaries have higher initial benefits, which reflect the growth in general wages during their careers. Today, the cost of the payroll tax is estimated to rise to at least 8 percent for the employee in the year 2000, and to 12 percent in the year 2025. Fourth, the distribution of costs and benefits is not necessarily identical with that assumed according to the distribution of payments. Most important, the side effects and impact on the economy have to be taken into account in any intelligent discussion of the program.

The discussion above was restricted mainly to that part of the Social Security System that works to insure individuals against the risks of old age and premature death. Other parts of the program will be discussed shortly, when the growth of health insurance programs is analyzed. The reader should also note that the Social Security System is just one (albeit the biggest) of many government programs designed to maintain the income of the individual. Unemployment compensation and other programs also insure individuals against a reduction in their income in case of catastrophe.

Social insurance programs under the narrowest possible definition include OASDHI, railroad retirement funds, public employee retirement, veterans pensions, and workers' compensation. The amounts of money paid by these programs increased from $22.7 billion in 1960 to $170.3 billion in 1977. By the end of 1980, the disbursements of the old age, survivors', disability, and hospital funds alone were nearly $14 billion a month (see table 4.1).

This phenomenon is not restricted to the United States. In other developed countries, too, income-maintenance programs are of relatively recent origin. At the beginning of this century they existed only in Denmark, Germany, and New Zealand; by the 1940s, some form of social security could be found in about a dozen countries. Since then, coverage has expanded and payments have increased at a fast pace. Between 1962 and 1972, average public income-maintenance expenditures for the European Economic Community rose from 8.2 to 10.6 percent of the gross domestic product (GDP). In the United States in that decade these same expenditures grew from 5.5 to 7.4 percent of GDP.[18]

Health Insurance

Another area of increasing government insurance is health programs. Since 1972, there has been a significant shift in the financing of health care from the private to the public sector in almost all member countries of the OECD.

TABLE 4.1. SOCIAL WELFARE EXPENDITURES, 1960-77
(in millions of dollars)

	1960		1970		1972		1973	
Program	Federal	State and local	Federal	State and local	Federal	State and local	Federal	State and local
Social Insurance	14,307	4,999	45,246	9,446	61,248	13,561	72,249	13,917
Old-age, survivors, disability, health	11,032		36,835		48,229		57,767	
(of which: Health insurance Medicare)			7,149		8,819		9,479	
Public employee retirement[1]	1,520	1,050	5,517	3,142	7,648	4,273	8,878	5,133
Railroad employee retirement	935		1,610		2,141		2,478	
Unemployment insurance and employment services[2]	474	2,356	1,036	2,783	2,487	5,164	1,869	4,197
Other railroad employee insurance[3]	284		100		128		80	
State temporary disability insurance[4]		348		718		784		848
Workers' compensation[5]	63	1,245	148	2,803	616	3,340	1,177	3,739
(of which: Hospital and medical benefits)	9	411	21	964	27	1,158	32	1,323
Veterans pensions and compensation programs	3,403		5,394		6,209		6,606	
TOTAL	17,710	4,999	50,640	9,446	67,457	13,561	78,855	13,917

TABLE 4.1. *(continued)*

Program	1974 Federal	1974 State and local	1975 Federal	1975 State and local	1976 Federal	1976 State and local	1977 Federal	1977 State and local
Social Insurance	82,832	16,169	99,715	23,298	119,594	26,010	134,741	26,514
Old-age, survivors, disability, health	66,287		78,430		90,441		105,410	
(of which: Health insurance Medicare)	11,348		14,781		17,777		21,549	
Public employee retirement[1]	10,785	5,893	13,339	6,780	15,664	7,777	17,833	8,770
Railroad employee retirement	2,693		3,085		3,500		3,819	
Unemployment insurance and employment services[2]	1,722	4,940	3,429	10,407	8,251	11,335	5,966	9,510
Other railroad employee insurance[3]	57		75		227		189	
State temporary disability insurance[4]		915		990		1,035		1,076
Workers' compensation[5]	1,287	4,422	1,357	5,122	1,512	5,864	1,524	7,158
(of which: Hospital and medical benefits)	36	1,574	50	1,825	66	2,099	70	2,531
Veterans pensions and compensation programs	6,777		7,579		8,280		9,082	
TOTAL	89,609	16,169	107,294	23,298	127,874	26,010	143,823	26,514

SOURCE: U.S. Bureau of the Census, *Statistical Abstract of the United States, 1979*, pp. 326-27.

1. Excludes refunds to those leaving service. Federal data include military retirement.
2. Includes compensation for Federal employees and ex-servicemen, trade adjustment and cash training allowance, and payments under extended, emergency, disaster, and special unemployment insurance programs.
3. Unemployment and temporary disability insurance.
4. Cash and medical benefits in five areas.
5. Benefits paid by private insurance carriers, state funds, and self-insurers. Beginning 1970, Federal includes Black Lung benefit programs.

Government-financed medical insurance in Canada, which in 1972 was limited mainly to one province, was extended to the entire population in 1973. Medicare and Medicaid were established in the United States. In Austria, Belgium, and Germany, health insurance programs have been extended to more and more people. In Finland, Ireland, and Japan, health schemes cover the entire population. Sweden added dental care to its public health insurance. Increased eligibility and other institutional changes accounted for a third of the growth in the ratio of public health expenditures to the GDP.[19] At the same time, public expenditures grew as a result of the swelling costs for health services. The chief growth areas during the period were hospital and medical services; the relative price of pharmaceuticals declined. Rising health costs have outpaced inflationary trends in the rest of the economy in all OECD countries. Most of the rise above price inflation is accounted for by the labor-intensive nature of modern medicine, the increasing use of expensive technology, and the increasing need for medical treatment caused by the aging of the population. By 1976, health care expenditures as a percent of GNP ranged from 5.8 percent in the United Kingdom to 8.6 percent in the United States.

Since the early 1960s, OECD countries' expenditures on public health as a proportion of GDP has increased from 2.5 percent to 4.4 percent. Total health expenditures in 1974 were, on the average, 5.5 percent of GDP. In the United States, total health expenditures were 7.4 percent, of which 3.0 percent represented public expenditures. Between 1960 and 1974, total health service consumption increased four times, but current public expenditure on health increased more than seven times. According to one OECD study, "A very real fear now appears to exist in the governments of the member states that the demand for health services is insatiable on the basis of any pricing system to consumers that is socially and ethically acceptable. And despite the increase in expenditures, there is no clear evidence of declining morbidity."[20] Indeed, health expenditures continued to rise. In the early 1960s it was expected that health care expenditures would absorb an additional 1 percent of GNP every ten years. Actually, the rate accelerated in the 1970s at an average rate of 2.5 percent of GNP for the period after 1970. Even when the annual rate of increase is adjusted for changes in the consumer price index, the yearly increase adjusted for inflation ranges from 5.13 percent in the United Kingdom to 11.3 percent in West Germany (and 5.93 percent for the United States).[21]

U.S. public expenditures on health insurance as a percent of the total national health bill are the lowest of all OECD countries. In fiscal year 1977, all levels of government (federal, state, and municipal) covered 40 percent of the total health bill; private health insurance covered 27.6 percent, and only 30 percent was directly paid by individuals. Although the U.S. public share of the health bill is lower than in other countries, it has increased enormously. In

1929, almost 87 percent of health care expenditures came directly out of the pockets of individuals.[22] Private third-party payment programs started in the 1930s. These private insurance programs have increasingly been provided as employee fringe benefits. In 1950, direct out-of-pocket payments still accounted for over 70 percent of national personal health expenditures. In 1965, merely fifteen years later, this had dropped to 52 percent, and by 1977 it had dropped to only 30.3 percent. These figures include all kinds of health care. However, direct payments by private individuals varied in different health services; individuals paid 91.9 percent of the costs of eyeglasses and appliances, 83.1 percent of drugs, 79.5 percent of dental care, 38.8 percent of physician services, and merely 5.9 percent of hospital costs.

The government entered the health insurance field as an employer when Congress enacted in 1959 the Federal Employees Health Benefit Program. This program operates through third-party private insurers. Government entered the health care field as an insurer in 1965, when the first health insurance provisions were added to the Social Security Act. Since then, federal involvement in the financing and delivery of health services has grown rapidly with the enactment of dozens of programs to improve access to health care. The Carter administration proposed the National Health Plan, which was to insure all Americans against the high costs of medical care and expected it to be implemented in 1983. In the interim, the administration added programs such as Adolescent Health Services, Child Health Assurance Program (CHAP), and the Pregnancy Prevention Program. In addition, under a new federal requirement, some 155 million full-time workers and their families will be covered by employer-provided insurance that limits annual out-of-pocket expenditures for covered services to $2500 per family; covers employees and/or their dependents for 90 days after termination of employment, death of the employee, divorce or separation; and provides the right to convert employer coverage to individual policies at reasonable rates. Employers will pay at least 75 percent of the premium costs for mandated coverage. Federal subsidies will be provided to these low-income working families to offset their share of premium costs and to employers whose payroll costs would be inordinately increased by the guarantee.

It is often claimed that health insurance systems, public or private, tend to increase health care costs. "Costs tend to be viewed as less significant when paid by an insurance company or governmental agency than if paid by the patient directly. Providers appear to be willing to incur substantial costs to improve the reliability of a diagnosis or chance of recovery only minimally."[23]

The existence of health insurance, as with all insurance, changes the "moral hazard" problem. In the health care field, in which it is difficult to judge the merit of increased "quality," this problem seems to be acute.

Between 1969 and 1978, hospital expenditures in the United States zoomed 198 percent, reaching $80 billion and accounting for 40 percent of all health care costs. Over the same period, the consumer price index increased by less than half that rate (80 percent).

Property Insurance

One reason for the increase in both government and third-party health coverage, paid at least partly by the employee, has been the general tendency to call for reductions of risk. There are pressures to transfer risks from the individual to a larger group. At the same time, this tendency reduces the willingness of private firms to assume risk. In many instances, when private insurers are not available, the government has to step in. Several property insurance agencies are examples of the trend. The insured loan agencies were established to insure or guarantee loans granted by the government. Thus, the Rural Development Insurance Fund established October 1, 1972, guarantees loans for water systems and waste-disposal facilities, community facilities, and industrial development in rural areas pursuant to Section 116 of Public Law 92-419. The Agricultural Credit Insurance Fund insures or guarantees farm ownership, soil and water, and farm operation *to individuals;* it also insures loans to *associations* for irrigation and drainage projects, watershed, and flood prevention. In 1979, its operations had a volume of $8 billion.

The Federal Deposit Insurance Corporation insures *deposits* in banks up to $100,000. FDIC may, in return, supervise and regulate member bank transactions. Most FDIC members are state banks, which are *not* members of the Federal Reserve System. The Veteran Loan Guaranty Revolving Fund is expected to guarantee or insure 362,850 loans in 1981. The Students Loan Insurance Fund subsidizes and insures loans granted to students under Public Law 96-123. The federal government pays up to 7 percent interest on the loans while students are in school and during a twelve months' grace period following graduation or withdrawal from school. In addition, the government pays lenders an outstanding loans allowance calculated at 3.5 percent below the 90-day Treasury bill rate. The federal government is also liable for costs associated with the defaults, death, disability, or bankruptcy of insured students. The default rate on the federal program in 1980 is estimated at 14.9 percent. Total costs for claims and interest subsidies amounted to about $1.7 billion. The figures in the Appendix represent only the insurance cost, not the cost of the interest subsidies program. The figures do not represent another program for health education assistance, administered by the Department of Health and Human Services.

A government-sponsored enterprise, the Students Loan Marketing Association (SLMA), was created in 1972 to expand funds available to students by providing a secondary market for insured students loans. Legislation has been proposed to create within the Department of Education a Government Student Loan Association (GSLA) to administer all student loan programs and convert the federal and state guaranteed loan programs into a supplemental loan program in partnership with state guarantee agencies.

The Federal Savings and Loan Insurance Corporation insures savings in federal savings and loan associations and in state-chartered institutions of the savings and loan type (as opposed to banks). Again, the deposits of savers are insured up to $100,000 per account. FSLIC can make loans to associates in financial difficulty. It functions under the Federal Home Loan Bank Board. In 1979 FSLIC insured 4043 member institutions, with a potential liability of $453.3 billion. The corporation is self-supporting; its revenues and other receipts have been sufficient to meet all insurance losses and expenses, leaving a reserve for contingencies of $5752.8 million as of September 30, 1979.

Federal Housing Administration funds are made up of four different mortgage insurances. The Mutual Mortgage Insurance Fund is a mutual fund that provides for the Department of Housing and Urban Development's basic single-family mortgage insurance program. The Cooperative Management Housing Insurance Fund is another mutual fund, providing mortgage insurance for management-type cooperatives.

The general insurance fund provides for a large number of specialized mortgage insurance programs including the insurance of loans for property improvements, cooperatives, condominiums, housing for the elderly, land development, group-practice medical facilities, and nonprofit hospitals. The special-risk insurance fund provides mortgage insurance on behalf of mortgagors eligible for interest-reduction payments who otherwise would not be eligible for mortgage insurance. In addition, the fund provides insurance on mortgages covering experimental housing as well as insurance for high-risk mortgagors who normally would not be eligible for mortgage insurance.

The Rural Housing Insurance Fund was established in 1965, pursuant to the Housing Act of 1949 as amended (Public Law 89-117). It insures or guarantees rural housing loans, loans for rural rental and cooperative housing, and farm labor housing loans. Beginning in 1978, rental assistance payments were also made from the fund, and a special Home Ownership Assistance Program (HOAP) was scheduled for implementation in 1981.

The Federal Ship Financing Fund guarantees construction loans and mortgages on U.S. flag vessels built in the United States. In 1979, the Maritime Appropriation Authorization Act increased the limitation on guaranteed obligations outstanding from $7 billion to $10 billion.

Credit Union Share Insurance Fund, authorized by Public Law 91-468, enacted October 19, 1970, is a similar body to the FDIC and FSLIC, for credit unions chartered by federal and state governments. The fund is supposed to be self-supporting through contributions from approximately 18,000 member credit unions. The Indian Loan Guaranty and Insurance Fund was established pursuant to the Indian Financing Act of 1974. Its purpose is to insure or guarantee loans made by commercial lending institutions to Indians. The interest rate is subsidized, thereby reducing the cost to the borrower. The estimated cumulative balance of guarantees outstanding at the end of 1980 is $68 million.

Aviation insurance is authorized under Title XIII of the Federal Aviation Act. The fund provides aviation insurance in wartime and under certain situations short of war. The government also provides insurance for U.S. air carriers used in connection with certain Department of Defense and Department of State contract operations.

The federal government insures farmers against losses due to insect and wildlife damage, plant diseases, fire and drought, flood, wind, and other weather conditions. Federal crop insurance in 1981 is estimated to be in force in 1676 U.S. counties, and the crop insured is estimated at about $2.7 billion. Crop insurance is handled by the Federal Crop Insurance Corporation. By law, premium rates do not reflect direct costs of loss adjustment, administrative or operating expenses, marketing, and collection. Crop insurance is taken by about 50 percent of farmers, and 13 percent have all-risk crop insurance. From 1948 to 1975, loss ratios in excess of 100 percent were incurred in about half the years, and underwriting gains were experienced in the remaining years. About half the total number of crops, 11 out of 23, produced aggregate loss ratios in excess of 100 percent over the 1948-75 period; but no single crop produced losses continuously over the period. Thus, farmers in some crops are subsidizing farmers of other crops; and it seems that farmers have a strong desire to transfer to others some of the risks of farming. Legislation proposed for a nationwide all-risk crop insurance program would combine insurance provisions of the Federal Crop Insurance Act and the U.S. Department of Agriculture low-yield payments program to protect farmers against losses when natural or uncontrollable conditions adversely affect yield.

Private insurers view flood risk as uninsurable because of adverse selection: only those subject to heavy losses from flood tend to take coverage, and catastrophic losses cannot be spread over a larger number of clients. Aware of the unavailability of private insurance against flood, Congress first passed a flood insurance bill in 1956, but later refused to finance it. After further studies, Congress passed the Housing and Urban Development Act of 1968. It created a government-controlled corporation, the Federal Insurance Administration, to work in cooperation with private enterprise. For a variety of reasons, relatively little insurance was purchased at first. In 1972, Hurricane Agnes caused over $2 billion of flood loss to the eastern seaboard of the United States; only $5 million was paid out in damages under National Flood Insurance. Congress then provided generous relief through its Small Business Administration disaster-loan program. Residents and businesses suffering damages were able to obtain forgiveness grants up to the first $5000 of loss, and loans at 1 percent annual rate for the remaining portion. The Small Business Administration approved $1.2 billion for victims of Hurricane Agnes, out of which over $540 million was in the form of forgiveness grants, which did not have to be repaid.

Hurricane Agnes had at least two results: first, a presidential Task Force was formed to compare the costs and benefits of federal disaster relief with those of an insurance program. Congress also conducted an extensive set of hearings and appraisals. The result of all this was the passage, in April 1973, of a new flood insurance law (the Flood Disaster Protection Act of 1973) in which subsidized coverage more than doubled. At the same time, the insurance became compulsory. Congress insisted that all construction in designated flood-prone areas receiving federal financial assistance be covered by flood insurance. Buildings in flood-prone areas constructed with federal financial assistance had to participate in the flood insurance program or be denied disaster-relief funds in federally related financing.

At the same time, the publicity brought about by Hurricane Agnes apparently increased the sales of federal insurance. Flood coverage increased from about $1.5 billion to $4 billion. By 1977, after the element of compulsion was added, the coverage increased to $7.5 billion, and more than 1.1 million policies were in force. In 1979, there were 1.7 million policies in force and the insurance in force was for $67.2 billion. In 1981, the number of policies is estimated to increase to 2.1 million while the insurance in force is estimated to be $81.2 billion. Insured flood losses and associated loss adjustment for 1981 are estimated at $209 million.

Up to 1978, the Federal Insurance Administration operated the flood insurance program in partnership with private industry. A pool of private insurers, the National Flood Insurance Association, underwrote the coverage with government bearing the subsidized premiums; private insurance agents distributed the coverage. This partnership was terminated in 1978, and a separate government corporation was set up to operate the program for the Federal Insurance Administration. In 1979, the Federal Insurance Administration was abolished and its functions transferred to a new agency—the Federal Emergency Management Agency. This agency is responsible for emergency planning, preparedness, and mobilization, including stock piling. It is responsible for different programs of hazard mitigation and disaster assistance, including among others those administered under the Flood Insurance Protection Act of 1968, Flood Disaster Protection Act of 1973, Urban Property Protection and Reinsurance Act of 1968 (as amended), Disaster Relief Act of 1974, Earthquake Hazard Reduction Act of 1977, and Federal Fire Prevention and Control Act of 1974. The programs established under the Urban Property Protection and Reinsurance Act of 1968 are described below.

Insurance Against Crime and Civil Disorder

In 1968 Congress authorized the establishment of special state plans, known as FAIR, which would qualify for federally sponsored reinsurance.[24] This program was designed to facilitate the establishment of a private insurance capacity at "affordable rates" against loss to property located in areas not eligible for coverage from private insurers on a regular basis. Congress felt that as a result of riots and other disturbances, private insurers withdrew from offering coverage at reasonable rates in large sections of urban areas in the United States. It hoped to restore private coverage by offering reinsurance. Following this legislation, twenty-six states adopted FAIR plans; the volume of premiums written grew steadily, reaching total premiums in 1976 of $193.5 million, a 75 percent increase over the 1974 level. Reinsurance premiums have declined from over $35 million to only slightly more than $1 million in 1976. In spite of subsidized rates, FAIR plans were unprofitable for commercial insurers. They lost a total of $260 million from 1968 to 1976, or about 28 percent of premiums collected on insurance under the FAIR plans. These losses were covered ultimately by larger premiums paid by the purchasers of fire and liability insurance. Private insurers apparently no longer wish to utilize the federal reinsurance program in significant volume. In 1979 the National Insurance Development Fund collected $1.9 million in premiums. Claims paid through riot and civil disorder reinsurance were estimated at $1.5 million.

When it created the FAIR plans, Congress also authorized the establishment of a federal government crime insurance to include robbery, burglary, and larceny insurance. Storekeepers' burglary and robbery, plus business interruption insurance, were also included if the Secretary of Health, Education, and Welfare so designated. In contrast to FAIR plans, crime insurance is sold directly to the customer. This was the first case in which Congress authorized the federal government to underwrite a form of property insurance, which previously had been exclusively handled by the private insurance market. The Federal Insurance Administration was directed to conduct studies to determine in which states crime insurance was not being offered at "affordable rates," defined as rates that "would permit the purchase of a specific type of insurance coverage by a reasonably prudent person in similar circumstances, with due regard to the costs and benefits involved."[25] The Federal Insurance Administration encountered difficulties in convincing insurance agents and brokers to sell these policies; they were often reluctant to attempt to sell coverage because other policies in these same areas were difficult to place in the commercial insurance market. In addition, the crime program required rather strict safety and loss prevention measures in order to qualify for coverage. Thus this program covers a very small percentage of the needs.

Crime remains one of the most underinsured risks in the United States. For example, the Federal Bureau of Investigation estimated property stolen in the United States in 1975 to be valued at $3.2 billion, only $961 million of which was recovered. In 1975 the total cost of violent crime was estimated by the FBI at $80 billion.[26] Yet the total premiums collected by commercial insurers under burglary and theft policies are estimated for that year to be $120 million. It is clear that only a small portion of total loss exposure is insured. A large percentage of the violent crimes is concentrated in large metropolitan areas, and the victimized are very often old people and the poor. Federal crime insurance does not insure against most violent crimes and did not solve the problem even on those crimes insured by it. It was offered in nearly half the states, but the volume of policies sold has been minimal and has been concentrated in only a few states. Crime insurance has been sold mainly in New York, Massachusetts, Pennsylvania, and Florida; these four states account for about 80 percent of the policies in force. In 1979 premiums earned were $12.3 million and are estimated at $14.8 million for 1980. The program suffered a net loss of $12.4 million in 1979 and the loss for 1980 is estimated at $13.9 million.

Crimes of violence have increased rapidly since the 1950s. According to the FBI, violent crimes increased 120 percent in the ten years from 1966 to 1975.[27] One can argue that it is the duty of the state to provide police protection to each citizen. If it fails to fulfill this obligation, it should indemnify the injured victim for the losses resulting from crime. Such compensation will reduce the lost output due to insecurity, unemployment, and social disruption caused by uncompensated losses. In addition, society will gain because victims of violent crime will be required to report crimes promptly and cooperate with the authorities, thus helping law enforcement officials to increase the rate of apprehension and reduce crime.

Yet, at the present time, there is no federal crime victim compensation program. Senator Yarborough of Texas sponsored such legislation in 1965; since then, bills have been introduced in every session of the Congress. Bill

S.750, sponsored by Senator Mike Mansfield and introduced to the Senate on September 18, 1972, was passed by the Senate but not by the House. Some states, however, have started such programs.

The first state laws designed to aid victims of violent crime and their dependents were enacted in 1966 in California and New York. Since then, an additional seventeen states have established some form of victim compensation program. Four additional states have limited statutes for this purpose. The state violence compensation laws compensate victims for medical expenses and loss of income. Property losses are not covered by any state. States limit the amount of compensation, generally to $10,000 and in some cases to $25,000. Maryland has a $45,000 limit and Ohio $50,000. New York and Washington laws impose no limits.

The life insurance agencies listed in the Appendix are mainly for veterans having service-connected disabilities or for other groups of servicemen. The federal government makes grants to state agencies, which pay unemployment compensation to eligible workers. It also pays the states for unemployment compensation to eligible former federal employees and adjustment assistance under the Trade Expansion Act of 1962 and the Trade Act of 1974. All state and federal unemployment tax receipts are deposited in the Unemployment Trust Fund and invested in government securities until needed for benefit payments or administrative costs. State and federal unemployment taxes and deposits by the Railroad Retirement Board were approximately $15 billion in 1979 and were estimated at approximately $17 and $19 billion respectively for 1980 and 1981.

There are several additional insurance funds in the U.S. federal government budget. Most of them are small and of an administrative nature. Thus, the Check Forgery Insurance Fund is for use by the U.S. Treasury in making settlements with payees or special endorsees of checks drawn on the U.S. Treasury that have been paid by forged endorsement. Many more insurance operations are registered in the budget as guaranty programs or in other names. These will be discussed separately.

Rationale for Government Insurance

The rationale of all federal insurance programs has been either that private insurance is unavailable or that an element of compulsion is needed.[28] George K. Bernstein, former director of the Federal Insurance Administration, stated:

> . . . the fact that government should resist assuming those responsibilities which can be executed more appropriately by the private sector, does not alter the fact that, in the area of insurance, governmental involvement has

been required with increasing frequency to meet the valid needs of our nation. And there is every indication that this involvement will grow, rather than diminish, in the years ahead unless fundamental marketing reforms are undertaken by the insurance industry itself.[29]

The alleged justification for compulsion is that individuals fail to appreciate the risks involved. As already shown, this argument is the major rationale for the Old Age and Retirement program and the flood insurance program. In other programs, the rationale seems to be political expediency, as with crop insurance, or existence of some social purpose, as with workers' compensation.

Government insurance is sometimes offered on an ad hoc basis. Flu vaccination is a case in point. Swine flu broke out in 1976 on a military post at Fort Dix, New Jersey. President Ford recommended to Congress a $135 million national vaccination program. Most of the government health experts believed that the probability of a large-scale swine flu outbreak was not more than 2 percent. Yet government officials felt that even that small chance should not be tolerated. A vaccination program was undertaken.

During the period in which the vaccination program was discussed, manufacturers perceived the risk of litigation in cases of adverse reactions to the vaccine as much too high. Private insurance firms testified before Congress that there could be between 3.8 million and 10.0 million adverse reactions to the vaccine, which could result in claims of between $9.5 billion and $25 billion in defense costs alone, not to mention actual damage awards. Private insurers were reluctant to offer complete liability coverage to manufacturers without government guarantees. The government finally agreed to accept most of the risk of product-liability suits.

Four drug manufacturers were required to accept $2.5 million each of initial liability, and private insurers accepted an additional $55 million of liability, or $220 million for all four manufacturers. Any amount above that was to be paid by the government, which bore the major risk of product-liability suits resulting from the program.

In fact, no outbreak of swine flu occurred, and the vaccination later proved to be unnecessary. It is therefore impossible to estimate the probable cost of this particular government insurance.

Another example is that of nuclear energy risks. In 1957, the Price-Anderson Act authorized government liability insurance in atomic energy installations in the amount of $560 million. This was established as the maximum liability for which private corporations would be held liable in a single nuclear accident. The act was challenged in federal court in 1977, and the $560 million limitation was declared unconstitutional. However, the lower court ruling was reversed by the U.S. Supreme Court in 1978.[30] Under the Price-Anderson Act, liability for nuclear energy risks is covered by a joint pool of private and government funds. Private insurance is limited to $5 million for each nuclear plant. As the number of new power plants increases, the private insurance capacity will equal or exceed the $560 million limit, and the government liability will be eliminated.

As of now, despite a high level of subjective risks in society concerning nuclear energy, the total amount paid because of nuclear accidents has been very low. Between 1957 and 1973, only twenty-four nuclear incidents were reported to insurance companies, none of which arose out of the operation of nuclear reactors. Over that period, total losses related to nuclear exposure paid by private insurers amounted to less than $1 million. The size of total liabilities caused by the Three Mile Island accident is not yet known.

The insurance programs discussed above are those in which premiums are calculated and the government finances the insurance from earmarked revenues. Again, in most governmentally operated insurance programs, premiums are neither collected nor calculated. Risks are shifted from the individual, and the program is financed through general government revenues, by budgetary deficits, or through invisible methods. As a result, government expenditures grow. A further consequence of the insurance state has been changes in laws and regulations, establishing minimum standards (e.g., for safety), shifting risks (e.g., product-liability laws), or protecting firms against the risk of new entrants (e.g., some regulatory commissions). These changes will be discussed later. Let us now look at the tip of the iceberg—the increase in governmental expenditures.

Increased Expenditures

In 1902 total expenditures at all levels of government in the United States amounted to $1.66 billion. Of this sum, $572 million was accounted for by federal and $1088 million by state and local government disbursements. By 1977, total government expenditures had multiplied 410 times, to $680 billion.

Of course some of this increase can be attributed to population growth and inflation, but certainly nowhere near all of it: per capita expenditures, for example, have gone up more than 127 times, from $21 in 1902 to $79 in 1932, $837 in 1960, $1625 in 1970, and $2674 in 1976. The absolute level of the increase in governmental expenditures may be a poor indicator. Let us focus, therefore, on the relations among expenditures and the GNP.

Leaving aside the sums spent on the expansion of public education, the government's share of the GNP expenditure had not grown substantially between the Civil War and 1932. Since then, it has increased dramatically: from 10.0 percent in 1929, it went to 18.4 percent in 1940, 21.3 percent in 1950, 27.0 percent in 1960, 31.7 percent in 1970, and 36 percent in 1977. Nor is this phenomenon restricted to the United States. In Germany the proportion of gross national product represented by government expenditure has gone from 30.4 percent in 1965 to 41.1 percent in 1976. In Belgium the share increased in the same period from 29.8 percent to 42.1 percent; in the Netherlands, from approximately 33 percent to 52.2 percent.

At the same time revenues have also risen. In some industrialized countries, taxes comprised more than half of gross national product at factor cost in 1974. According to estimates prepared by the British Treasury, taxes (including social security payments but excluding capital taxes) were 53.4 percent of the GNP at factor cost in Denmark, 52.9 percent in Norway, 50.6 percent in the Netherlands, 49.1 percent in Sweden, 41.1 percent in France, 39.7 percent in Canada, 38.7 percent in the United Kingdom, and 32.0 percent in the United States. Based on the slightly different classification of the UN system of national accounts, West Germany collected 42.5 percent and Japan 24.6 percent.[31]

In the United States, national defense expenditures were the major reason for the increase in government expenditures in the 1950s. As a result of the cold war and the Korean war in 1950, defense expenditures grew from 4 percent of GNP in 1948 to 13 percent in 1953. Nondefense expenditures remained stable at the 1948 level. To be sure, due to the military buildup, government purchases of goods and services increased from 12 percent of GNP in 1948 to 22 percent in 1953. From 1954 to 1966, government expenditures were around 27 or 28 percent of GNP; defense expenditures around 9 to 10 percent; nondefense expenditures were around 19 percent. Government purchases of goods and services for that period were around 21 percent of GNP.

Since 1965, however, government expenditures have zoomed from 27 percent of GNP to about a third of GNP in 1976. Over the same period, defense expenditures have been reduced to about 6 to 7 percent of GNP, and government purchases of goods and services have stayed around 21 percent. The big jump has occurred in transfer payments, which were around 7 percent of GNP until the mid-1960s. In 1970, they were 9.5 percent, and in 1977 they reached almost 12 percent of GNP.

Transfer payments are payments made to individuals from taxes collected by government, generally as risk-reduction devices designed to mitigate hardship. The most important and most familiar of these in the United States are unemployment compensation, Aid to Families with Dependent Children (AFDC), social security, Medicaid, Medicare, and food stamps. These transfer payments are categorized as government expenditures but are not included in estimates of GNP. Still, while it is sometimes useful to differentiate between productive (goods and services) expenditures and transfer payments, it is well to remember that the real costs of a government's operation ought to include the value of private goods and services foregone to secure public benefits. Since transfer payments are made out of taxes imposed on some members of the community and therefore represent goods or services foregone, they should for all practical purposes be counted as part of the public sector. The dominance of insurance activities in the federal government domestic transfer payments is illustrated in table 4.1.

The increase in transfer payments is only one manifestation of the change in government's role. Far more dramatic has been the shift in the relative proportions of governmental budgetary outlays. In the United States, the most traditional category of outlay—law enforcement and justice—amounted to less than 1 percent of the federal budget in 1981; defense and international affairs declined from 51.6 percent of the total actual federal budget in 1960 to only 25.3 percent of the estimated total for the fiscal year 1981; education, manpower, and social services, health, income security, and veterans benefits and services rose from 27.3 percent in fiscal year 1960 to 54.6 percent of the estimated budget for fiscal year 1981. Income security alone accounted for 35.7 percent of the estimated 1981 budget.

The extent of the shift in governmental activities is even more vividly demonstrated in table 4.2, in which expenditures are shown according to major functions.

From 1969 to 1979, the federal budget of the United States increased 271 percent, from $184.5 billion to $500 billion. During the same period, the income security part of the budget swelled 429 percent, from $37.3 billion to $160 billion or from 20 to 38 percent of the total budget. This is only a partial picture of the increase in insurance. Thus, payments to retired military personnel are shown in the budget as part of the defense budget. From 1969 to 1979, these payments jumped 421 percent, from $2.4 billion to $10.1 billion. Disaster relief and insurance, less than $.1 billion in 1969, increased 10 times, to more than $1 billion. Consumer and occupational health and safety increased 450 percent, and so did the budget for health care; these last two items were $10.2 billion in 1969 and $46 billion in 1979. If one adds to these items the farm income stabilization, pollution control, and income security for veterans (classified officially under veterans benefits), the total for 1969 was $61 billion, or 33 percent of the budget, while the 1979 total was $236.2 billion, comprising more than 47 percent of all federal outlays.

Still other costs of insurance are shown as part of other governmental departments and agencies, such as the National Transportation Safety Board,

TABLE 4.2. FEDERAL BUDGET OUTLAYS BY FUNCTIONS, 1969-81
(percent of total budget)

	1969	1973	1976	1979	1980	1981
National Defense and International Affairs	45.5	31.8	26.0	23.7	23.5	24.9
Income Security	20.2	29.5	34.6	33.4	34.0	35.0
Health	6.4	7.6	9.1	9.4	9.2	9.9
Veterans Benefits	4.1	4.9	5.0	3.4	3.2	3.2
General Science	2.7	1.6	1.2	1.0	1.0	1.0
Energy	0.5	0.5	0.8	1.3	3.5	1.0
Natural Resources and Environment	1.5	1.9	2.2	2.3	1.9	1.9
Agriculture	3.1	2.0	0.7	1.6	0.8	0.8
Commerce, Housing, Transportation	3.8	4.0	4.7	4.4	4.5	4.1
Community and Regional Development, Education, Social Services and Employment	4.9	5.3	6.4	7.4	6.0	6.2
Administration of Justice and General Government	1.3	1.9	1.7	1.5	1.4	1.3
Interest	8.6	9.2	9.5	9.2	9.7	9.4
General Purpose Fiscal Assistance	0.2	3.0	2.0	1.4	1.3	1.3
TOTAL	100.0	100.0	100.0	100.0	100.0	100.0

SOURCE: Calculated from federal budgets.

the Nuclear Regulatory Commission, the Occupational Safety and Health Administration, Mine Safety and Health Administration, the Environmental Protection Agency, the Occupational Safety and Health Review Commission, and the Consumer Products Safety Commission—all of which started operations in the last decade.

The federal budget is, of course, only part of total governmental expenditures. The breakdown of all these expenditures is shown in tables 4.3 and 4.4. Again, the increasing insurance operations can easily be seen. Defense and international relations dropped from more than a quarter of total governmental expenditures in 1950 to 18 percent in 1976 (and further to 15.5 in 1977). The social security expenditures grew at the same time from less than 1 percent of total expenditures to almost 16 percent. When unemployment compensation and employee retirement are added, the percent jumps from 1 percent in 1950 to almost 25 percent of the total in 1976. Further, all public income-maintenance programs were 6.5 percent of personal income in 1960. That ratio almost doubled, and in 1976 income-maintenance programs were more than 11 percent of personal income. As another indicator, social insurance programs were less than $5 billion in 1950, or $75 per capita in constant 1976 dollars. In 1960, these programs cost $19.3 billion, or $192 per capita. By 1970, the costs swelled to $54.7 billion, or $375 per capita. In 1976, the costs of these programs zoomed to almost $147 billion, or $669 for each man, woman, and child in the United States. Public social insurance thus increased nine times in a quarter of a century, and has been growing since then.

Again, social insurance programs are only a minute portion of the total costs of public insurance coverage. For example, all social welfare expenditures were 8.9 percent of GNP in 1950 and 10.5 percent in 1960. They doubled in 1976, to 20.6 percent of GNP. In addition, government operated in the last two decades many more economic insurance programs: stabilization of farm prices, safety standards, and protection of firms against the risks of competition. Most of these insurance programs are not registered in the budget or in official statistics of governmental expenditures.

In other industrialized countries, the budgetary share of the GNP was even higher, and the change in the composition of expenditures was at least as dramatic. In the United Kingdom, military defense as a percentage of governmental final consumption expenditure dropped from 37.9 percent in 1960 to 23.2 percent in 1977; in the same period, health and education increased from 35.2 percent to 42.8 percent, and social security and other social services from 7.0 percent to 11.2 percent. From 1960 to 1977 in the Netherlands, health and education expenditures increased as a percentage of governmental final consumption expenditure from 27.4 percent to 37.7 percent and in Belgium from 30.5 percent to 39.6 percent while national defense expenditures dropped from

TABLE 4.3. GOVERNMENTAL EXPENDITURES FOR MAJOR FUNCTIONS, 1950-77
(in billions of dollars)

	1950	1960	1965	1970	1973	1974	1975	1976	1977
Defense and International Relations	18.4	48.9	55.8	84.3	83.0	85.4	93.9	98.0	105.6
Education	9.6	19.4	29.6	55.8	74.9	81.7	95.0	106.3	110.6
Insurance Benefits and Repayments	6.9	17.6	24.9	48.5	75.3	86.7	109.2	129.4	144.1
(of which: OASI & Health Insurance)	.7	10.8	16.6	35.8	56.4	64.7	76.6	86.3	n.a.
Interest on General Debt	4.9	9.3	11.4	18.4	25.1	30.1	33.8	39.6	44.7
Public Welfare[1]	3.0	4.5	6.4	17.5	27.0	31.0	39.4	45.1	49.5
Health and Hospitals	2.8	5.2	7.7	13.6	18.7	21.7	24.9	27.5	30.0
Natural Resources	5.0	7.1	11.0	11.5	16.7	17.4	18.1	19.4	23.4
(of which: Stabilization of Farm Income)	2.7	3.4	5.8	4.3	6.0	4.1	2.4	1.3	2.2
TOTAL EXPENDITURES	70.3	151.3	205.6	330.0	389.7	478.3	560.1	625.1	680.3

SOURCE: U.S. Bureau of the Census, *Statistical Abstract of the United States, 1978*, p. 288; *1979*, p. 284.

1. Including old-age assistance, aid to families with dependent children, aid to the blind, aid to the disabled, cash assistance for general relief, medical and other public welfare programs.

TABLE 4.4. GOVERNMENTAL EXPENDITURES FOR MAJOR FUNCTIONS, 1950-77
(by percent of total)

	1950	1960	1965	1970	1973	1974	1975	1976	1977
Defense and International Relations	26.2	32.3	27.1	25.3	19.0	18.2	17.2	16.0	15.5
Education	13.7	12.8	14.4	16.8	17.1	17.1	17.0	17.0	16.2
Insurance Benefits and Repayments	1.0	11.6	12.1	14.6	17.2	18.1	19.1	20.8	21.2
(of which: OASI & Health Insurance)	1.0	7.1	8.1	10.7	12.9	13.6	13.7	14.1	n.a.
Interest on General Debt	7.0	6.1	5.5	5.5	5.7	6.3	6.1	6.2	6.6
Public Welfare[1]	4.3	3.0	3.1	5.3	6.2	6.5	7.1	7.2	7.3
Health and Hospitals	4.0	3.4	3.7	4.1	4.3	4.5	4.5	4.4	4.4
Natural Resources	7.1	4.7	5.3	3.5	3.8	3.3	2.9	2.7	3.5
(of which: Stabilization of Farm Income)	3.8	2.2	2.8	1.3	1.4	.9	.4	.2	.3
TOTAL EXPENDITURES	100.0	100.0	100.0	100.0	100.0	100.0	100.0	100.0	100.0

SOURCE: Calculated from table 4.3

from 29.2 percent to 16.4 percent in the Netherlands and from 37.7 percent to 16.2 percent in Belgium. In Australia during the same period, national defense expenditures increased from 17.7 percent to 19.9 percent of governmental final consumption expenditure, but health and education expenditures increased from 33.9 percent to 50.8 percent.[32]

The figures above include education services together with insurance programs. But even if we confine ourselves to expenditures connected only with reduction of risk, we find the same trend. In all developed countries insurance coverage has been extended, a larger percentage of the costs have been covered by publicly financed programs, and program costs have been increasing. The increased cost of reduction of risk to individuals is the major reason for the swelling size of government.

It has recently become fashionable in the United States to attack "big government" and blame it for all evils. Government is perceived as inefficient, corrupt, and unable to lead the nation in making hard choices. Many have called for a return to the days of laissez-faire, for the restoration of the American dream, or for a constitutional amendment forcing limits on government spending. Some of these calls are written in forceful language, questioning almost all governmental operations. Yet many of those who preach a shrinking government are precisely those who demand more services, more benefits, and protection against more risks. Americans have to realize that even the United States is not a land of boundless resources. If the government is forced to supply more insurance services, it has to collect the "premiums." The results are not only high taxes but rampaging inflation and receding productivity. The pernicious price spiral in the last decade has been one of the direct results of the increasing demands for protection. In the insurance state, competitiveness has declined and efficiency has been reduced. Attempts to increase insurance have resulted in government deficit spending and an increasing money supply—the surest way to create inflation.

Americans are facing a very important choice. To what extent do they feel they have become affluent enough so that risks should be reduced and chances avoided, and how far do they believe in the old ideals of rugged individualism and competitive spirit? If risk reduction is preferred, then government must be bigger and taxes must be high. Productivity will be lower, costs will increase, and growth will stop. For example, if Americans do not want to have nuclear energy, be exposed to the health dangers of coal mining, or be dependent on oil imports, the only solution is a drastic cut in the use of energy, with all its ramifications in the daily life of each and every American. Moreover, reduced risks means support for ailing industries and troubled firms, perpetuation of inefficiency, and an ever increasing government.

On the other hand, if more production, more growth, and stable prices are desired, then many costly government insurance programs have to be scrapped. A few catastrophic risks can be reduced through incentives provided by the marketplace—for example, by offering lower private insurance rates to those who follow certain safety rules. However, many of the standards, regulations, and programs of risk avoidance and shifting will have to be abolished. In particular, all regulations protecting producers against competition should be curtailed. A country that wants to grow cannot afford to pay its farmers hundreds of millions of dollars for not planting crops, nor can it tolerate regulations allowing incompetent and inefficient producers to flourish in a public hotbed, nor can it insure individuals against their own folly. Accelerating growth requires boosting productivity, stimulating research and development, and a surge in savings.

Savings can be stimulated by offering savers higher rates of interest, as well as by exempting interest on savings accounts from taxes. The rate of savings in the United States is lower than that of any other Western country; it declined from 7.4 percent in 1970 to 5.2 percent of after-tax income in 1978. This savings rate might be compared with the Japanese 20 percent. It is sometimes claimed that the low rate of savings has been caused by excessive social security. Although true to some extent, this is only a part of the picture. Europeans save 13 to 17 percent of their disposable income despite highly developed social welfare systems. The reason for lower American savings is much simpler: the low interest rate paid on savings accounts makes it irrational to save in the United States.

All attempts to reduce risk or insure against its consequences bring certain benefits but also exact direct and indirect costs. Both benefits and costs are not evenly distributed; finding the exact distribution of costs and benefits is not easy, partially because those who pay the "insurance premiums" attempt to shift these costs to others. The final incidence of costs (and benefits) is not always clear. Further, the more people are protected, the more salient the "moral hazard." Some indirect costs exacted by insurance schemes are higher expenditures for goods assumed to be free, or less interest in the efficiency of operations. This last point holds true for workers whose jobs are guaranteed and for employers whose market share is protected against competition. Insurance schemes, whether public or private, sometimes cause a deterioration of the moral fibers of society, or they may cause a substantial reduction in the propensity of individuals to save, which may result in shortage of capital for investment. Finally, too much insurance and risk-reduction does not allow the Schumpeterian "constructive destruction" to operate; there is much less incentive for innovation either in new products or in cost-cutting methods. All these costs must be weighed carefully against the obvious, even laudable, benefits of many schemes, and the distribution of the costs and the benefits must conform with the values of the individuals in any specific society. Unfortunately, rights are often interpreted as the right to collect, not the right to pay. Each individual tries to shift the costs to others, while tilting the benefits to himself or herself.

The result of all these demands for insurance has been an increase in government expenditures. However, since rising expenditures are resented, government is forced to add invisible methods to outright budgetary allocations. One characteristic of the modern state is precisely this use of "invisible government" to hide the distribution of economic costs and benefits, to shift the burden of risk, and to influence the allocation of resources.

NOTES

1. FDIC derives its income principally from insurance assessments paid by insured banks and from interest on investment in U.S. government securities. As of 30 September 1979, the deposit insurance fund amounted to $9.6 billion.
2. Mark R. Greene, "The Government as an Insurer," *Journal of Risk and Insurance* 43, no. 3 (September 1976): 393.
3. Total premium income collected by private property, health, and liability insurance in 1977, according to *Insurance Facts, 1978*, was $72.4 billion. Private life insurance premiums were $72.3 billion (*Life Insurance Fact Book, 1978*). Total for all private insurance therefore was $144.7 billion. The federal government collected in that year premiums of $123.3 billion.
4. Mark R. Greene, *Risk and Insurance* (3rd. ed.; Cincinnati, Ohio: Southwestern Publishing, 1977), table 5-1.
5. Washington, Ohio, West Virginia, North Dakota, Nevada, and Wyoming.
6. Greene, "The Government as an Insurer," p. 394.
7. Alicia H. Munnell, *The Future of Social Security* (Washington, D.C.: Brookings Institution, 1977), p. 1.
8. *The Budget of the United States,* Fiscal Year 1980, Appendix pp. 472, 474; 1981, Appendix pp. 485, 488.
9. Robert I. Mehr, "Changing Responsibility for Personal Risks and Societal Consequences: Premature Death and Old Age," *Annals of the AAPSS* 443 (May 1979): 6.
10. Ibid., p. 8.
11. For a technical discussion, see Munnell, *Future of Social Security,* chap. 3 and pp. 144-45.
12. The social security wage base is increased annually in line with increases in the average wage. In 1981, the wage base was $29,700.

13. If they work a minimum number of quarters in an OASDI-covered employment, they may collect both social security and a government pension.

14. See Richard A. Musgrave and Peggy B. Musgrave, *Public Finance in Theory and Practice* (New York: McGraw-Hill, 1973), pp. 390-95.

15. John A. Brittain, *The Payroll Tax for Social Security* (Washington, D.C.: Brookings Institution, 1972), pp. 60-81. For a criticism of this study, see Martin S. Feldstein, "The Incidence of the Social Security Payroll Tax: Comment," *American Economic Review* 62 (September 1972): 735-38. Brittain's reply is in the same issue, pp. 739-42.

16. For a summary, see Munnell, *Future of Social Security*, pp. 62-83.

17. Martin S. Feldstein, "Social Security, Induced Retirement, and Aggregate Capital Accumulation," *Journal of Political Economy* 82 (September-October 1974): 905-26. Feldstein estimated savings in 1969 in the absence of social security to be $89.4 billion as against actual savings of $38.2 billion. On the other hand, Alicia H. Munnell estimated savings in the absence of social security for the same year to be only $41.8 billion. See her *The Effect of Social Security on Personal Savings* (Cambridge, Mass.: Ballinger, 1974), chap. 4. The impact of social security on private savings has been a subject of both theoretical and empirical debate among economists. Barro disagrees with Feldstein, maintaining that social security has had no effect on savings or may have even induced more private savings. See Robert J. Barro, *The Impact of Social Security on Private Saving: Evidence from the U.S. Time Series* (Washington, D.C.: American Enterprise Institute, 1978). See also George M. von Furstenberg, ed., *Social Security versus Private Saving* (Cambridge, Mass.: Ballinger, 1979.).

18. OECD Working Party Number 2, *Public Expenditures on Income Maintenance Programs,* OECD Studies in Resource Allocation Number 3 (Paris, July 1976), p. 89.

19. OECD Working Party Number 2, *Public Expenditures on Health,* OECD Studies in Resource Allocation Number 4 (Paris, July 1977), pp. 28-29.

20. Ibid., p. 86.

21. Joseph G. Simanis and John R. Coleman, "Health Care and Expenditures in Nine Industrialized Countries," *Social Security Bulletin* 43, no. 2 (January 1980): 5.

22. Robert M. Gibson and Charles R. Fisher, "National Health Expenditures, Fiscal Year 1977," *Social Security Bulletin* 41, no. 7 (July 1978): 5.

23. Robert A. Zetten, "Consequences of Increased Third-Party Payments for Health Care Services," *Annals of the AAPSS* 443 (May 1979): 32.

24. Sec. 1102(a) and (b) of Title XI, Urban Property Protection and Reinsurance Act of 1968.

25. Urban Property Protection and Reinsurance Act of 1968, as amended, Sec. 1203(a)(1)(1).

26. Federal Bureau of Investigation, *Crime in the United States,* Uniform Crime Reports 1975 and 1977 (Washington, D.C.: U.S. Government Printing Office, 1976, 1978). The FBI defines violent crime to include murder, forcible rape, robbery, and aggravated assault.

27. Ibid.

28. Greene, "The Government as an Insurer," p. 395.
29. George K. Bernstein, "The Federal Insurance Agency Administrator's Recommendations on High Risk Insurance," a Special Report for the *Journal of Commerce* (undated), p. 20, cited in Greene, "The Government as an Insurer," p. 395.
30. *Carolina Environmental Study Group, Inc.* v. *U.S. Atomic Energy Commission,* 431 F. Supp. 203.
31. Naturally, when social security contributions are excluded, the tax burden is reduced. In 1974, the proportion of taxes excluding social security was 52.4 percent in Denmark, 37.7 percent in Norway, 30.4 percent in the Netherlands, 39.4 percent in Sweden, 24.9 percent in France, 35.9 percent in Canada, and 24.3 percent in the United States. The United Kingdom's proportion was 24.3 percent, according to the revised (1968) method of UN system of national accounts, and 31.4 percent according to the old method as compared with 29.0 percent for West Germany and 20.0 percent for Japan. The figures are quoted from a news item in the *London Times,* 9 September 1977, based on the September edition of the British *Economic Progress Report.*
32. Calculated from OECD, *National Accounts of OECD Countries, 1960-77* (Paris: OECD, 1979), vol. 2.

5. The Invisible Government

Social scientists like to study measurable phenomena so that they can rely on data readily at hand and susceptible to quantification. When the growth of the public sector is discussed, they almost automatically turn to data on such variables as governmental revenues and expenditures as a percent of GNP, or on the distribution of these expenditures among different functions such as defense, welfare, health, education, and housing. Important as these measurements might be, however, they often miss the real issues. Public policy is much more than the size of governmental expenditures or revenues. Most policy goals of government are implemented not through direct budget allocation but through a combination of regulations, laws, and changes in institutional setting.

Suppose, for example, the government wants to increase the income of a certain group of citizens, say, war veterans. One way of doing this would be to pay them educational allowances, such as those granted under the GI Bill. These allowances would be part of the governmental budget and would appear in its published expenditures. Another way would be to restrict some jobs to veterans only. The government could pass a law, regulation, or directive saying that no one would be allowed to operate a taxicab without a license and then issue licenses only to veterans. Since the number of licenses would be restricted, this would produce an artificial scarcity and increase the income of the license holder. But the rise in income would neither appear in the budget nor be recognized as a government expenditure; it would simply be part of the increased price of taking a taxi. The demand for taxi services is relatively elastic, so a monopoly on taxi licenses is certainly no guarantee of unlimited income; nevertheless, it guarantees a reasonable income without adding to the government budget, and it seems fair to assume that most people would be much less disturbed by this licensing policy, if they noticed it at all, than they would be if taxes were raised to pay for a veterans' bonus.

Any requirement for licensing limits entry into a field and is consequently an extremely effective way of adding to the income of chosen individuals or groups. They receive "quasi-property rights," which in some cases cannot be transferred, but in others are perfectly marketable. A citizen of the United

States cannot sell his citizenship, but he can sell his taxi license legally on the open market. The going rate for a medallion allowing the operation of a taxicab in New York City some time ago was more than $25,000. This is not meant to imply that medallions to operate a taxicab in New York are granted only for political tribute or as government largesse. The point is that they could be used in that way. In Israel, for example, both taxicab licenses and licenses to operate gasoline stations are controlled by the government and allocated as a part of a rehabilitation program for disabled war veterans.

At the same time, the remorseless growth of government in Western countries has caused apprehension and uneasiness, mainly manifested in complaints about "big government," particularly among more conservative citizens. But the pressures for more protection do not cease, and in fact often originate among those who complain most bitterly about government interference. The government's bureaucracy and legislators meet with conflicting claims and pressures and have somehow to come up with a policy.

Faced with the impossible task of protecting more citizens against a growing array of risks, while avoiding more taxes that the same citizens complain about, even though the taxes are needed in order to pay for all these insurance schemes, government is compelled to use its coercive power to shift the burden of risk and redistribute costs and benefits in ways that will not affect its measurable size. To do so, it disguises taxes in the form of increased costs of compliance with government regulations rather than boosting tax rates or levying new taxes, and it substitutes hidden forms of aid in lieu of outright budget-recorded subsidy. The measures work as subterfuges, but they also increase the interdependence between the public and the private sectors and blur the distinctions between the two. They have also created a new kind of entrepreneur in the form of the regulation manipulator, whose methods for maximizing profits rest on extracting benefits from government rather than the efficient management of resources.

Quasi Property Rights and Disguised Taxes

In a simple economic model of social choice, all services supplied by the public sector are financed through taxation. In a democratic society, both public revenues and public expenditures are assumed to appear in the budget, and this budget is assumed to be thoroughly scrutinized. Detailed congressional examination and critical decision making are thought to precede approval by the elected representatives of the people in the United States. In reality, this assumption is simply untrue. Many services supplied by the public sector are financed not by taxes but by other, nonfiscal means, and are carried out through the coercive powers of the government exercised consciously and un-consciously by the bureaucratic apparatus. They are also willingly accepted by a public that grows daily less reliant on its private moral and economic re-sources. Some of these costs are incurred involuntarily in the sense that, in the absence of law, regulation, quota, or license, they would not have been in-curred at all.

As Adam Smith sang the praises of the "invisible hand" that miraculously led to a higher order of economic welfare for all via the free market system, so future students of national wealth may see fit to sing of the "invisible govern-ment" that mysteriously provided for the allocation of resources and distribu-tion of income and risks in the second half of the twentieth century.

Here is an example of how all this works. Since 1970, the government has required all cars to be equipped with safety belts. This measure was intended to reduce the cost of accidents. That is, assuming the belts are actually used, the loss of life and property from accidents is demonstrably lower, and the cost of each belt is reduced because the belts can be mass produced. Neverthe-less, the safety belt requirement, whether or not it is beneficial or justified, cer-tainly adds to the cost of the car. Belt costs are incurred involuntarily, for had the government decided not to enact a law, car manufacturers would not have installed safety belts in all cars. The costs are shifted to the consumer, and the majority of consumers also incur belt costs involuntarily insofar as they may not have paid the additional charge of the belts had they been free to choose. Most consumers purchase safety belts only because they cannot buy a car without them.

Several studies of the U.S. Department of Transportation show that most drivers do not bother to wear the belts even when they have them.[1] According to one figure, only 20 percent of drivers wear safety belts, despite devices such as buzzers and lights that remind them to wear the belt. Whatever the benefits to the economy from safety belts, the costs are hidden inside the general cost of purchasing a car. But as long as most people do not wear the belts, and therefore are not protected when driving, the nonwearers incur costs but no benefits. Primarily those who like safety belts, and pay less for them because they are mass produced, benefit from the law. Of course, once the government insures against all sorts of risks, then the saving of life may reduce the cost of life insurance. But both costs and benefits were achieved through regulation and not allocated in the budget.

To be sure, invisibility is a somewhat exaggerated term. It is perfectly possible for a diligent economist to search through mountains of government documents and discover the myriad methods used for invisible operations. Economists have already made quite a few inquiries into the incidence of, say, tariff protection and reduced water prices for farmers. Although it is theoretically possible to uncover all the methods used, it is not likely that it will be done, and uncovering the distribution of costs and benefits is even more difficult. The ability of the bureaucracy to refine its methods so that it can direct its attention to a designated group, plus the huge number of methods used, make a comprehensive cataloging of them too daunting to contemplate—and for our purposes fortunately also unnecessary.

The important points for this discussion are as follows:

1. Almost any allocation of resources, distribution of income, or shifting of risk that the government wants to make can be accomplished by means readily at its disposal—a subtle change, for instance, in the legal framework surrounding a government activity, or the power to impose disguised taxes on selected segments of the population through regulations, prohibitions, quotas, or licenses. The use of government guarantees can reduce costs and affect risk-bearing, price structure, allocation decisions, and changes in income distribution.

2. Invisible methods increase the dependency of citizens on government.

3. Invisible methods can usually (though not always) reduce the effectiveness of the parliamentary process by insulating certain operations of the bureaucracy from parliamentary control, reducing the availability of information to the public, elevating the importance of various large interest groups, and increasing the opportunity for bureaucratic abuse and waste.

4. Invisible methods enable the government to pursue policies (e.g., help to specific interest groups) that are contrary to its avowed goals.

To win elections, candidates for government office can promise to increase transfer payments, such as a rise in social security benefits just before an election.[2] Once elected, they can distribute benefits and allocate costs as politics dictate, favoring some and punishing others, by using invisible methods. They can help a town through the erection of a military base nearby, aid homeowners through a subtle change in the tax laws, reduce the risk to one firm through guarantees of loans or transferring to this firm the proceeds of tax-exempt bonds, bail out a declining firm by loan guarantees or invigorate another firm by granting it a large government contract. By the same token, government officeholders can reduce the profits of one firm by withholding from it these same forms of aid or increasing the firm's costs by adding a variety of regulations.

Invisible methods also lend themselves to more refined intervention. Some countries help private industry by granting loans to specific firms at subsidized rates of interest. The opportunity cost of the subsidy is not shown in the budget (or in the national accounts). As a result, it does not appear in statistical analyses of government size, and occasionally even allows the dodging of international agreements. Subsidized loans in particular are often used to boost exports because other incentives violate international conventions.

Sometimes, invisible methods are recorded in the budget, but without revealing the true nature of the transaction. Suppose, for example, that the government helps a certain firm out of bankruptcy by purchasing its output at a high price. Obviously, the purchase will be recorded in the budget, but the reason for the purchase and the above-market price will not. The U.S. defense procurement is alleged to have been used to help ailing firms this way; and military installations unnecessary for defense purposes have been kept in operation solely because of political pressure to avoid the increased unemployment that would have occurred in the area had they been closed. As Ronald Fox remarked in a study of U.S. defense procurement, "Most members of Congress favor reductions (in defense spending) only in districts other than their own."[3]

Invisibility also avoids accountability. Accountability means that "those who wield power have to answer in another place and give reasons for decisions that are taken."[4] Invisibility means that the true costs, beneficiaries, and relationships between costs and the decisions leading to them are not immediately clear. Government expenditures recorded in the budget are not necessarily "better" than expenditures shifted to the private sector. Pollution, for example, can be combated by collecting taxes from the polluters and paying subsidies to those who suffer from pollution, or it can be fought by legislation requiring antipollution devices whose costs are added on with other costs of production and may or may not be shifted to consumers. Each system has its advantages, its side effects, and its distribution effects on both income and risks. The point is simply that any study of public expenditures and revenues that restricts itself to pollution control accounted for by the budget will grossly underestimate the total cost of that program.

Keeping the cost and scope of attempts to achieve a no-risk society as invisible as possible seems to be what government bureaucrats and legislators prefer. Hidden costs and revenues give rise to fewer protests, confrontations, and conflicts than do revenues and expenditures that are publicly recorded, if only because the public is often totally ignorant of the former's existence. It is also easier to reconcile belief in a free-enterprise system with the increasing amount of government-directed costs when those costs seem to disappear.

State-Owned and Government-Sponsored Enterprises

Over the past decade or two, state-owned enterprises have assumed an increasing role in the world economy. In many developing countries they have become a principal vehicle through which the state hopes to achieve its development objectives. Advanced industrialized countries including Canada, Great Britain, France, Italy, and Sweden have used state-owned enterprises as a tool for advancing a wide variety of national goals. In many cases, whatever the original reasons for establishing state-owned enterprises, the enterprises soon shifted risks to the public sector by protecting declining industries, by bailing out ailing firms and protecting their owners and workers against losses, by various guarantees of input prices to the private sector, or by shielding workers against unemployment. Many state-owned enterprises have suffered heavy losses, in part, at least, as a result of their function as protector and insurer.

In the 1940s and '50s, state-owned enterprises were formed mainly to regulate public utilities and collect taxes. In the 1960s and '70s, they often were used to shield workers from unemployment and save private entrepreneurs from suffering losses in declining industries. Dozens of private enterprises were acquired by governments in Germany, France, Italy, the Netherlands, Sweden, and the United Kingdom to save them from bankruptcy; others were organized to assure guaranteed employment to thousands of workers. Often, the plants built suffered heavy losses but were not allowed to reduce their workforce.

In 1976, for example, a committee nominated by IRI, Italy's largest state-owned enterprise, reported that the company employed at one of its plants (Maccaresse) two or three times as many people as it needed and that the plant was losing about $4500 per employee—an amount equal to half its sales. In 1977, state-owned steel firms in Italy lost $550 million, but only 900 of 104,000 workers were laid off. At Alfasud, the unions were even demanding that a new plant be built to create 1400 more jobs, although the existing plant was losing about $7000 per employee and working at little more than half its production capacity. In the Netherlands the government bought dozens of enterprises to fend off their collapse. The hard-coal industries in Britain, France, Italy, Spain, and West Germany were brought into state ownership to avoid closure, as was three-quarters of the Swedish shipbuilding industry.

Railroads all over the world lose billions of dollars annually, yet their workforce has not been materially reduced. In the United States the government established in 1976 the Consolidated Rail Company (Conrail) to acquire six bankrupt railways. Although Conrail is legally a private company, it is able to continue its services and employment despite huge losses only because it receives large public subsidies. Conrail's losses make it extremely unlikely that the company will be able to repay its debt or pay dividends on its preferred shares; in fact, it might even have to draw another $7.5 billion from the Treasury before 1988.[5] Conrail workers are protected by the government under the Regional Rail Reorganization Act of 1973. Certain retirement benefits of railroad workers are subsidized by the federal government under the Railroad Retirement Act of 1974. Additional assistance was provided for new career training assistance and supplementary unemployment insurance under the Milwaukee Railroad Restructuring Act of 1979. The huge losses sustained by all these state-owned enterprises for employment guarantees are covered sometimes by government and sometimes by the profits of other enterprises, mainly in oil and energy.

Presumably because of ideological reasons, the United States tends to shield workers against the risk of unemployment by granting contracts to private enterprise, or by the creation of a pseudo-private enterprise such as Conrail, rather than by resorting to state-ownership.

After World War II, the United States found itself the owner of hundreds of producing enterprises run by the military, from rope factories to laundries and supermarkets. The federal government was also the largest insurer in the country, the largest producer of electric power, the largest lender and the largest borrower, the largest landlord and the largest tenant, the largest holder of grazing land and timberland, the largest shipowner, the largest warehouse operator, and the largest fleet operator. The Defense Plant Corporation alone owned over 2000 factories. By 1945, fifty-eight publicly owned corporations held combined assets worth $30 billion.

In the mid-1950s, the National Association of Manufacturers, the U.S. Chamber of Commerce, and the investor-owned utility association campaigned for "privatization" to reduce what they regarded as government competition that endangered the American way of life. The second Hoover Commission report on the reorganization of the government echoed these feelings: "The genius of the private enterprise system," it said, "is that it generates initiative, ingenuity, inventiveness, and unparalleled productivity. With the normal rigidities that are part of government, obviously, the same forces that produce excellent results in private industry do not develop to the same degree in government business enterprises."[6] The commission ended by recommending that as many government activities as possible be phased out or reorganized under contract with private firms. Between 1949 and 1956, the U.S. government liquidated wartime corporations and withdrew its investment from twelve federal land banks. By 1956, the major remaining federal corporations were those subsidizing farmers and homeowners and removing private risks from banking and trading operations.[7]

In the 1960s, the federal government began to incorporate government-sponsored enterprises that were not subject to the Government Corporation Control Act and therefore not included in the budget nor subject to budgetary ceilings in their net corporate outlays. Clearly these enterprises were often devices to allow for the financing of government programs outside the budget, usually by earmarking taxes and mortgaging future revenues. All these enterprises were chartered by the federal government and are supervised by a government agency. Yet they are privately owned and their budgets are not reviewed by the President.

Since Americans are by and large suspicious of government ownership or "interference," there was no public objection when many large public independent enterprises and autonomous agencies were established to circumvent government influence in the form of civil service regulations or statutory and constitutional decrees. This autonomy also proved to be a handy device for avoiding limits on public borrowing and reducing the budget. Secretary of Housing and Urban Development Robert Weaver justified the proposal to convert the Federal National Mortgage Association from a mixed-ownership government corporation to a government-sponsored enterprise by the need to avoid the "vagaries of the budget situation." The U.S. Post Office was turned into a separate Postal Service to exempt it from budgetary control; it was authorized to sell bonds to avoid the "annual battle between the Post Office Department and the Bureau of the Budget, which notoriously results in limitations upon funds available to be appropriated." Since 1971, when the Export-Import Bank was excluded from the U.S. unified budget (and from any limitations imposed upon it by the budget), the number of public agencies not classified by law as U.S. government agencies has grown steadily.

Once the government came upon the idea of forming these autonomous government enterprises, they proliferated. Such bodies as the National Park Foundation and the Securities Investors Protection Corporation belong to the category of government agencies legally attached to the private sector. They are authorized to borrow funds from the U.S. Treasury and from the public through loans guaranteed by the Treasury. Undersecretary of the Treasury Paul Volcker testified before the Senate Banking and Currency Commission in May 1972 that "such rapid expansion of Federal Credit demands should be of paramount public concern, especially because most of them are beyond the pale of budgetary review and control; while others involve awkward, expensive, and discriminatory financing arrangements."

Autonomous agencies are not limited to the federal government. State governments also use them to avoid "archaic" constitutional limits on public debts. Bonds for these authorities "are held to be exempt from all the dollar ceilings, requirements for special elections, interest rate limits, and other constitutional encumbrances on general obligation debt. . . . They also allow elected officials to escape the political burdens of imposing the charges or taxes that are needed for debt service and operations."[8] Bonds are issued to finance schools and hospitals through leasing arrangements; to finance site development or construction of plants that are then leased to the companies for the life of the bond and afterward transferred to private ownership, and to finance pollution-control equipment in private industry with the benefit of lower rates of interest on the tax-exempt bonds. "The resort to public authority revenue bonds backed by the state's moral obligation [is] explicitly intended to circumvent election procedures and to neutralize a powerful segment of public opinion running against the project."[9]

Industrial revenue bonds are said to be more shielded from public scrutiny than are other aspects of public enterprise, certainly more so than the government's budget: "Financial arrangements for most public authorities insulate them from even the normal regulatory measures applied to investor-owned corporations. The operations of the municipal bond market are exempt from direct SEC regulation. Indenture provisions governing authority rate setting often preclude government regulation of utility prices. Tax exemption, of course, keeps the Internal Revenue Service out of the public enterprise's books. Private bank mortgages are more stringently regulated than those purchased by public authorities. Public corporations also are exempt from most labor regulations."[10]

By now, there are more than 7000 public authorities in the United States, and the funds they have raised have tripled in a decade—state and local authorities alone spend more than $14 billion a year.

Off-Budget Items

Another direct governmental expenditure that does not have to be reported in the budget is the so-called off-budget items. As the name implies, these public sector operations are excluded from the budget for either legal or accounting reasons. Many government-subsidized insurance programs or loan guarantees fall into this category. Both lower the cost of capital to the borrower because the risk of default is borne by the government, but the amount of these guarantees is shown neither in the budget nor in the statistics of government expenditures.

An example of an off-budget item is the Pension Benefit Guaranty Corporation, a wholly owned government corporation. It was established by the Employee Retirement Income Security Act of 1974 (Public Law 93-406) within the Department of Labor but outside the budget total. The corporation's mission is to administer insurance programs to prevent the loss of pension benefits to participants if pension plans terminate and are unable to pay insured benefits. The corporation is required by law to be self-supporting. It is financed by insurance premiums from defined benefit pension plans, and its total assets in FY 1981 are estimated at $730 million. Neither the premiums nor the claims paid appear in the budget. Another example of an off-budget entity is the Rural Electrification Administration. It finances insured electric and telephone long-term loans, bearing 2 or 5 percent interest. In 1980 cumulative net loans in both programs were more than $18 billion and loan guarantee commitments were more than $20 billion.

Another often used off-budget mechanism are loans granted to individuals or firms at subsidized rates of interest. The loans can be granted from the public purse directly or through publicly owned financial institutions, or simply by guaranteeing a loan made by commercial agents. The Farm Credit Administration supervises 13 banks for cooperatives, 12 federal intermediate credit banks, and federal land banks, operating through 520 federal land bank associations. Between them in 1980 they had $61 billion out in loans to farmers, and it expects to increase its portfolio to $100 billion by 1985 — a third of the total farm loan market in the United States. Federal credit programs are shifting risks from the private sector to the government. They are given through such programs as the Maritime Administration Ship Construction Guarantee Program, the Small Business Administration, as well as through federal financial institutions.

According to the comptroller general of the United States, credit outstanding under federal credit programs totaled well over $300 billion. In FY 1979, total direct loans were $137.2 billion, and in addition the government guaranteed $223.6 billion in loans. Since 1970, federal and federally assisted programs have comprised about 13 percent of funds advanced in the U.S. market. Moreover, from 1968 to 1978, federal credit programs grew at an annual rate of 9.6 percent; at the same period, the overall federal budget grew by 9 percent annually. However, the composition of the program has changed. In 1956 almost all guaranteed loans were for home mortgages. By 1976 these loans had extended to areas such as transportation, energy, and assistance to municipalities.

There are two main reasons for this increased growth and diversity, according to the comptroller general. First, these programs are subsidy programs for projects that "are too risky for private lenders to undertake at reasonable interest costs." Second, "some direct loan programs are statutorily excluded from the budget. That is, the amounts spent for these programs are simply not counted when the budget is added up. With respect to guaranteed loans, outlays show up in the budget only when federal dollars are paid out, usually resulting from a default and generally long after the decision to guarantee the loan has been made. In either case, therefore, *the costs of credit assistance tend to be hidden* and programs do not compete for budget resources like direct expenditures programs do."[11]

The U.S. Senate Committe of the Budget for the 95th Congress wrote: "Few people are familiar with all of the activities included in the discussion of off-budget agencies. [Since the unified budget concept was adopted in 1968] some programs were removed from the budget by legislative action, although they differed in no significant way from other programs which are included in the budget."[12] The committee did not even report on many programs making use of guaranteed loans, but they did recognize them as a "rapidly growing form of federal activity that is only partially or not at all included in the federal budget."[13]

In some cases, the budget document supplies information on "annexed budgets," mainly of financial institutions owned or controlled by the government. The annexed budgets include those of the Export-Import Bank, Federal National Mortgage Association, banks for cooperatives, federal intermediate credit banks, federal land banks, federal home loan banks, and federal home loan mortgage corporations. None of them is included in the statistics showing the government's share in the economy. Because most government-sponsored corporations are engaged in making loans or facilitating the flow of credits, the proliferation of government programs has produced a correspondingly rapid growth in federal credit activities. In 1966 11.7 percent of the credit in the U.S. capital market was raised or assisted by the federal government; by 1975 the federally supported share had risen to 36.4 percent.[14]

A special analysis of the 1981 budget states that federal and federally assisted borrowing is higher than a decade ago and that much of the increase parallels the growth in the economy and in total funds raised by the nonfinancial sector through the sale of debt securities and other forms of borrowing and through the sale of corporate equities. However, to some extent total federal and federally assisted borrowing seems to have increased as a proportion of total funds raised. This proportion increased from 18 percent during 1960-69 to 25 percent during 1970-79. On the average, government programs recently seem to have influenced the allocation of funds raised in financial markets more than they did in the immediately preceding years, even though federal debt relative to total debt has decreased.

Table 5.1 gives some details on federal participation in domestic credit markets. The table includes not only the direct on- and off-budget loans but also two federally assisted borrowings: government guaranteed borrowing and borrowing by government-sponsored enterprises. The first consists of loans for which the federal government guarantees the payment of the principal and/or the interest in whole or part. This government insurance reduces the cost of borrowing since the government accepts the risk of default. The major use of loan guarantees has been to support housing programs, but in recent years this use has widened. Note that loan guarantees are not reflected in the budget. They result in a budget outlay only when there is a default. Thus, their widespread use is one sign of an increase in the invisible government. The government insured farmers through the guaranty of loans to such entities as the Commodity Credit Corporation, Farmers Home Administration, and Rural Electrification Administration. It subsidized students through the guaranty of the Student Loan Marketing Association and the Student Loan Insurance Fund. It also guaranteed debt for energy security reserve, medical facilities, urban renewal, rail programs, aircraft loans (used to aid the export of aircraft), and New York City notes, as well as a $1.5 billion loan to aid the ailing Chrysler Corporation. All this aid came over and above other invisible methods, such as borrowing by government-sponsored enterprises. This borrowing increased from $7 billion in 1977 to $24.1 billion in 1978 and $25.7 billion in 1979.

Contracting

Contracting is yet another important financing mechanism of the invisible government. Government contracts are used mainly for defense acquisitions and the program management activities of the National Aeronautics and Space Administration (NASA), the Atomic Energy Commission (AEC), and the Federal Aviation Agency (FAA); but contracts are becoming increasingly important in the activities of the Department of Health and Human Services, the Department of Education, the Department of Transportation (DOT), and the Department of Housing and Urban Development. Their advantage, according to Annmarie Walsh, is that

TABLE 5.1. FEDERAL PARTICIPATION IN DOMESTIC CREDIT MARKETS, 1970-81
(in billions of dollars)

	1970	1971	1972	1973
Total funds advanced in U.S. credit markets[1] (includes equities)	93.6	125.7	163.5	207.7
Advanced under federal auspicies	16.1	16.5	22.9	27.2
Direct loans:				
On-budget	3.0	2.0	2.7	0.3
Off-budget	...	...	0.2	0.7
Guaranteed loans	8.0	16.1	19.8	17.7
Government-sponsored enterprise loans	5.2	−1.7	0.1	8.5
Federal participation rate including government-sponsored enterprises (percent)	17.2	13.1	14.0	13.1
Total funds raised in U.S. credit markets[1]	93.6	125.7	163.5	207.7
Raised under federal auspices	17.9	32.5	39.5	45.5
Federal borrowing from public	5.4	19.4	19.4	19.3
Borrowing for guaranteed loans	8.0	16.1	19.8	17.7
Government-sponsored enterprise borrowing	4.5	−3.1	0.2	8.5
Federal participation rate (percent)	19.1	25.9	24.2	21.9

SOURCE: *The Budget for Fiscal Year 1981*, Special Analysis E, p. 144.

they offer a detour around conservative belief systems. . . . They permit elected officials to claim balanced budgets and conservative economic policies while distributing projects and contracts funded by public debt. . . . Incentives for efficiency, productivity, and management improvement are weak in that portion of the private sector for which the government is the major customer and in which the cost-plus contract and variations of it are commonplace. . . . These efforts put "free enterprise" rhetoric to work in extracting private profit from government expenditures.[15]

In other words, federal contracting can be used to reduce the official measures of the size of government without reducing its actual size or impact. It can also relieve suppliers of all risks attached to costs, since the contract is based on one kind or another of cost-plus arrangement. At the same time the number of possible contractors is limited, which makes the government dependent on the contractor. The two are locked together in a bilateral monopoly; and prices, costs, profits, and performance are continually renegotiated.

Defense contracts are particularly riddled with problems of cost increases, schedule slippages, and poor technical performance. But despite thes

	Actual						Estimates	
1974	1975	1976	TQ	1977	1978	1979	1980	1981
193.4	181.3	251.8	66.1	314.4	385.3	410.7	(2)	(2)
25.5	27.0	26.8	6.7	37.2	58.7	73.3	71.3	71.2
1.9	4.3	3.3	0.9	2.5	8.4	6.0	6.1	−0.6
2.2	8.5	7.6	2.9	9.0	11.4	13.6	16.6	16.6
10.5	8.7	11.2	−0.1	14.0	13.9	26.1	33.4	41.4
11.0	5.5	4.7	3.1	11.6	25.0	27.5	15.1	13.8
13.2	14.9	10.6	10.1	11.8	15.2	17.8	...	...
193.4	181.3	251.8	66.1	314.4	385.3	410.7	...	...
24.2	64.8	98.2	19.3	79.5	94.2	81.2	91.9	86.4
3.0	50.9	83.4	18.0	53.5	59.1	33.6	44.3	33.1
10.5	8.7	11.2	−0.1	14.0	13.9	26.1	33.4	41.4
10.8	5.3	3.6	1.4	11.9	21.2	21.4	14.2	11.9
12.5	35.7	39.0	29.2	25.3	24.4	19.8	...	...

1. Nonfinancial sectors. Source: Federal Reserve Flow of Funds Accounts.
2. Not estimated.

faults and failings, top defense contractors are by now almost entirely sustained by government; most of their working capital is supplied by government, and their products are sold to it at noncompetitive prices. Several studies of defense contracting have clearly shown that the method is wasteful and has been used to achieve aims that have little to do with defense. Fitzgerald reports that Major General Zoeckler, the F-111 system program director, referred to inefficiency in the operations of military contractors as a national policy necessary for the attainment of "social goals." Contractor inefficiency, he said, provided for such things as equal employment opportunity programs, seniority clauses in union agreements, programs for employment of the handicapped, apprentice programs, aid to small business, aid to distressed labor areas, and encouragement of improvements to plant layouts and facilities.[16]

Thus, some of the high costs of defense procurement can be accounted for as part of the cost of invisible government social insurance programs. The Department of Defense uses its budget to provide or sustain employment in certain regions, and to avoid bankruptcy or otherwise bail out ailing firms. All these considerations leave little incentive to trim the budget or cancel out or cut back programs even if they are useless or unduly expensive.[17]

Federal contracting zoomed in the latter part of the Eisenhower administration. In its Bulletin 60-2, the Bureau of the Budget formally set down the government position, according to which goods and services that could be obtained from private sources should be obtained this way rather than in-house. Since then, this became the official policy of the U.S. government. As a result, certain contracting organizations have flourished by doing business solely and exclusively with the government or other public agencies, usually on a cost-plus-fixed-fee basis. These organizations perform purely public functions but are officially designated as private firms (many of them nonprofit). Some of them are the so-called FFRDCs (Federally Funded Research and Development Centers). According to the National Science Foundation, FFRDCs numbered 67 in 1967 and had a volume of almost $1.5 billion.[18] There were also government owned but privately contracted facilities (GOGOs); the government reduces the risks to the private firm by acquiring the necessary facilities and investing the needed capital, but enters into a contract with a private firm to administer the work (usually under a cost-plus contract).

There may be very good reasons why all these entities should be organized outside the government structure. It may well be that grouping talented people in privately organized firms to expend their efforts on public activities is a better organizational design than having them serve in the civil service. Certainly it is plausible that if these organizations were run under the general rules of fiscal behavior established for government agencies and managed by top management nominated by public officials, they would be less effective in doing their job. Yet, without attempting to answer this crucially important question of organization, one thing is clear: these organizations work only for the public sector and do not compete as a matter of policy. From this point of view, they are actually part of the public sector. Indeed, the same work would be organized in Europe as a state-owned enterprise.

Forced Costs of Compliance

Another major expenditure not shown in statistical measures of government is the outlays of the private sector made solely and exclusively to satisfy the requirements of government. Both federal and state governments in the United States collect taxes by requiring all individuals and enterprises to withhold taxes at the source; as a result, a substantial proportion of the cost of tax collection is buried in the books of the private sector as salaries paid for accountants and other collection expenses. Other costs (e.g., the time it takes an individual to prepare a tax return) would have to be measured in terms of foregone opportunities, a reduction of leisure time, or, if a tax accountant is used, an out-of-pocket expense. But most costs are paid for directly. Whoever pays the bookkeeper to calculate the tax, withhold it, and send it to the government subsidizes the public sector, since the after-tax cost of the salary to this book-keeper is shown as a private and not a public expense and is calculated as a part of the private sector's share in the economy. If tax collection were under-taken directly by government agencies, as in France, these expenses would ap-pear as part of the public sector's expenditures.

Some already significant and still increasing portions of private sector costs are "forced costs" of this nature. Forced costs include, in addition to tax withholding, reporting to various governmental agencies, the employment of tax lawyers or antitrust lawyers, the cost of SEC registration, and all other costs of compliance. Since these costs are listed as part of the private sector's expenditures, their magnitude is not known; they may not be taken into ac-count in cost-benefit analyses of governmental operations or of the efficiency of certain tax collection or regulatory methods.

These costs are not borne by taxpayers in general but by consumers of the specific products; since businesses will shift their burden on to consumers, it is they who ultimately pay the costs. Sometimes the burden involved is quite clear, as in a regulated industry where all expenses for tax withholding, com-pliance with government information requirements, and so on are part of the cost of doing business and are taken into account in the rate structure. In these cases the cost (minus tax reduction) is borne by consumers of, say, electricity or telephone services rather than by taxpayers as a whole. The consequences of this state of affairs for the equity of tax-burden distribution are worth more attention than has hitherto been accorded them.

Thomas Jefferson in his inaugural address called for "a wise and frugal government, which shall restrain men from injuring one another, which shall leave them otherwise free to regulate their own pursuits of industry and im-provement." In fact, government has always exerted some influence on busi-ness decisions. As its involvement with solutions to social problems and the mitigation of private risks continued to grow, the number and scope of its reg-ulations mushroomed. The government cannot control the national economy as a whole, but regulates it piecemeal. As demands mount for equal opportu-nity for minorities and between the sexes, and for protection of the environ-ment, of workers from occupational hazards and unemployment, of consum-ers from shoddy merchandise, of depositors from banks' failures, of investors from fraudulent sales of securities, and of business from foreign competition, so does government regulation and government control. The old federal regu-

latory agencies were concerned with reducing the risk of competition in certain industries; the new agencies are concerned with the abolition of risks
across industry lines. Both kinds of regulation are achieved mainly through invisible methods.

By now there are hundreds of federal departments, agencies, bureaus,
and divisions that regulate business activities to one degree or another. Thirty
years ago, the *Federal Register,* which publishes government regulations, con-
tained merely 2400 pages. Its length expanded, according to *Business Week* (4
April 1977), from 54,105 pages in 1970 to 72,000 pages in 1975, or 18,000 pages
worth in only five years. The visible costs of the major regulatory agencies
were estimated for fiscal 1979 at $4.8 billion; the invisible compliance costs
were far more staggering.

The amounts spent by business to comply with new and old regulations is
difficult to determine, but Dow Chemical, for example, estimated their 1975
bill at $147 million. The entire chemical industry is said to have spent $5.3
billion in 1977 just to meet new national clean water quality standards. The
U.S. steel industry projects a cost of $14 billion through 1983 to meet air and
water quality standards on the statute books as of 1975. According to J. G.
Vorhes, vice president of General Motors, during the calendar years 1974,
1975, and 1976 General Motors spent more than $3.25 billion to comply with
regulations imposed by all levels of government. Mr. Vorhes estimated that
compliance required the equivalent of full-time effort by 22,000 to 25,000
employees each year, or approximately 5 percent of that corporation's workforce in the United States.

According to *Time* magazine (19 March 1979), economist Colin Loxley of
Wharton Econometrics estimates that the three large car manufacturing firms
will spend about $18 billion between 1979 and 1985 to comply with the various
pollution, mileage, and safety goals required by the government. These costs
will increase inflation, and most of them will be borne by car buyers. The price
of an average car in 1985 will be $945 more than it would have been without
these regulations. In 1978 the costs of federal regulations paid for by the average car buyer were more than 10 percent of the average price of a car ($668 out
of $6475).

A recent Library of Congress study found that 439 federal laws affect
postsecondary education. Another study, by the American Council on Education, estimated the cost of campus compliance with federally mandated programs at between 1 and 4 percent of an institution's operating budget. Although the colleges are reimbursed to some extent for the administrative costs
connected with the six different federal student-aid programs, most costs are
not reimbursed, and the nationwide costs to colleges for following federal

rules was said to be roughly the same amount as these campuses attract in voluntary donations.[19]

A Bureau of Economic Analysis review of new plant and equipment showed that expenditures for pollution abatement accounted for 4.8 percent of total plant and equipment expenditures in manufacturing. In particular industries, however, the percentage was much higher: it reached 12.6 percent in steel and nonferrous metals; 8 percent in chemicals, petroleum, and electric and other utilities; and 7 percent in paper, stone, clay, and glass industries. The Council on Environmental Quality has estimated the total pollution abatement and environmental quality expenditures for 1978-87 period in 1978 dollars to be $711 billion, of which $498 billion is borne by the private sector. If toxic and hazardous substance regulations yet to be issued are added, the total cost to the U.S. economy will be more than a trillion dollars diverted from other possible uses.

The administrative costs of the forty-one regulatory agencies for which data are available in the U.S. budget rose from $2.2 billion in 1974 to $4.5 billion in 1978, to $4.8 billion in fiscal year 1979. Murray L. Weidenbaum and Robert DeFina tried to develop a method for estimating the costs of complying with all these regulations and came up with estimates that show this invisible portion of governmental operations as twenty times bigger than direct budgetary costs. According to them, for fiscal year 1976, the administrative costs were $3.189 billion, while the compliance costs were $62.309 billion. Assuming the same ratio of compliance to administrative costs, total regulatory costs in the United States for 1979 can be estimated at $100 billion.[20] The U.S. Department of Commerce estimates the direct cost of regulations, in terms of reallocation of the nation's resources, at $160 billion per annum, or 6 percent of the Gross National Product.[21]

The various estimates of the costs of regulation are crude. Moreover, they include only the compliance costs of regulations administered by U.S. regulatory agencies. Not included are the high costs to the consumer of protecting certain industries (steel, shipbuilding, textile, footwear, color television, and many more) from foreign competition. Also excluded are the costs of the Buy American provision (recently eliminated in the Multilateral Trade Negotiations), which affected U.S. government procurement policies, or the benefits to certain industries of R & D programs or different aid provisions. Incremental regulatory compliance costs also fail to take into account the heavy influence of many governmental directives on corporate investment decisions.

Weidenbaum and DeFina do not offer any calculations for the invisible benefits to business from government largesse. Yet surely the invisible part of regulation includes not only many and varied costs but also many benefits to different groups. Obviously, the major benefits of regulation result from the correction for market failure or achievement of some social or political objective. Thus, regulation of natural monopoly is expected to allow the efficiency of scale economy without suffering the undesirable practices of unregulated monopolies. Unfortunately, these benefits are very hard to measure, and no reliable estimates of them can be computed, given the current state of the art.

Some benefits of regulation are simply transferred from one group to another. Thus, requirement of compulsory insurance results in a transfer from consumers and firms to the insurance companies—which are beneficiaries of the regulation. When ailing firms are kept in business in order to allow employment to their workers, there are benefits to these workers and to the shareholders of the company, while the price is paid by the consumers. In short, many benefits of regulation are in the nature of transfer; costs to one group mean benefits to another.

Put differently, to assess the impact of regulation one has to compare not only the total costs and benefits but also their distribution. Unfortunately, the distribution of costs and benefits does not conveniently appear in some budgets or ledgers. Even if it is known, the problem is far from solved because it is almost impossible to compare costs and benefits when they accrue in different magnitudes to different parts of the population.

The costs of the regulation can be classified into several categories. The easiest cost to identify is the directly observable cost to the government: the budgeted regulatory activities of the administrative governmental bodies doing the regulations. Costs cover such diverse activities as nuclear plant inspections by the Nuclear Regulatory Commission, visits of OSHA inspectors, hours taken in writing regulations by the National Consumers Safety Council, investigation of an accident by the Federal Aeronautics Administration, or hearings held by the National Highway Traffic Safety Administration on the feasibility of installing the airbag. In a second category are the administrative costs to the private sector: staff hours spent on filling out all sorts of forms required by the government. Yet another category is the costs of compliance with regulations imposed on private firms. These include the costs of safety equipment, drug-testing programs, or the additional costs in manufacturing a car either because of the need to add pollution-reduction equipment or because of requirements to install stronger bumpers or safety belts. These are part of the invisible costs, but they are relatively easy to identify because they are recorded in the books of the private firms affected by the regulations.

More difficult to identify, and therefore more controversial, are static and dynamic efficiency costs. If government regulation prompts private firms to combine resources in an inefficient way, these are static inefficiency costs. Dynamic inefficiency results when private firms reduce their rate of innovation, productivity, or technological change as a result of regulation. Many studies have demonstrated that regulation creates different kinds of static inefficiencies. The obvious one is that prices are often higher in regulated industry than they would have been if market forces allowed more competition: if the regulation reduces the number of the firms in a certain industry, does not allow new entrants, and forbids exits, the firms in the industry essentially form a cartel, charging higher prices. Restrictions on entry allow inefficient firms to persist in their operations. Also, rate-of-return regulation sometimes causes inefficient utilization of capital because of the so called Averch-Johnson effect: since rate-of-return regulation allows the regulated firm to earn a normal rate of return on its capital, it encourages the firm to increase the amount of capital.

Regulation may also cause excess capacity; for example, ICC regulation of motor freight certificates of approval, specifies areas to be served, routes to be taken, commodities to be carried, and rates to be charged. Route certificates often exclude service to intermediate points and promote empty back hauls by limiting the commodities and destinations each firm is allowed. They have thus produced substantial excess trucking capacity. The Civil Aeronautics Board operation provided another example of regulations alleged to cause excess capacity until the 1979 deregulation. Since airlines were not allowed to compete over fares, they competed in service quality, which was defined as the number of scheduled flights on a given route. As a result, planes flew half empty, vast amounts of fuel were consumed, and the airlines were saddled with excess capacity while the skies over major airports were congested.[22]

In the railroad industry, ICC regulates prices and rates on the "formula for use in determining rail freight services costs," called Rail Form A. This formula is based on historical average cost. It arbitrarily allocates the substantial fixed costs of the rail operation to various categories, with no allowance for peak and off-peak demand. As a result, the costs of serving light-density routes are understated, and those of serving high-density routes are overstated. This has resulted in many inefficiencies and has induced the movement of goods from low-cost to high-cost modes.[23]

Another example of inefficiency is reported by a study on pollution regulation. EPA standards require every firm to reduce pollutants by the same percentage. If standards will be replaced by effluent charges, however, some firms would remove more of the discharges into the environment and others would remove less. The charges could be designed so that, on the average, the same level of environmental quality is achieved. If the decrease of costs for the first group is greater than the increase in costs to the second group, this system could be more efficient.[24] Social regulation relating to environment, safety, and health, according to the Council of Economic Advisers, caused a decline in productivity in mining and utilities in the 1967-77 period. Safety and environmental regulations (including crime prevention) accounted for 0.4 of the 3.2 percentage decline in productivity between 1948 and 1973 and 1973 and 1976, as calculated by Edward Dennison.[25]

The major inefficiencies caused by regulation are dynamic ones: reduction of entrepreneurial creativity, innovation, and technological change. A firm competing in the market has to be innovative in order to continue in business. It often tries to increase its market share at the expense of others. A regulated firm has much less incentive for innovation. In fact, one study of the Brookings Institution reaches the conclusion "that the performance of regulated industries falls far short of the ideal and even of a reasonable target for public policy."[26] The regulatory process usually discourages research and development and retards the rate of technological change. This is so because neither entry nor exit is allowed, and prices and rates of return are regulated. As one example, many rail firms prefer piggyback configurations that use small flatcars designed to carry a single van or container. Piggybacking in many cases is less costly than the larger freight cars designed to carry two vans. However, Rail Form A led to the adoption of the more costly configuration because the same average cost of fleet car per mile was used to compute ICC-approved rates for both alternatives. Because of this regulation, the freight rate per van riding on a single-van flatcar would be greater than the freight rate per van riding on a double-van flatcar, although it is less costly in a strict economic sense.

The cost of inefficiencies does not end at the level of the regulated industry alone. When the ICC regulates shipping costs, this also affects the iron ore industry or any other industry that moves goods around the country.

Other costs imposed by the regulation do not involve inefficiency or wasteful use of resources. Instead, risks are transferred from one group to another. For example, OSHA regulations shift the expected loss due to injury or illness from the worker to the firm.

Most works on regulation are confined to a calculation of costs, mainly compliance costs. One such study was made by Stephen Seidel for the Center of Urban Policy Research. Seidel documented and analyzed the full range of governmental regulations at all levels of government that affected the housing industry.[27] Based on his findings, Kristina Ford calculated the cost of what she calls "over-regulation" for that industry. She found that 19.7 percent of the purchase price of the $50,000 house she used as an example could be related to governmental regulatory excesses of one form or another. In a period in which housing costs have been increasing much faster than inflation, costs attributable to excess government control can certainly be called too high.[28] Ford's study also showed the many difficulties in singling out the costs attributable to government controls. In every instance Ford herself used an extremely stringent definition of "excess regulation," namely "those forms or variations of governmentally imposed controls which exceed minimum health, safety, and welfare considerations in the provision of housing." She also did not offset any benefits against these costs; for example, all initial costs of energy conservation regulations were taken into account, but the savings in heating bills allowed by these energy-saving devices were not.

The private housing industry is only one illustration of the degree of invisible government's involvement and the difficulty in untangling the maze of cost-increasing regulations, on the one hand, and subsidies on the other. No significant aspect of the housing market is unaffected by government action in one form or another. Faced with the collapse of the housing industry in the 1930s, Congress completely restructured the private-house financing system under the New Deal through the establishment of the savings and loan industry to supply the mortgages and the Federal Housing Administration to insure them. In addition, all deposits of commercial banks, mutual savings banks, and savings and loan associations were insured through the Federal Deposit Insurance Corporation, the Federal Savings and Loan Insurance Corporation, and others.

In the Housing Act of 1949, in which a "decent house and suitable living environment for every American family" was proclaimed a national goal, several mortgage insurance programs were added, conferring benefits on special groups including veterans, farmers, and the elderly. Since then, still more programs have been initiated to help meet this ambitious goal, including more subsidy assistance, especially since 1968. Some benefits were curtailed. For example, thrift institutions have been paying higher taxes since 1962 as a result of a change in an obscure provision of the tax law. Before 1962, these institutions could shelter almost all their net income from home mortgages by deducting a "reserve against bad debts." The Tax Reform Act of 1962 lowered the maximum deduction to 60 percent and thus raised the tax rate for thrifts; the Tax Reform Act of 1969 further eroded their tax advantage by providing for the gradual reduction of the deduction to 40 percent by 1979 and some recapture of the deductions in excess of actual losses. This change boosted the tax rate for thrifts to a point where savings and loan associations now pay federal taxes at rates above those paid by commercial banks.[29]

What we now have is an enormously complex, confusing, and some claim wasteful, aggregation of housing programs. The growth of public sector programs has decreased the ability to offset housing slumps that usually ac-

company credit-tight money periods. Economists attribute many of the difficulties to interest rate ceilings on the amounts thrift institutions receive in
deposits and pay in mortgages.[30] One of the major hidden subsidies in the
housing market is in fact the lower rate of mortgage and this subsidy may
cause a perception of funds shortages:

> A major factor shaping Federal Housing subsidy programs has been the
> desire to structure the subsidy mechanism so as artificially to minimize
> the immediate impact of the program on the federal budget. Accordingly,
> interest subsidy programs that spread the budget impact of the subsidy
> over periods as long as 40 years are often favored over other types of sub-
> sidies whose budget impact is more immediate. . . .
> The device of hidden (or partially hidden) subsidies in housing—in
> contrast to overt subsidies—is common in housing programs as well as
> other government operations. An early use of this device in housing was
> through the Federal National Mortgage Association special assistance
> operations—now being continued by Government National Mortgage
> Association—where the subsidy is provided by purchasing mortgages at
> prices above their value at the time—often at par. This contrasts with the
> direct loan and the subsidized interest rate housing programs. The use of
> the Tandem Plan in a variety of ways is one form of subsidy that is suffi-
> ciently covert to avoid the controversy that would result from a direct
> subsidy of equal amount.
> Another hidden subsidy exists under the rural housing insured loan
> system of FmHA. The Housing Act of 1965 established that system and a
> Rural Housing Insurance Fund to finance it. This was done mainly to
> avoid the budget consideration that had restricted direct loans under the
> FmHA's original authority.[31]

The federal government is involved in the housing market through its tax
policies, mortgage insurance, regulation of mortgage financing, subsidy payments, welfare assistance, credit policy, labor policy, equal housing opportunity policy, environmental policy, and numerous other ways. The states, too,
regulate the market through zoning laws, subdivision laws, safety requirements, and other regulations, many of which increase private costs while be-
stowing invisible benefits to the industry.

The report of the National Housing Policy Review estimated that in 1972
the cost of homeowner deductions for income tax purposes was $6.2 billion;
of federally subsidized housing programs, $2.5 billion; of federal welfare as-
sistance payments for housing, $2.6 billion; and of other taxes foregone (e.g.,
capital gains on home sales) $3 billion to $4 billion. The cost of ceilings on interest, known as Regulation Q, is harder to quantify; but small savers are certainly short-changed. They receive a rate of interest on their savings that is
much worse than the loss of purchasing power because of inflation. Worse

still, several studies have shown that holding down interest costs on savings accounts has not had much effect in reducing the cost of mortgage loans. Instead, most of the benefits have gone to shareholders of commercial banks.

Economic and social regulations are undergoing scrutiny by American policy makers. Deregulation has been pursued in airlines and trucks, and price controls on oil and gas have been phased out.

Cross Subsidization

Cross subsidization is another private subsidy of public expense. The cost of many services, in rural areas for example, exceeds the revenue the various governmental regulatory bodies allow, but the regulators force the supplier to provide the services anyway and recoup the losses in more profitable areas. Because competitors often will try to enter only lucrative markets, a regulatory agency usually does not allow these entrants to compete at a lower price. As a result, everyone who uses the services of the profitable route is subsidizing those who use the services of the losing one. This arrangement is routine in airline routes, telephone operations, mail services, railroad lines, and so on. In all cases, the subsidy is neither shown nor calculated officially.

Conceptually, almost all public sector interventions in the price mechanism can be looked upon as some sort of cross-subsidization or tax-subsidy scheme. An overvalued rate of exchange taxes exporters and subsidizes importers; tariff protection is a tax on consumers and a subsidy to the producers; losses of a state-owned enterprise caused by a government order to freeze prices is a subsidy for the users of its product; a law requiring producers to install safety devices in a car is conceptually a tax on those buyers of cars who would rather have less safety and a lower price; prevention of the sale of saccharin because of potentially harmful side effects limits the freedom of the consumer to eat sweets and stay thin. The freedom of doctors to prescribe new drugs whose benefits, in their opinion, exceed the possible risks is limited by the Food and Drug Administration, whose complex controls greatly impede the flow of new food additives and drugs onto the market: 47 new licensed prescription drugs were introduced in 1960 in the United States, only 12 got over (FDA) hurdles in 1975.

Tax Expenditures

Taxation schemes can be looked upon as yet another manifestation of the private sector's paying for "invisible government" attempts to shift the burden of risk and the benefits to society. In nearly all these schemes the government takes funds from one group and redistributes them to another, outside the spotlight of budgetary review. Homeowners, for instance, can take deductions on mortgage interest and property tax payments, and imputed rent is exempted from income tax; a company's contributions to workers' pension plans (as well as the retirement plans of individuals) are tax deductible and are also not included as taxable income. Tax loopholes favor a variety of groups and enterprises and reduce U.S. Treasury tax revenues by more than $140 billion a year.

Luckily, the Congressional Budget Act of 1974 (Public Law 93-344) requires a listing of tax expenditures in the budget. The calculation of tax expenditures involves all sorts of theoretical and technical difficulties related to the definition and measurement of income. Moreover, simply adding tax expenditures produces inaccurate totals because tax expenditures affect the value of other tax expenditures. Indeed, the tax expenditure estimates prepared by the Treasury department are not totaled. To give an idea of the magnitude of these expenditures, the effects of certain provisions can be cited (all estimates are for FY 1981): capital gains involve a tax expenditure of $23.6 billion; exclusion of interest on state and local debt, another $9.4 billion; deductibility of state and local nonbusiness tax, $24.8 billion; deductibility of charitable contribution, almost $10 billion; itemized deductions, $44.5 billion. The net exclusion of pension contributions alone is a tax expenditure estimated at more than $17 billion; deductibility of mortgage interest and property tax on owner-occupied homes, $22.3 billion; exclusion of social security and railroad retirement plus the additional tax credit and exemption for the elderly, $10.2 billion. The total of these expenditures, as calculated by the Treasury department, if the effect of one tax expenditure on another is ignored, is estimated for FY 1981 at $146 billion.

Since resources are always scarce, and wants are apparently insatiable, the traditional class struggle has by now taken the form of conflict over the distribution of tax incidence and risk bearing as well as the receipt of public benefits. Unable to satisfy all the public's wants or reduce the level of its expectations, governments simply satisfy some wants at the expense of others, and insofar as possible, they do so in unseen ways. Contrary to common myth, this redistribution has by no means always favored the poor. What Boulding and Pfaff call "implicit public grants"[32] — special provisions of the tax law, public policy, or administrative practices — more often than not end in even greater inequities.

Ever since the enactment of the Poor Laws in Elizabethan England, governments have felt compelled to add a "distributional corrective" to soften the burdens that market forces bring to some people. As many more groups in society acquired power, the distributional neutrality of competitive markets was further weakened as they succeeded in using it to tilt benefits their way. By the twentieth century, social reforms were no longer expressions of noblesse oblige but demands — backed by political power — of the more recently enfranchised for greater equality in income, opportunity, and, quite often, results. Poverty and disease are no longer accepted simply as unfortunate manifestations of the natural order of things. Governments have stepped in to deal with economic hardship, alleviate social problems and pressures, and reduce risk. In the process they have been pushed into at least pledging to meet more and more demands, and to mitigate a growing number of risks by shifting them from individuals or groups to the society at large.

Since the aggregate demand for protection far exceeds the resources available to government through taxation, the invisible government takes over. The extent, scope, and impact of these different risk-reduction and risk-shifting methods have been increasing, while the techniques to make them invisible have grown more and more refined. Some are so complex, subtle, and clandestine that the public need not even be considered when they are devised or implemented. Invisibility makes possible a disbursement of various grants and benefits in ways that are not immediately obvious, and allows a distribution that would not be socially acceptable if it were fully known. The flood of new legislation that has emerged in response to diverse concerns, and a growing percent of the visible government, can be explained by attempts to increase protection, prevent losses, and expand insurance.

Some of the growth of both the visible and invisible public sector can be attributed to the growing complexity of an urban society, as well as to the added provision of public services such as education or sewage. However, especially over the last two decades, most of the increase has been in risk-reduction and risk-shifting: unemployment insurance, pollution abatement, social security benefits, health insurance, product safety, flood protection, and no-fault workers' compensation are well-known examples. Insurance against losses in declining industries or against a loss of status are less often recognized but equally widespread. Since many methods used to shift risks have been invisible, no attempt to quantify the total size of the invisible government or the portion of the risk-shifting in its operations has been made. The examples above should be sufficient to illustrate the trend.

In many cases, there are good theoretical arguments for shifting the burden of risk to the public sector; for example, the shifting of risks in research activities is very likely to be profitable from society's point of view. In other instances, it is more difficult to show theoretical economic arguments for the increase in risk-shifting. Thus, the only rationale in an individualistic society for a mandatory requirement of safety belts is that, in an insurance society, the costs of accidents are not borne by the individual but by the public. Indeed, the increase of the public sector tends to further augment the list of things in which government intervention may be justified. The more the government protects the individual, the more it feels justified to resort to direct control over the insured. Yet, less insurance and less protection might be preferred by the public to preserve more individual freedom.

The doctrine that society should achieve optimality by nonmarket means if it cannot achieve them in the market is pervasive.[33] This doctrine, however, sometimes fails to recognize the side effects and costs of the increasing involvement of the public sector and its failures. Increasing protection to one individual is often possible only by decreasing protection to another. In addition, the reduction of risks may lead to increased dependence and also uncertainty, as can be seen with the government contractors already discussed. Moreover, increasing protection is a major cause of inflation.

Political parties exist to support different economic and social policies. Parties to the left generally favor large government budgets, low unemployment even at the cost of high inflation, equalized income distribution, and immediate relief from need. Conservative parties are more concerned with the state of national finances. They favor a low rate of inflation, low taxation, smaller and balanced government budgets even at the cost of somewhat higher unemployment; and they oppose income equalization. In all industrial countries, government control over taxes, money supply, spending, and regulations changing the structure of property rights allows government to determine the short-term movement of the economy to a significant degree. In countries with a strong leftist bias, control is maintained openly and without scruple.

In more conservative countries, or in the United States where the belief in the natural rights of the individual and the free enterprise system is still strong, governments are more apt to resort to invisible methods. In the United States this invisibility has allowed subsidies to the U.S. shipbuilding industry, tariff and quota protection to the textile and shoe industries, trigger prices to alleviate the plight of the steel industry, lower effective interest rates to homeowners, depletion allowances to mineral producers and other extractive industries, the granting to ranchers of grazing rights on public lands at fee levels well below comparative rights on private lands, the disposal of surplus property like ships and manufacturing plants at below-market values, and grants and contracts to educational and cultural programs. It has allowed increased allocations to favored regions, chosen on the basis of political expediency or debts. In short, it has created opportunities for the left and the conservative alike to circumvent public debt ceilings, to disburse both costs and benefits in ways that are not easily traceable.

What, then, is the answer? How can Americans halt the apparently unending spread of this invisible mechanism for which they pay more and more and over which they have less and less control? By now almost everyone will agree that the days of laissez-faire capitalism are over, that government must assume responsibilities for its citizens to guard them against at least some of the more pernicious complexities of modern life. On the other hand, people must also begin to recognize that there is no such thing as a risk-free society, or cost-free insurance, and begin to sort out which responsibilities they are willing to exercise and which they would rather pay others to assume. Finally, Americans in particular must begin to accept that big government is here to stay, and that the important thing it not to shrink it—an impossibility in any case as long as so many demands are made upon it—but to control it.

Control is easiest when activities are clearly visible. But complaints about high taxes and government interference and simultaneous demands for broader services effectively drive these activities underground, where government can function without interference in a manner that better serves the interests of politicians and manipulators than the public at large. A totally visible government also makes more meaningful our choices at the polls. Politicians in a visible government would be more accountable for their promises, and the government we vote for would be the one we see, not an invisible leviathan that grows in its own haphazard way from one administration to the next.

NOTES

1. L. Robertson, *Urban Area Safety Belt Use in Automobile with Starter-Interlock Belt Systems: A Preliminary Report* (Washington, D.C.: Insurance Institute for Highway Safety, 1974).
2. See John F. Manley, *The Politics of Finance* (Boston: Little, Brown, 1971), pp. 277-80; and Edward R. Tufte, *Political Control of the Economy* (Princeton, N.J.: Princeton University Press, 1978), pp. 28-35.
3. Ronald Fox, *Arming America: How the U.S. Buys Weapons* (Boston: Division of Research, Harvard Business School, 1974), p. 150.
4. Arthur S. Miller, "Accountability and the Federal Contractor," *Journal of Public Law* 20 (1971): 473.
5. *The Economist,* 30 December 1978. For many more examples, see William Keyser and Ralph Windle, eds., *Public Enterprise in the EEC* (Alphen aan den Rijn, The Netherlands: Sijthoff & Noordhoff, 1978).
6. U.S. Commission on the Organization of the Executive Branch of the Government, *Business Enterprise: A Report to the Congress* (Washington, D.C., May 1955), p. xxi.

7. Annmarie H. Walsh, *The Public's Interest: The Politics and Practices of Government Corporations* (Cambridge, Mass.: MIT Press, 1978), p. 31.
8. Ibid., p. 24.
9. Ibid., p. 144.
10. Ibid., p. 157.
11. *Federal Credit Assistance: An Approach to Program Design and Analysis,* U.S. General Accounting Office, PAD-78-31, 31 May 1978, p. 4. Italics added. Loans made by the Federal Financing Bank (FFB) do not always appear in the budget.
12. Committee on the Budget, United States Senate, *Off-Budget Agencies and Government-Sponsored Corporations* (Washington, D.C.: U.S. Government Printing Office, 1977), p. vii.
13. Ibid., p. viii.
14. Ibid., p. 6.
15. Walsh, *The Public's Interest,* p. 37.
16. A. Ernest Fitzgerald, *The High Priests of Waste* (New York: Norton, 1972), p. 159.
17. Some of the debilitating problems of the weapons acquisition process are analyzed in Morton J. Peck and Frederick M. Scherer, *The Weapons Acquisition Process: An Economic Analysis* (Boston: Division of Research, Harvard Business School, 1962); Murray L. Weidenbaum, *The Military/Space Market: The Intersection of the Public and Private Sectors* (St. Louis: Department of Economics, Washington University, 1967); Seymour Melman, *The Permanent War Economy: American Capitalism in Decline* (New York: Simon and Schuster, 1974); and C. Merton Tyrrell, *Pentagon Partners: The New Nobility* (New York: Grossman, 1970).
18. NSF 71-9, *Scientific Activities of Independent Non-Profit Institutions, 1970,* February 1971.
19. *Christian Science Monitor,* 4 April 1977.
20. Murray L. Weidenbaum, "On Estimating Regulatory Costs," *Regulation,* May/June 1978, pp. 14-17. The detailed study by Weidenbaum and DeFina is entitled *The Cost of Federal Regulation of Economic Activity* (report of the Center for the Study of American Business at Washington University, n.d.).
21. Jerry J. Jasinowski, "A Report on U.S. Industrial Policies" (paper presented at the International Symposium on Industrial Policies for the 1980s, Madrid, 5-9 May 1980).
22. George W. Douglas and James C. Miller III, *Economic Regulation of Domestic Air Transport: Theory and Policy* (Washington, D.C.: Brookings Institution, 1974), p. 97.
23. See James C. Nelson, "The Changing Economic Case for Surface Transport Regulation," in *Perspectives on Federal Transportation Policy,* ed. James C. Miller III (Washington, D.C.: American Enterprise Institute, 1975), p. 22.
24. A. V. Kneese and Charles L. Schultze, *Pollution Prices and Public Policy* (Washington, D.C.: Brookings Institution, 1975).
25. Quoted in Jasinowski, "A Report on U.S. Industrial Policies."

26. W. M. Capron and R. G. Nold, "Summary and Conclusion," in *Technological Change in Regulated Industries,* ed. W. M. Capron (Washington, D.C.: Brookings Institution, 1971), p. 221. For similar conclusions, see Burton H. Klein, *Dynamic Economics* (Cambridge, Mass.: Harvard University Press, 1977).
27. Stephen R. Seidel, *Housing Costs and Government Regulations* (New Brunswick, N.J.: Center for Urban Policy Research, 1978).
28. Kristina Ford, "Afterword—A Guide to Cost Conversion," in Seidel, *Housing Costs,* p. 317.
29. Robert M. Buckley, John A. Tuccillo, and Kevin E. Villani, *Capital Markets and the Housing Sector* (Cambridge, Mass.: Ballinger, 1977), pp. 106-7.
30. For an analysis and many recommendations, see Leo Grebler, "An Assessment of the Performance of the Public Sector in the Residential Housing Market 1955-1974," in ibid.
31. National Housing Policy Review, *Housing in the Seventies, A Report of the National Housing Policy Review* (Washington, D.C.: U.S. Department of Housing and Urban Development, 1974), p. 290.
32. Kenneth E. Boulding and Martin Pfaff, eds., *Redistribution to the Rich and the Poor* (Belmont, Calif.: Wadsworth, 1972), p. 2. See also Joseph A. Pechman and Benjamin Okner, *Who Bears the Tax Burden?* (Washington, D.C.: Brookings Institution, 1974).
33. See, for example, W. J. Baumol, *Welfare Economics and the Theory of the State* (Cambridge, Mass.: Harvard University Press, 1952).

6. Risk in International Perspective

Interdependence: A Constraint on Risk Reduction

The trend toward protecting more individuals against more risks continually runs into conflict with another major trend in the post-World War II period: the growing interdependence between nation-states in the Western world. Until recently, international interdependence was actively encouraged by governments through such policies as the convertibility of currencies, voluntarily reduced tarriffs, and sometimes the increase of mobility of capital and labor across national borders. Most national leaders, still haunted by memories of the trade wars of the Great Depression, are trying to stem another tide of protectionism at all costs. But, though it increases the wealth of nations, interdependence also limits the freedom of each government "by embedding each country in a matrix of constraints which it can influence only slightly, often only indirectly, and without certainty of effects."[1]

As a result, each nation has become vulnerable to forces in the international arena and to the impact of the economic and social actions of other countries. It would in fact be very difficult to design a political strategy in one country that would not have repercussions on the economies of others. Policies in any given country must take into account the ramifications bound to result from them elsewhere. The greater the interdependence, the smaller the amount of discretion left to any one government. Policies designed to achieve results in the domestic economy that do not take into account the policies of other nations are doomed to failure or at most to a slow and only partial success. Spillover effects from other economies can result from changes in interest rates, prices, costs, income, and governmental tax policies, any one of which rapidly affects the local factors of production.

Reducing risks in one country can also have spillover effects and cause the country's international economic position to deteriorate. Policy measures designed to aid industry or strengthen exports increase tensions on the international scene, they can also be thwarted easily by moving capital, or the firm itself, to another jurisdiction. If the German government compels its electricity firms to buy expensive coal to ward off unemployment in the Ruhr Valley, other countries will reduce their export orders from Germany. Such a subsidy impedes the ability of the German steel industry to compete in the world market because the industry is paying more for coal. In fact, the German government forbade the import of coal to Germany, and the cost of that embargo to the German steel industry in the 1960-70 period was estimated at $600 to $700 million. If the Bundesbank increases its discount rate to fight inflation, foreign capital seeking the higher rate of interest may flow into Germany and foul the good intentions of the German central bank. If taxes are raised, profits can be shifted to another country by intracompany pricing. If regulations increase the cost of production, the regulated firm can promptly move out. If a firm finds wage demands exorbitant, it simply moves production somewhere else.

Governments of the Western world have been confronted with the dilemma of reconciling growing demands for a reduction of risk with the mounting difficulties that arise from trying to isolate their economies from those of the rest of the world. How can they achieve national objectives when economic interdependence materially reduces their freedom to apply policy measures? Clearly, attempts to shield workers from having to change jobs will be futile if barriers to foreign trade are lifted. Safety devices, antipollution measures, work guarantees, or any one of the variety of regulations imposed on business firms to reduce risk all entail mounting costs and evoke reactions that will weaken the measures instituted and thwart attempts at risk reduction. Higher production costs can cause firms to move to another jurisdiction, and the remaining firms may not be able to compete against the foreign firms that are not subject to all these cost-increasing regulations. If the problem is "solved" by imposing the invisible tax of inflation, the inflation will cause capital to move to other countries and will create a deteriorating balance of payments and an effective devaluation. A government cannot protect its citizens from all consequences of economic policies of other countries, exogenous shocks (such as an abrupt increase in oil prices), or the vicissitudes of world markets; but it can dilute the consequences of these factors, although always at the cost of reduced freedom in the execution of its domestic policies.

Immediately after World War II, governments chose interdependence. Although totally free movement of all factors of production and trade has never been allowed, attempts to increase freedom and integration have been made. International bodies have been created to avoid a repetition of the devastating "beggar-thy-neighbor" policies adopted by many countries between the wars. In the 1920s and '30s, each country tried to dump its unemployment problem onto other countries through protectionist measures and repeated devaluations. Germany reduced the burden of its war debts by inducing an inflation of horrendous dimensions. After World War II many countries pledged to lay off protectionism; the General Agreement on Tariffs and Trade

(GATT) was signed in 1947, pledging avoidance of customs protection and tariff wars; and the International Monetary Fund (IMF) was designed as a way of avoiding competitive devaluations. Free trade was thought to benefit all concerned, and therefore efforts should be made so that goods and services can flow freely among nations. Helping the industrial development of the Third World was another aspect of these policies. Most developed countries enjoyed a sustained economic growth, which they assumed would go on forever, and that growth would allow them to finance whatever social insurance programs they thought they needed.

Some efforts to reduce the free flow of certain goods and services continued, to be sure. Labor movements, so prevalent in the nineteenth century and early twentieth, were much more restricted. The migration of millions of people to the United States, Canada, and Australia before World War I was arrested in the 1920s by a variety of immigration laws and barriers. In the European Economic Community, Article 48 of the Rome Treaty required complete labor mobility within the Common Market, but very little movement actually took place. Still, the possibility existed for those who chose it. U.S. immigration laws tended to reject laborers in favor of scientists, engineers, doctors, and the like, and this caused a "brain drain" in countries that paid its professionals less well.

Restrictions on the free flow of capital were gradually lifted, and huge amounts of money moved from one country to another. Technology transfers were also unrestricted, although more recently a movement is afoot to restrict them as well. Gilpin, for example, claims that technology transfers by multinational firms work against the interest of the United States and should be curtailed.[2]

Immediately after World War II, it was said that when America sneezed, Europe caught pneumonia; in the 1970s and 80s, the converse appears to be true. But whoever actually catches the pneumonia, all industrialized market countries are much less immune to the economic ailments of others than they once were. One source of this growing interdependence is technological advances; another is the acceleration in the growth of international trade and international production encouraged by the first. International travel makes people in one country much more aware of the customs, cultures, and habits of others, an awareness that movies and television reinforce. Interdependence is promoted by policy makers; the creation of the European Common Market and the concomitant reduction of tariffs and lowering of barriers to the free flow of labor is one example.

It is sometimes worth reminding ourselves that most of the technologies that have made this world smaller are of quite recent origin. Materials such as titanium, polyethylene, argon, a whole family of plastic products, antibiotics, microwaves, electronics (television, calculators, tape and video recorders, cassettes, transistors, citizen-band tranceivers), and self-developing cameras are all innovations of the last forty or fifty years. The first radiotelephone was installed in 1926, the first satellite for telephone communication in 1965; the first electronic computer started operating in 1946; commercial airlines started sixty-five years ago, and a jet aircraft made its first transatlantic flight as recently as 1958. Talking movies were widely available only after 1926, and the first commerical program was televised in 1941. As a result of these new technologies, the world became smaller; and differences between consumers in different parts of the world narrowed.

Information is spread quickly and efficiently all over the globe. The way people behave, dress, and live in different parts of the world, and the technologies that determine it, become more and more homogeneous. The art of remote-control management of operations was improved; and suspicion of the unfamiliar, unknown and, therefore risky and uncertain foreign investment began to disappear. The efficiency of information transmission has reduced the reaction time to any specific policy in any one country. A change in interest rates will cause an almost spontaneous flow of funds into that country, if the rate of interest increases, or out of it, if the rate of interest falls. Communications allow a faster response both to changing market opportunities and to changing government regulations and policies and the efficient operation of large firms organized on an international scale. The flow of goods and services across national boundaries has grown, and the share of foreign trade out of total private sector activities has been increasing.

International Trade and International Production

In 1928, the value of total world export was $31.7 billion. This value went down to an average of $22.9 billion in 1937-38. In 1953, world trade reached $71.4 billion. It climbed to $128 billion in 1960, to $312 billion in 1970, and to $1020 billion in 1976. By 1978, the dollar value of international trade was $1300 billion. Even when inflation and the deterioration of the dollar are taken into account, this represents an impressive growth in world trade, particularly in the last thirty years. The rate can be illustrated by comparing the years from 1913 to 1948 to the period from 1948 to 1973. In the first period, the volume of world production increased by approximately 2 percent a year; population growth and increase in productivity each accounted for about 1 percent growth. The volume of world trade grew by one half of 1 percent a year, or less than the population. By contrast, in the second period, world production rose by an average annual rate of about 5 percent, more than double the rate of population growth. The aggregate volume of world trade grew by an annual average rate of about 7 percent. Manufacturing exports grew from 39 percent of world trade in 1928 and 40 percent average for 1937-38 to 45 percent in 1953. They reached about half of total exports in 1960, and more than 60 percent in the 1970s.[3]

Despite the recession after the 1973 oil crisis, world trade continued to grow, albeit at a lower rate. During 1973-78, world exports expanded at an average yearly rate of about 4 percent, and world production by 3.5 percent. In most of the post-World War II period, world trade grew at a much faster rate than production.

There were also other changes in the composition of world exports. The newly industrialized countries were able to increase their share. In 1976 the old industrial countries had only 63 percent of the world total, a substantial drop from the 69 percent they had maintained in the years preceding the oil crisis. Industrial production in those countries between 1973 and 1979 stagnated; in the developing countries, industrial capacity, production, and exports continue to grow. The populous Third World countries have claimed a growing share in future increments of world production and trade. The South has become less and less content with providing outlets for western manufacturers and supplying cheap raw materials. Instead, the developing countries have developed their own industries, and some of them have become industrialized. Excluding the eastern bloc's industrial production, developing countries' share of total industrial production grew from 14.1 percent in 1963 to 19.1 percent in 1977. At the same time, the U.S. share declined from 40.2 to 36.9 percent.[4] This shift means that adjustment in the structure of various economies has become necessary. The burden of adjustment, however, has not been evenly distributed: it has strongly been felt in low-skill labor-intensive sectors like wearing apparel, footwear, leather goods, and shipbuilding; but, later, also by such capital-intensive heavyweights as steel, chemicals, and automobiles.

The Pains of Adjustment

Adjustment affects mainly that part of the economy faced with international competition. In 1978, according to U.S. Department of Commerce figures, the total output devoted to merchandise exports was 6.7 percent in the United States, 10 percent in Japan, 15.6 percent in France, 23.2 percent in Britain, 23 percent in Italy and Canada, 22.3 percent in West Germany, and 41.4 percent in the Netherlands.[5] The integration of certain factors in the economies is in fact greater than is implied in these figures. With the larger size of the public sector, in which foreign trade activities are minimal, the burden of direct adjustments to world conditions is borne mainly by the private sector, and within that sector, only by those industries that are faced with international competition. Despite continually lower transportation costs (which in itself increases interdependence), not all private industries are confronted with international competition. Real estate and construction are generally domestic activities. So are wholesale and retail trade, transportation and communication, and to a lesser extent banking and insurance. Other industries are traditionally heavily protected. Agriculture is a well-known example; defense industries are a lesser-known one. When the ratio of foreign trade to the total output of the internationally exposed private sector is calculated, the strong impact of international trade on any one country's industry is apparent.

The United States has a relatively small share of foreign trade in its GNP, but this share is rapidly growing: exports increased from about 4 percent of GNP in 1960 to nearly 8 percent in 1978. Imports in the same period grew even faster, from 3.0 to 8.7 percent.[6] In certain industries, the change has been much more dramatic: foreign manufacturers of cars pushed their share in the U.S. market to an unprecedented 28 percent in 1979, compared to around 15 percent in the previous recession;[7] steel imports to the United States zoomed from 3.7 percent in 1961 to 17.2 percent of the total market in 1978.[8] Not surprisingly, car manufacturers in Detroit, formerly staunch free traders, and the United Auto Workers are lobbying for a curb on Japanese imports and join other business leaders calling for protection.[9] U.S. steel manufacturers are campaigning for tax concessions, and file antidumping suits against European steel manufacturers.

Since the 1960s, lobbies of powerful interest groups have been pressuring government to aid ailing industries against foreign competition so as to avoid the risk of reduced income or unemployment by owners and workers alike — the more the industry declined, the greater the pressure. In the mid-1970s, advocates of a liberal trade policy were hard pressed to preserve it in the face of recession, unemployment, and structural adjustment. Demands for curbing imports and protecting local industries began to grow to the point where the GATT secretariat found it necessary to warn that "the spread of protectionist pressures may well prove to be the most important current development in international economic policies, for it has reached a point at which the continued existence of an international order based on agreed and observed rules may be said to be open to question."[10]

Clamor for restrictions against imports of labor and goods is one consequence of the no-risk society mentality. Governments are hard pressed to achieve full employment, or at least to fend off higher unemployment, without reducing social insurance programs. Pressure is exerted to restrict employment to a country's own citizens. Demands mount to protect citizens against the need to change a job, retrain in a new profession, or accept a lower income. But at the same time linkages between national economies prevent them from erecting buffers against the economic policies of other countries.

Some of the reasons for interdependence are initiated by government, but most are not. Most economic analysts attribute the expansion of world trade and the unprecedented economic growth until the mid-1970s to the deliberate freeing of the world economy from the shackles imposed by the protectionist and nationalist policies of the 1930s and the gradual elimination of direct controls on trade and payments, supported by reduced transportation costs and the higher incomes and growing demands of populations more and more familiar with foreign lands and foreign habits.

International trade in services has been growing too. Travel and tourism have become among the world's fastest growing industries. The real expenditures of U.S. travel abroad grew at 6.9 percent per year between 1965 and 1973; globally, foreign tourism expenditures grew 6.7 percent annually between 1967 and 1978. They are expected to grow significantly faster — at a rate of 9.5 percent in 1985.[11] Other trade in services, from earnings on foreign investments to international banking and insurance, has been rising. In 1977 total invisible receipts in the Western world — that is, receipts from trade in services — were $300 billion, compared with $1031 billion of merchandise exports.

Since labor movements across borders were restricted, capital moved instead, seeking out the cheapest, most skilled, or most docile labor. These flows of capital, coupled with technological advances and better management of large, geographically dispersed organizations, have brought about international production controlled by huge, oligopolistic, multinational enterprises. Sophisticated business firms have increasingly become international in their operations and their outlook, partly because it allows them to circumvent government controls simply by moving production to another jurisdiction.

Multinational enterprises have been growing at a much faster rate than world trade. In the United States, about 60 percent of industrial production is controlled by enterprises with a multinational structure; in Europe, the proportion is about the same. Multinational enterprises have a much smaller share in the Japanese economy, but that share, too, is rising rapidly.

The tremendous growth of multinational firms has been a cause of concern to most national governments. The managers of these enterprises view nation-states as anachronistic institutions and national regulations as ruinous to worldwide business efficiency. Governments, however, see themselves as guardians of their own citizens and are not very interested in "world welfare." They have a hard enough time governing their own countries. They intervene, urge, subsidize, tax, or deny entrance to protect their citizens and domestic firms. They sometimes also try to ban international movement of capital or certain goods and services, or even of information, on political grounds (e.g., the export of technology to the Soviet Union or arms to South Africa).

Technology transfers are more common as well. A decade ago, the technology gap between the United States and the rest of the world was regarded as virtually insurmountable. By now, many people are afraid that the United States is losing its technology lead and entering a phase of economic decline. The technology lead the United States once possessed is dwindling in machine tools, automobiles, petroleum refining, metallurgy, and steel. In newer technologies—aerospace, electronic computation, and telecommunication—the United States appears to have retained a significant lead over virtually all other nations, but these are precisely the industries European governments are investing in to reduce the gap.

The freedom of movement of factors of production has grown in some respects: capital flows more freely, and labor within the European Common Market can move from one country to another, though in practice workers still prefer to remain where their ancestors lived. Large numbers of workers have come from less-developed areas of Europe to more prosperous lands. At times, 5 percent of all workers in Germany and a whopping 25 percent in Switzerland have been "guest workers." The numbers may well grow when the vast number of Spanish and Portuguese workers are free to move within the Common Market.[12]

Most of these guest workers are transient, coming for a few years to save their nest egg and return home. They do hard, menial, and boring work on assembly lines or in other industries, work that the country's citizens are unwilling to do, usually because a more interesting, challenging, or higher-paid job is available. Guest workers provide an unemployment buffer, since governments find it much easier to let foreigners bear the brunt of economic adjustment than to let local citizens go without jobs. The use of *Gastarbeiter* in Germany may well have been one reason why the German government refused to sustain Volkswagen, with its largely foreign workers, while the British government poured hundreds of millions of pounds into aid for its ailing motor industry. Another reason may have been the internationalization of production in the automobile industry. Most firms in this industry have a global strategy and manufacturing plants all over the world. Although the industry is labor-intensive, there have been few international diplomatic conflicts over market shares, despite the large-scale invasion of Japanese cars to the United States. The only calls for aid came from a British National Champion — British Leyland — which opted for national rather than international production. In 1975 British Leyland, supported by U.S. automobile subsidiaries in Britain, succeeded in getting a voluntary export limitation agreement from the major Japanese corporations.[13]

Goods, services, factors of production, technological expertise, and production itself were internationalized in the first twenty-five years after World War II, though movements over frontiers were never as free as some liberal economists might have wished. Some restrictions remained on the movement of capital, more on migration. Nonetheless, coupled with technological innovations, even this freedom managed to produce a new era of interdependence, which in turn complicated the successful pursuit of national objectives.

The higher levels of international trade and the bigger volume of movements of capital, technology, and production across national borders were generally encouraged as a way of augmenting the consumers' well-being, invigorating growth, and broadening opportunities for profit. With time, though, the difficulties of pursuing domestic goals have led some people to question the benefits of free trade.

Increased trade flows, coupled with movements of capital and multinational production, make each nation's economy sensitive to developments outside the country. Governments in industrial countries continue to proclaim their adherence to economic growth and free trade, but their economic policies are affected by their desire to reduce risks and their reluctance to allow unwelcome adjustments in the economy that reflect changes in world trade and production. At the same time, the ability of multinational enterprises to make transactions within their system has sharply curtailed the power of government to intervene with any effect, and this exacerbates the problem of concurrent jurisdiction and the limited ability of governments to control capital and trade flows. Governments are reduced to impotence in their international economic policies, while mounting demands for protection rely on government actions to tilt benefits to the domestic economy.

Industrial Policies

In the 1970s, industrialized countries experienced many structural, political, and financial crises, which have dampened their industrial growth and world competitiveness. The decade was characterized by a slowdown of investment, an acceleration of inflation, a realignment of currencies, and the energy crisis. Since 1974, oil prices in terms of U.S. dollars zoomed by 1000 percent. These were followed by a substantial reduction of GDP growth and reduction in employment in certain industries. The major casualties of the crisis have been in investment goods industries, chemicals based on oil, motor vehicles (owing to adverse effects of the rise in oil prices), and industries such as textile and steel in which the competition of newly industrialized countries (NIC) have been stiffest. In the 1980s, according to most experts, the experiences of the recent past are likely to continue: low and unstable economic growth, continued accelerated inflation, volatile and uncertain financial markets, strong pressures on energy prices, and North-South polarization. To reduce the hardships caused by these shocks, governments must adopt policies that will accelerate growth, and these will entail certain risks. The political realities, however, are that governments will be pushed to grant protection to industries, to alleviate the pain of adjustment.

When recessions loom large, governments and interest groups are made unhappy by uncontrollable situations that result from free movements of the factors of production. International trade brings many benefits, but it also entails threats to local industries when they are unable to compete with the more efficient, or cheaper, foreign manufacturer. Theoretically, an adjustment process can push the world's economies toward a new equilibrium, but the cost of this adjustment is often regarded by the independent economies involved as too high. Angry voices then demand greater protection of local industry and domestic employment. Recently, the path toward freer trade has been reversed.

In the last two decades, governments have emphasized "industrial policies." An OECD study published in 1975 defines industrial policy as "concerned with promoting industrial growth and efficiency."[14] To implement such policy, the study notes, governments use "financial and fiscal incentives; technical assistance, training and a wide range of consultative and advisory activities; policies within the framework of government procurement and contracts for technological development (R and D contracts); and direct State participation in industry." To this, the study adds: "Certain types of institutional arrangements, although logically distinct from the measures enumerated above, may also be important instruments of industrial policy: e.g., industrial development agencies or similar bodies concerned with the systematic identification of industrial problems and possibilities and the stimulation of action with regard to them; and special agencies set up to promote the development and adaptation of small and medium-sized businesses."

In fact, industrial policy in the 1970s was increasingly concerned with preserving employment in a particular industry or region, by artificially protecting employment against foreign competition. Government policies were aimed at maintaining high wages and obsolete capital equipment, and it passed the costs to consumers and taxpayers.

Governments try to buffer themselves against the economic policies of other nations and to protect their citizens from the hardships of adjustment, but for the most part they are unable to do so. International vertical integration of production—both through long-term procurement contracts and as a result of ownership ties—have weakened the effects of tariffs. True, effective tariff rates (i.e., tariffs calculated on the basis of value-added) are much higher than the nominal rates, but it is nonetheless still exceedingly difficult to protect industries through tariffs because elevating tariffs to very high levels is often forbidden by international agreements. Even if tariffs are raised, their effectiveness is less sharp than governments would like because when firms are vertically integrated internationally, they will continue to buy from their own subsidiaries. For essentially the same reasons, the hope that flexible exchange rates will reduce the linkages between national economies has not been realized: the power of capital controls is on the wane partially owing to technological breakthroughs in communication. Taxes on foreign income or control of remission of profits have also lost their bite. Multinational enterprises avoid these controls through devices such as transfer prices, interest payments, debt repayments, licensing fees, and management charges. In short, with the reduction of arm's length transactions and the ability of capital and production to move across national borders, many policy tools are dulled, and efforts to control the economy or protect industry are correspondingly ineffectual.

Governments are aware that their domestic policy objectives can be thwarted by their international obligations. Attempts to protect the environment, augment safety, guarantee pensions, protect existing employment structure, or aid minorities do not always jibe with the goals of increasing world trade or the realities of international production. Government then becomes a maze of conflicting bureaus attempting to achieve conflicting goals. Some policies bring uncertainty to the export industries; others aid exports to shield ailing industries from the need to adjust.

Caught in the bind between interdependence and the promises to maintain full employment and social protection, many governments have felt that Keynesian aggregate demand policies have become insufficient in achieving their contradictory national aims. One country after another has searched for specific modes of intervention, hoping to find some method that would allow them to achieve both goals. Most interventions are designed to avoid the need for adjustment.

In the United States in 1977, tariffs on shoes, color television sets, and sugar were demanded. In all these cases, the International Trade Commission (empowered by the 1974 Trade Act to recommend relief to domestic industries threatened by imports) found justifiable grounds for protective tariffs. In the shoe industry, foreign shoe manufacturers had increased their share of the U.S. market from 22 percent in 1968 to 46 percent in 1976. This competition was said to have cost 70,000 jobs in 300 U.S. shoe factories. Foreign manufacturers of color television sets were able to capture 42 percent of the U.S. market, and sugar imports pushed the price of that commodity down to the point where domestic manufacturers claimed they could not cover their costs. The net result was loud calls for protecting domestic industry and jobs. Luckily for the consumer, the President rejected the recommendation of the International Trade Commission. Nevertheless, pressures for protection continue, by the steel industry and car manufacturers, as well as by shipbuilders.

Theoretically, if imports are cheaper than local products, consumers profit from imports, and local producers find more fruitful fields to do business. One proposal of the International Trade Commission—to increase tariffs on incremental imports of shoes to the United States from 10 percent to 40 percent—would have added approximately $500 million to the cost of shoes to the U.S. consumer; the proposed increase in tariffs on color television sets from 5 percent to 25 percent would have resulted in a hike in the price of each set of about $40; and the proposed cut in sugar imports of about 33 percent would have added $110 million to the total cost of sugar to U.S. consumers. Consumers, in short, end up paying the costs of protection as well as the price of stronger inflationary pressures and retaliatory moves by other nations. In spite of this, demands for more protection continue. Nor is the United States alone in facing strong pressures for protection. All OECD member countries, not to mention the Third World countries, have been pushed into giving more and more protection to their citizens and industries. Trade restrictions proliferate when a nation is unwilling to adjust the structure of industries to the changing conditions of the world; governments start looking for ways to aid their industries without breaking the international treaties they have signed.

When technological change is allowed, some people will always lose jobs. Skills become obsolete and industries go under as they cease to be competitive because other firms can produce the goods more cheaply. A neoclassical economist would simply shrug his shoulders and say that such moves increase the wealth of all nations and that any necessary adjustment will come automatically through the rate of exchange. If Japanese productivity grows faster than U.S. production and if its exports grow as well, then the rate of exchange of the Japanese yen to the U.S. dollar will change. The yen will be appreciated and the dollar depreciated until a new balance is reached.

Nevertheless, adjustment based on rate of exchange alone means that certain industries will still be in trouble, and if governments do not aid these industries, the adjustment might be instant, chaotic, and harmful. Orderly adjustment, however, often turns into perpetual protection because there is no automatic mechanism to withdraw it. In agriculture, protectionist policies have been used for many years, because the industry sees itself as perpetually threatened. Though the labor force in agriculture has shrunk in the last hundred years, no country seems to think that the protection of farmers can be stopped. As a result, the population as a whole has been faced with higher prices for food even though the government stockpiles a tremendous amount of surpluses.[15]

"Orderly Adjustment"

Despite numerous declarations supporting unfettered international trade, most countries have been adding on trade restrictions in an effort to protect jobs in the least efficient sectors of their economy. While continuing to pay lip service to free trade, they restrict the movements of goods and services in all sorts of ways. The French talk of "organized free trade"; the United States initiates "orderly marketing agreements" and forces other nations to use "voluntary restraints." Other countries have a whole arsenal of weapons designed to break the spirit, although not the legal structure, of the General Agreement on Tariffs and Trade.

International organizations concerned with trade matters—such as the GATT, OECD, and the European Community—"have functioned increasingly not as the administrators or executors of internationally agreed regimes but rather as would-be legitimizers of deviant or strictly self-serving behavior."[16] Such behavior was particularly apparent in those manufacturing industries in which recession coupled with the increased competition of other countries caused surplus capacity and threatened employment. When production is heavily concentrated geographically, the ability of producers and labor unions to exert pressures on government is multiplied by the concentration of voting power.

Consider the textile industry. In certain Asian countries—Hong Kong, Japan, India, Taiwan, Pakistan, and South Korea—the textile industry has been expanding and has become more efficient and competitive. The price of imported textile goods would have been falling in an unfettered market and, in due course, those with a stake (investors, owners, and workers) in the textile industry outside those countries would have incurred severe losses. Some firms would have gone bankrupt and some workers would have lost their jobs, learned a new trade, joined the unemployed, or moved someplace else. Others would have accepted lower wages and remained in the same business. In the meantime, workers and investors in Asian countries would have increased their real income, and all consumers would have been able to buy cheaper clothing. Workers in Asian countries, however, do not vote in the United States, Germany, or the United Kingdom, and the risks of the losses are always looked upon as more severe than the probable gains in lower prices. The government comes to the rescue of its textile industry; in one country after another, policies attempt to shield the textile manufacturers from international competition.

Textile imports have been restricted by multilateral agreements (first the Long Term Textile Agreement of 1962, then the Multi Fibre Agreement of 1974), by bilateral "voluntary" agreements and by all kinds of other restrictions of international trade. Textile industry in all developed countries has been given protection, as well as state aid, to rationalize and modernize. The developing countries were expected to restrict their exports in order to slow down the declining employment in the textile industry in OECD countries. To achieve this goal, the United States has agreements with about thirty countries, the European Economic Community with twenty-two. In addition, different countries, including France and Britain, imposed their own unilateral import quotas. Consumer interest in cheap textiles and the humanitarian need to allow developing countries to grow have been much weaker than the interests of the industry and its workers.

To be sure, governments were unable to shield their declining industries completely. Textile and clothing output in the OECD area slowed and employment fell at a rapid pace. Annual average rates of growth of production in textile, 4.5 percent in the OECD area before 1973, stagnated to a minus 1 percent. Since 1973, more than 1.3 million employees left the textile industry — about 15 percent per annum of the entire labor force. At the same time, these totals conceal important differences in governmental policies: Japan and the Netherlands provided financial assistance to firms to systematically dispose of excess capacity,while other countries used ad hoc measures to curtail imports. As a result, the Japanese textile industry reduced its employment force from 1.3 million in 1963 to 753,000 in 1978. The United States, on the other hand, employed 863,000 workers in its textile factories in 1963 and more than a million in 1978.[17]

Steel provides another example. For a number of reasons, the world demand for steel has recently been declining. The immediate reaction of steel manufacturers when evidence of decline first appeared was to cut prices and dump steel in the world market. Local producers of steel demanded protection against imports. Even when they were simply faced with competition from a more efficient producer they claimed unfair advantage. Japanese steel takes half the man-hours to produce what American steel does. U.S. steel manufacturers, however, claim they are forced to spend much more capital because of environmental protection laws. In fact, Japanese capital expenditures on environmental protection have been higher than those of the United States both absolutely and as a percent of total capital expenditure.[18] Economic theory says that the least efficient producers of steel should gracefully give way to the more efficient producers. But in practice the least efficient steel producers simply pressured their governments into protecting them. Labor, afraid of unemployment, added to these pressures.

U.S. special steel producers now receive protection in the form of quotas; carbon-steel producers receive a system of "trigger prices" (any import below the trigger price automatically results in an "antidumping" investigation). Europeans are given tax rebates, subsidized loans, and a variety of grants. In 1968, the United States negotiated voluntary steel export restrictions with Japan, binding the United States to impose no further restrictions until the end of 1971. Despite this agreement, the United States imposed import surcharges in August 1971. Another agreement was signed in 1976, again imposing import quotas, and in 1977 trigger prices on Japanese steel imports to the United States were imposed. The Europeans followed suit with "indicative prices" barring Japanese steel imports if prices were lower than these indicative prices by at least 6 percent. A new triangular agreement on market restrictions between the EEC, the United States, and Japan was signed on November 30, 1977. The GATT secretariat, in its 1976-77 report, rightly pointed out that there is an irreconcilable conflict between the attempts to improve the steel industry's profits and efforts to promote the industry in general. "Steel-using industries," they say, "find themselves at a competitive disadvantage vis-à-vis foreign firms obtaining steel at world market price. If the industries competing with imports are in turn granted additional protection, the danger of retaliation increases."[19] Yet, the price of steel is now manipulated by the European Economic Community (which ironically was founded to foster free trade), as well as by individual countries. The same sorry state of affairs is found in a growing number of other countries.

In 1945 America's steel industry was the most powerful in the world. In 1965 U.S. steel production was 26 percent of world production. By 1977 the U.S. percentage of world production had declined to 17 percent. The basic underlying reason for this decline has been a loss of competitiveness because of increasing costs of production caused in part by high labor costs and in part because equipment is old and inadequate. Modern basic oxygen furnaces account for 80 percent of Japanese steel production, as opposed to 61.6 percent in the United States, 72 percent in Germany and 52 percent in the United Kingdom. Japan possesses 31 percent of the crude output in continuous casting;

West Germany 24.3 percent, and the United States only 9.1 percent (the UK share is even lower, 8.5 percent). In 1956 Japanese unit cost per metric ton of steel produced was $119.83, compared with $110.84 in the United States. In 1976 the picture was reversed: Japanese costs were $151.93, compared with $294.65 in the United States.

The U.S. steel industry has regularly pleaded for protection against imports. It also has filed antidumping suits against foreign suppliers. In Europe, the steel industry—largely publicly owned—has been protected by expensive government support and financing. This aid has led to delays in the closing of obsolete or less efficient plants and the construction of what has proven to be excess capacity. The plight of the steel industry has prompted even more government action: nationalization of steel and later a community-wide "rationalization" plan that eventually led to a creation of a producers' cartel (Eurofer) in 1977. In addition, the community negotiated steel import limitations with many of the "disruptive" suppliers including Japan, South Africa, Mexico, and South Korea.

Demands for protection are as understandable as the response to them of popularly elected governments who must face the voter. As long as people believed that governments could not tilt, change, or otherwise alter economic phenomena—as long as unemployment, for example, was conceived of as an unavoidable calamity—people did not expect the government to protect them from such events.

Advances in science encourge the belief that cures can be found for all ills, and governments ought to supply the cure. If the solutions shift the burden to foreigners, all the better. After all, national governments are elected by a domestic, not international, citizenry; their responsibilities at home overshadow their responsibilities to the outside. One puzzle remains: Economic theory tells us that protectionism acts against the interest of the majority of citizens because most citizens profit from international trade. In an open trading system a country will export goods it can produce at lower costs than other countries and import goods that other countries can produce at lower cost than it does. Countries thereby gain from trade that makes possible higher levels of consumption and investment. Unfettered international trade also contributes to price stability because it forces the domestic economy to restrain prices and wages so that it can compete effectively with foreign producers. Since the gains are so obvious and widespread, why are there so many pressures for protectionism, and why do governments succumb to them?

The sources of the pressures are two: First, although the liberalization of trade unquestionably increases the aggregate national income, some industries gain and others lose. As markets, technology, and tastes evolve, some products lose their advantage and others gain. Firms that have lost markets to foreign competitors have capital that cannot immediately be changed, and workers in these industries have specialized skills that cannot be used. They have to learn new skills or move to a different region to find employment in another industry. These transitory effects create problems, since the costs of adjusting the economy to changing conditions have to be borne by these individuals and groups, and they are the ones who demand the protection. Second, in times of recession and unemployment, displaced labor and capital are less likely to be absorbed in industries in which the country has a comparative advantage. The adjustment is more difficult to the individual and perhaps more costly to the society. In many cases, increasing foreign trade makes countries vulnerable to economic and especially political changes in the international scene. The larger the share of imports, the greater the vulnerability to embargoes or the difficulties of getting or producing an item in the event of war.

Most actions protecting local firms, however, are not in defense-oriented or strategically essential industry. For example, the United States protects footwear, steel, and color television sets; the United Kingdom restricts imports of Japanese cars; France protects wine; and Germany protects processed goods. The list is long and growing; it includes not only the above items but also furniture, ball bearings, refrigerators, and ethylene. Except perhaps for the aerospace industry, whose protection is sometimes justified in terms of national pride, and shipbuilding, vaguely related to defense needs, the third argument does not hold.

The first two arguments are connected with adjustment costs. It can be shown that adjustment costs are almost always lower than protectionist costs, particularly when the probability of retaliation is taken into account. The risk of adjustment can also be softened somewhat by government through assistance to workers, firms, and communities. The United States provides readjustment allowances, relocation payments, and training to displaced workers; technical and financial assistance to affected firms; and public works money to communities. Other countries have similar and even more wide-ranging programs.[20]

Why, then, if the gains to consumers from open trade outweigh the costs of adjustment to domestic firms and workers, is the voice of the consumer hardly heard and that of those demanding protection to achieve economic security so loud, clear, and effective? The answer illustrates one basic problem of politically determined distribution.

Assume that a certain trade liberalization will increase national income to the point where every U.S. citizen gains $10 from the tariff reduction.[21] The total gain will be $2.3 billion—a lofty amount indeed. The adjustment costs most of which will be transitional, come to $500 million. Under these assumptions, there will theoretically be a net gain to society of $1.8 billion. Society could compensate the losers and still be better off.

The problem is that $10 is seen by each individual as negligible, not worth informing oneself further or writing to one's congressman. The cost of $500 million, on the other hand, is borne by a smaller number of individuals—say, 100,000—an average of $50,000 each, and this group will certainly bring pressure on government to save themselves. Though, in addition to the $10, some workers might get jobs in an export-oriented industry that could grow as a result of the liberalization, no one knows this for sure. The losers, in contrast, know who they are.

In most cases of trade liberalization, increase in free trade can be shown to bring about greater benefits than costs. Because of the asymmetry of costs and benefits, however, the pressures for protectionism still mount. In many cases the benefits are not only diffused but they come in the form of future flows of funds—increasing employment and income opportunities in an export industry or lower costs to the consumer. The costs, on the other hand, are very concentrated and very real: people out of jobs, machines idle. In such a situation, it is understandable, politically, if not from a purely economic point of view, that governments will turn to protectionism to slow down adjustments and minimize disturbances in a certain industry or region regardless of future gains beyond the horizon of the next election. To the economists, the whole area of protection and related problems is riddled with inconsistencies and incoherence if they are not trained to take political considerations into account. Yet it is precisely politics that leads to attempts to shift the risk and the burden of adjustment and that makes it difficult to establish the legitimacy of any international agreement. Trade liberalization has always been heralded by strong traders: France and Britain in the mid-nineteenth century and the United States in the mid-twentieth.[22] Once free trade causes inconvenience to the strong nation, that nation tries to find ways around its commitments to ensure economic security to its producers and workers.

The shipbuilding industry is one of the most telling examples of the widespread use of government subsidies to keep a declining industry afloat. No government is willing to let its shipbuilding industry be closed down by market forces. In the United States, subsidies, special tax exemptions, crewing restrictions, safety regulations, government procurement for the U.S. Navy and sealift, and preferential treatment for the domestic fleet are used to protect the industry.[23] In Sweden, successive governments have rescued so many yards that the state now owns virtually all of the shipbuilding industry. Total government aid to shipbuilding over the past three years reached $4.3 billion.

The Swedish government is now making an effort to slim the industry by 1985, at which time only three large yards will be in operation.[24] Britain has done the same, and its nationalized shipyards lost $200 million in the first nine months of operation. When British shipbuilders wanted to lay off 12,000 out of 40,000 workers, the unions dug in for a fight. France spent $200 million on subsidies to its shipyards.[25] Domestic yards in Germany were about to lay off 5000 workers in the first ten months of 1977 when the German government came to their rescue through direct subsidies and the export of ships through tied-aid arrangements to developing countries for a total of almost DM 600 million. It also nationalized the Schleswig-Holstein yards. By 1978, the total amount put out in subsidies to shipbuilders was estimated by the OECD at $50 billion. This is double the total education, training, employment, and social services allocation, and more than the total allocation to health services of the U.S. federal budget. To be sure, the U.S. shipbuilding industry's share of the market is kept secured by invisible subsidies. The full force of adjustment to recession had to be worked out between Europe and Japan.

Within the European Community, France forbids the importing of Italian wines and limits advertising on bourbon and scotch, but not on its own cognac and apertifs. Britain limits imports of television sets, and all nine member countries restrict imports of textiles. The Europeans have been preaching "organized liberty of exchange," which is a variant on the U.S. idea of "orderly marketing agreements" — both are simply government-to-government negotiated quotas. Between 1971 and 1974, there were 24 actions filed by EEC countries to restrict imports through claims of dumping. Between 1975 and 1978, claims rose to 171; 41 were for 1977, and 94 for the first eight months of 1978.[26] The United States has negotiated such agreements limiting imports of Japanese color television sets, Korean and Taiwanese shoes, and Asian textiles, in addition to its "trigger prices" to protect steel. It also created a $550 million steel loan guarantee program.

Subsidies and Other Invisible Protection

Governments also try to dump unemployment on others through exports by using all kinds of subsidies. The European Economic Commission complained to GATT that the operation of the Domestic International Sales Corporations (DISC) is actually a disguised tax incentive to U.S. export activities and violated GATT rules on subsidies. A report of an independent panel of experts presented in November 1976 agreed with the EEC: "After reviewing the operation of the DISC scheme in the light of the provisions of GATT, the panel concluded that the scheme should be regarded as an export subsidy and that in some cases it had effects which contravened United States obligations under Article XVI:4 of the General Agreement. The panel found there was a *prima facie* case of nullification or impairment of benefits which other GATT member countries were entitled to expect under the General Agreement."[27] The DISC scheme is one example of the roundabout ways used by governments. As in the domestic economy, in the international arena the hand of the government is often invisible.

Facing recession and unemployment, countries have been emasculating liberal trade agreements through all kinds of invisible methods: subsidies, guaranteed government procurements, incentives and taxes, the employment of a whole array of nontariff barriers (ingeniously manipulating licensing systems, safety regulations, health requirements), and so on. The use of subsidies for encouraging production, employment, and investment, the design of government procurement policies to create a protective umbrella for local industry, and mounting requirements for tie-in arrangements in foreign aid are all mechanisms that have become much more sophisticated and selective and are designed to help an industry here, prod a firm there, or help a region somewhere else. In the process, the respect paid to international agreements, charters, and declarations has been eroded. No careful analysis exists to explain how subsidy programs work; nor is there a list of all subsidies. Individual subsidy programs were introduced without taking into account their repercussions on other parts of the economy.[28]

In the 1950s and '60s, it was claimed (and believed) that governmental aid should be restricted to the needy. Subsidies were widely used, but they were officially regarded as a tool for the more equitable distribution of benefits. Industrial subsidies were used mainly to lure investors to depressed or underdeveloped areas: the Mezzogiorno in Italy, the north of England, the province of Brittany in France, Appalachia in the United States, or certain regions in Scotland and Ireland. The Irish combine an extremely favorable corporate tax regime with a highly selective and interventionist industrial strategy masterminded by the Industrial Development Authority (IDA) to create jobs. In the 1970s, following the woes of the dollar and the oil crisis and the larger volume of imports from the developing world, all kinds and forms of subsidies were used to protect jobs in declining industries and avoid the risk of even temporary unemployment.

Even when a subsidy is given through the budget, it is not always easy to recognize. If taxes on fuel used by trucks and factory machines are lower than taxes on gasoline, used mainly by private cars, is the difference a subsidy? If the government substitutes a direct tax (such as an employment tax) for an indirect tax that raises the same amount of revenue but is not paid on exported goods, is this an export subsidy?[29] In 1966 the British government introduced a so-called selective employment tax, which was to be paid by all industries. Manufacturers, however, received a rebate of 130 percent of the tax paid; and the public sector, including the transportation industry, received a rebate of 100 percent. It was claimed that since purchase taxes were not paid by the service sector, the 130 percent rebate helped offset the balance. At the same time, a large percentage of the manufacturing output was exported. The tax refund certainly aided export, but this policy was considered consistent with GATT provisions on export subsidies.[30]

The crux of the matter, again, is that governments are forced to intervene in order to reduce the risk borne by certain groups and shore up troubled segments of their economies or protect industries with a high potential for politically unpopular disruptions. Firms often present their problems as abnormal, temporary, or caused by the noneconomic behavior of foreign firms. Economic experts may advise the government that the aid should not be forthcoming because the problems are structural rather than abnormal, and chronic rather than temporary, but governments still go by their political instincts as much as by economic arguments. They step in to save votes. As a result, there is a trend toward more dependence of firms on government to reduce the risk of competition.

The Dangers of a New Mercantilism

To some extent, the economic system is drifting into a new mercantilism, but one with a different power structure from that which prevailed in the sixteenth and seventeenth centuries. In its earlier formulation (as in the new one) mercantilism was characterized by a symbiotic relationship between the state and private economic favorites. It was based on a quest for power in its foreign relations utilizing publicly granted monopolies in foreign trade and characterized by a maze of intricate government orders regulating the supply of labor, conditions of land tenure, and the financial flow in the economy. Industries deemed critical or strategic were granted a monopoly in production and protected against foreign competition.

This social agreement served a vital role in strengthening the nation-state, but also left important endeavors undeveloped. The French cry of *"laissez-faire, laissez-passer!"* called for the right of the capitalist class to enjoy a system in which the free market alone would determine what should be produced, how it should be produced, and who would produce it. Capitalism realized the elimination of all crown-granted monopolies and all restrictions on trade, as well as the transformation of labor and land into commodities.

Today, the policy tools used by governments of the industrialized countries have become at least as varied as in the old mercantilist system. Acutely conscious of the decline in their capacity to use conventional economic policy to influence international economic relations, governments aim their support at particular sectors, one industry, or even one specific firm in their country. Canadian and European governments and state governments in the United States negotiate specific and detailed contracts with firms, laying down the subsidies these firms will receive if they agree to invest in a specific region or town. In some instances, such as that of Volkswagen in Pennsylvania and the Ford Motor Company in Ontario, the booty has amounted to tens of millions of dollars.

Japan is sometimes referred to as "Japan Inc." because of the close interaction and coordination among its private industrial firms, its financial system, and its government. One method often used in Japan to help favored firms is to allow the banks to grant them loans in times of difficulty and to maintain intimate and (reciprocal) relationships with the banks. The banks, in turn, can afford such policies mainly because the central bank tolerates them, for example, by not demanding "writeoffs" of risky loans. When the growing computer industry had liquidity problems as a result of its rapid growth, the Japanese government organized a leasing company to buy computers and handle the leasing, and in this way injected capital into the firm.[31]

Yet, these notably close relationships between private firms and government in Japan are not unique. In all industrialized market economies, the government has increased its involvement in the economy and designed elaborate methods for aiding private industries and reducing their risks. These methods range all the way from acquiring the firm outright to covering its losses through general taxation revenues to allocating government purchasing contracts used to favor local manufacturers or pay them invisible subsidies by paying higher prices for those products it supplies to government. In between, governments use state guarantees, subsidized loans, differential tax treatment, lenient surveillance of "troubled" situations, purchase of shares, grants, allowances, direct subsidies, or subsidies of the major inputs. Governments also provide aid to industry through procurement of its products, specifications of the product for foreign aid, development grants, training assistance, research facilities, advisory services, and intelligence gathering. Many of these aids shift the risk of unemployment and the burden of adjustment on to other countries. Others are triggered by the belief that domestic firms have become less competitive as a result of other risk-reduction regulations: tougher environmental standards, high costs of health insurance, or tighter safety requirements. Needed structural changes are avoided or not allowed, and decisions are based on political considerations. The scope of these activities can be expected to grow sharply, making it more difficult to reach any meaningful international agreement that can be enforced.

In the struggle to keep jobs, delay the need of economic adjustment, and boost exports, state-owned enterprises have changed their original scope of activities. Just after World War II, state-owned enterprises were established, or private firms nationalized, to keep the "commanding heights" of the economy in public hands and subject to governmental directives. In the 1960s and even more frequently in the 1970s, state-owned enterprises were created and private firms acquired, not to protect the commanding heights, but to avoid the sinking sands—to rescue firms from bankruptcy.

The use of state ownership to rescue ailing industries and reduce unemployment and business failure has not been adequately researched. Americans who believe in the "free enterprise system" perceive every acquisition of a private firm by the state as socialist expropriation. The facts present a rather different picture. In hundreds of cases, governments acquired all or some of the shares of companies in order to shift the burden of the losses incurred by the firm on to the public purse. Firms were acquired with full payment, and the payment was sometimes much higher than the fair market value of the firm, particularly when the probable flow of future funds is taken into consideration. Nationalization was forced on government to rescue the firm and fend off unemployment. In the United Kingdom, the government acquired Rolls Royce, Upper Clyde Shipbuilders, Beagle Aircrafts, Cable and Wireless, British Leyland, and many other firms.[32] In other cases, it acquired part of the shares; in still others, it guaranteed loans or financed production losses.[33] In Sweden, all state holdings are managed by one holding company, the Statsföretag. This firm is expected to earn a return to the taxpayers on its investments. It prides itself on resisting governmental pressures to bail out ailing firms without compensation. Still, despite the resistance, it does exactly that.

In the Federal Republic of Germany, generally considered a bastion of free enterprise and free trade, dozens of firms have been acquired by the government or by the Länder (the provincial governments). The reason, again, is to subsidize private industry and save jobs, mainly in structurally weak, low-income regions: iron, steel, and coal mining in Saarland and Lower Saxony, coal mining in the Ruhr area, and shipbuilding in Schleswig-Holstein.

In Italy, too, state-owned firms have acquired private firms to save them from bankruptcy. In the 1970s, the number of firms acquired by the state holding system was so large that at the request of the Istituto per la Ricostruzione Industriale, the major state holding firm, another state holding firm, Società di Gestioni e Partecipazioni Industriali, was established to rescue them. The funds required were large, and the government of Italy resorted to a less visible

method of financing. Instead of granting its firms the pseudo-equity investment of the *fondi di dotazione,* it financed them through the granting of subsidized long-term loans. The rate of interest is subsidized through a very simple,
and invisible, device: they are allowed to borrow from the central bank at
lower than market rates of interest.

In Belgium, the "State decided to help a number of individual companies
in distress. These companies, such as ACEC, Val-Saint Lambert, Materne and
Glaverbel, were hard-hit by the recent economic down-turn. The State considered them to be of great importance, especially in terms of employment, and
initiated rescue operations."[34] It asked the National Investment Company
either to help these enterprises or acquire them outright. The Belgian government spent $2 billion to rescue the top half dozen private steel firms in 1979.
France and Sweden also acquired private steel firms, and similar rescue operations saved most of the European shipbuilding industry, several textile firms,
and scores of other firms.

The same story can be repeated for other European countries. The U.S.
federal government, presumably for ideological reasons, is not able to buy up
manufacturing firms, but neither is it allowed to sit on its hands while they de-
generate. It had to find other ways to rescue them. It guaranteed a loan to
Lockheed and supports the railroads. Other cases—the granting of defense
procurement contracts, acquisition of redeemable preferred shares, "buy
American" policies, and the negotiations of "voluntary" quotas with other
countries—are less known.

The U.S. government also helped firms by specifying their product for
foreign aid. Foreign aid has been used to sell American tobacco, even though
the surgeon general declared cigarettes to be dangerous to health. The United
States bailed out its tenth largest industrial firm, when Congress granted the
Chrysler Corporation a $1.5 billion loan guarantee and mandated an addition-
al $2 billion to be supplied by banks, suppliers, and state governments. In ad-
dition, those states in which Chrysler plants are in operation gave the firm
hundreds of millions in loans.

Contrary to popular belief, protection of local industry dates back long
before the 1973 Arab oil embargo and the dislocations and economic stagnation that followed. World recession after 1973 intensified the demands for protection, but the present crisis in international economic relations came earlier.
Movements of labor across national boundaries have been restricted for decades, attempts to liberalize world trade in agricultural products have persistently been blocked, and "declining industries" have persistently been protected. The first international agreement to circumvent the rules of international
economic conduct, including the nondiscrimination rule, was signed in 1962.
This was the Long Term Agreement on Cotton Textiles, which restrained in-

ternational trade in textiles.[35] Nations have resorted to a whole battery of nontariff barriers. Governments impose cumbersome safety standards, packing and labeling regulations, and customs procedures to discourage importers. Japan, for example, insists on its own chemical analysis of imported cosmetics. The United States uses countervailing duties in the increasing number of cases where foreign countries have aided their exports by direct or indirect subsidies (such as excessive or "unjustified" tax rebates on export loss indemnification). Between 1959 and 1967, the U.S. Treasury had no countervailing duties; seventeen were issued between January 1, 1967, and the end of 1974. What are "legitimate" and what are "illegitimate" subsidies is a perennial issue facing all governments. The 1973 crisis heightened this problem by enlarging the number of industries and firms for which protection was sought. By the mid-1970s, according to GATT calculation, an additional 5 percent of world trade was subject to restriction.

If one believes that the government is pressed into protectionism by strong pressure groups and that such intervention works against the interest of the majority of the people, one should recommend an international agreement that would tie government's hand by making protectionism subject to retaliation by other countries. Governments would then be interested in giving up some of the autonomy they now have, because only in that way could they achieve the best interests of the electorate as a whole, rather than a small but vociferous interest group. The multilateral trade negotiations known as the Tokyo round[36] were probably not that Machiavellian, but their attempts to reach agreement on export subsidies were inspired by the possibility of retaliation by other countries to domestic protection and the debate over "legitimate" and "illegitimate" export subsidies. The negotiations resulted in two agreements: on tariff reduction and/or the binding of tariffs at the prevailing rate and on import licensing procedures. They also resulted in an agreement on nondiscrimination in central government procurement, as well as on certain nontariff barriers such as regulations related to health and safety, and on domestic subsidies.[37]

The extent to which governments of the world will be able to restrict themselves by solemn and generally agreed upon codes of conduct in the international economic scene remains to be seen. Past experience suggests that even solemnly agreed upon principles will be breached or circumvented in the face of pressures from home.

When government is made to directly assume the brunt of external shocks and then distribute the burden over the whole national economy, it ensures one sector of the economy against international disturbances. Fixed exchange rates are a good example of this phenomenon—the risk of fluctuations in the exchange rate to exporters and importers is mitigated. Another example may be the use of governmental guarantees and insurance to foreign trade and investment.

International spillovers follow, quite naturally, from attempts to shift costs of adjustment. If imports from fledgling manufacturing enterprises in developing countries are threatening the precarious performance of domestic enterprises, such imports are banned or at least made noncompetitive. The drift into a new mercantilism has resulted from attempts by interest groups to reduce the risks borne by them and by the changing structure of political power that backs the demands for a reduction of risks. These demands are justified not only by the need to maintain high levels of employment but by the conviction that international competition is unfair because attempts to reduce risk through invisible means cause a surge in production costs and investment funds are channeled into pollution-abatement equipment, causing the competitive position of some U.S. manufacturing industries to deteriorate. As in the case of purely domestic problems, the government is again viewed as the all-provider. But the maladies are more visible on the international scene, and the impotence of governments is also much greater.

Experience has already demonstrated the enormous costs that are borne by all countries, once beggar-thy-neighbor policies are adopted. Entities that interact in the international arena are even more diverse than those seen in the domestic arena; international consensus is more difficult to achieve than domestic consensus. More alarmingly, international acquiescence is also more difficult to achieve. What might be tolerated in a closed system constrained by national boundaries may not be tolerated in a world of sovereign, often selfish, and always proud, nation-states. The danger of the system's collapsing is infinitely greater on the international level; hence, there is a more urgent need for better policies. The major problem for the 1980s, therefore, is whether economies will be able to shift the composition of employment, output, and international trade to new growth industries.

The difficulties encountered in the last decade may have awakened governments to the dangers of continuously attempting to reduce all risks, and it may well be that they will finally reverse the trend. Governments that reduce risks in one place increase uncertainty in another. Rising expectations cause citizens to demand much more from their governments, but responsible governments need not pledge to meet all these aspirations, particularly when the willingness to pay for them is not forthcoming. Governments should lead their nations to an understanding of the dangers inherent in attempting to block essential changes, to an appreciation of the limits to their ability to shield any citizen from any change, and to the need for promoting and facilitating adjustments. It is hoped that governments will be able to carry out their responsibilities. If they are, they might stop using invisible methods to hide the real problems and learn to educate the public to the dangers of pushing beyond their capabilities, that is, beyond the limits of the public interest.

NOTES

1. Richard N. Cooper, *The Economics of Interdependence: Economic Policy in the Atlantic Community* (New York: McGraw-Hill, 1968), p. 4.
2. Robert Gilpin, *U.S. Power and the Multinational Corporation* (New York: Basic Books, 1974).
3. See Cooper, *The Economics of Interdependence*, p. 61; and GATT, *International Trade, 1976-77* (Geneva, 1977).
4. OECD, *The Impact of the Newly Industrializing Countries on Production and Trade in Manufactures* (Paris: OECD, Report by the Secretary General, 1979). Employment in manufacturing in developed countries is estimated to have fallen between 1973 and 1976 at 2 percent annually, against an annual average growth of 3 percent in developing countries. Gross capital formation fell by 2 percent in developed countries and rose in developing countries by 9 percent. See R. Blackhurst, N. Marian, and J. Tumlir, *Trade Liberalization, Protectionism and Interdependence* (Geneva: GATT, November 1977).
5. U.S. Department of Commerce, *International Economic Indicators,* June 1979, pp. 60-61. Figures for the Netherlands and Italy are for 1977 and for France are for 1976.
6. U.S. Department of Commerce, *International Economic Indicators,* December 1978, pp. 60-61; June 1979, pp. 60-61.
7. *The Economist,* 28 June 1980.
8. Economic Commission for Europe, *The Steel Market in 1978* (Brussels, The Committee).
9. *The Economist,* 12 July 1980, p. 70.
10. GATT, *International Trade, 1976-77.*
11. Anthony Edwards, *International Tourism Development: Forecast to 1985* (London: Economist Intelligence Unit, May 1976), pp. 7, 63.
12. The following comparison of net immigration as a percentage of population increase is noteworthy:

NET IMMIGRATION AS A PERCENTAGE OF POPULATION INCREASE

	1950-54	1955-59	1960-64	1965-69	1970-72	1950-72
Western Europe						
Belgium	7%	18%	34%	27%	47%	25%
France	9	32	48	30	31	33
Germany	-48	25	49	63	83	47
Luxembourg	40	77	65	60	84	66
Netherlands	-16	-2	4	7	19	3
Sweden	19	21	31	44	34	30
Switzerland	39	49	52	24	18	39

	1950-59	1960-69	1970-78
Northern America			
Canada	27%	17%	n.a.
United States	11	16	21%

SOURCES: John Cornwall, *Modern Capitalism: Its Growth and Transformation* (New York: St. Martin's Press, 1977), p. 86; Department of Economics and Social Affairs, *World Population Prospects as Assessed in 1973* (United Nations, 1977), table 26 and annex 1, table 28; and U.S. Bureau of the Census, *Current Population Report,* Series P-25, no. 802, "Estimates of the Population of the United States and Components of Change, 1940 to 1978," U.S. Government Printing Office, Washington, D.C., 1979.

13. Susan Strange, "The Management of Surplus Capacity: or How Does Theory Stand Up to Protectionism 1970s Style?" *International Organization* 33, no. 3 (Summer 1979): 328.
14. Organization for Economic Cooperation and Development, *The Aims and Instruments of Industrial Policy* (Paris: OECD, 1975), pp. 132-33.
15. The costs of the European Economic Community's Common Agricultural Policy (CAP) reached $10 billion in 1979 because of tremendous surplus. See Werner J. Feld, "Implementation of the European Community's Common Agricultural Policy: Expectations, Fears, Failures," *International Organization* 33, no. 3 (Summer 1979): 335.
16. Strange, "The Management of Surplus Capacity," p. 307.
17. U.S. employment in the textile industry reached its peak in 1973 with 1.18 million employees. See Wilhelm Kurth, "Textile and Clothing: A National and International Issue" (paper presented at the International Symposium on Industrial Policies for the 1980s, Madrid, 5-9 May 1980).
18. Palani G. Periasamy and Paul Little, "Analysis of Structural Problems in the Steel Industry and Policies for Reconstruction: An International Perspective" (paper presented at the International Symposium on Industrial Policies for the 1980s, Madrid, 5-9 May 1980.
19. GATT, *International Trade, 1976-77,* p. 23.
20. The U.S. adjustment program is available to firms, workers, and communities adversely affected by import competition. In other countries, adjustment assistance is provided on a wider basis. For details, see U.S. General Accounting Office, *Considerations for Adjustment Assistance Under the 1974 Trade Act: A Summary of Techniques Used in Other Countries, Report of the Comptroller General to the Congress of the United States* (Washington, D.C.: U.S. Government Printing Office, 18 January 1979).
21. For a much more rigorous exposition, see Blackhurst, Marian, and Tumlir, *Trade Liberalization, Protectionism, and Interdependence,* pp. 32-33. All figures are in present values.
22. See Karl Polanyi, *The Great Transformation* (New York: Farrar & Rinehart, 1944); Charles P. Kindleberger, "Government and International Trade," *Essays in International Finance* (Princeton: Princeton University Press, 1978).
23. See R. Keohane and J. Nye, *Power and Interdependence: World Politics in Transition* (Boston: Little, Brown, 1977).

24. *The Economist,* 21 June 1980, p. 78.
25. *The Economist,* 30 December 1978, p. 48.
26. Patrizio Bianchi, "Structural Changes in Industry" (paper presented at the International Symposium on Industrial Policies for the 1980s, Madrid, 5-9 May 1980), p. 3.
27. GATT, *Activities in 1976* (Geneva, 1977), pp. 78-79.
28. For a beginning of a theory, see W. M. Corden, *Trade Policy and Economic Welfare* (Oxford: Clarendon Press, 1974). For a catalog, see Organization for Economic Cooperation and Development, *The Aims and Instruments of Industrial Policy* (Paris: OECD, 1975). See also Irving Leveson and Jimmy Wheeler, eds., *Western Economies in Transition: Structural Changes and Adjustment Policies in Industrial Countries* (Boulder, Col.: Westview Press, 1980).
29. Such a policy was used by France in 1968. See Harald B. Malmgren, "The Border Tax Problem," *Canadian Tax Journal,* January-February 1969.
30. See the chapter on "Industrial Policy in the United Kingdom," in *Trade Effects of Public Subsidies to Private Enterprise,* ed. Geoffrey Denton, Seamus O'Cleireacain, and Sally Ash (London: Macmillan, 1975).
31. Harald B. Malmgren, *International Order for Public Subsidies,* Thames *Essay Number 11* (London: Trade Policy Research Centre, 1977), p. 24.
32. Parenthetically, despite the public ownership, these firms, for some obscure reason, are considered in the national accounts statistics as part of the private sector. Only the so-called nationalized industries are shown as part of the public sector.
33. For many details, see Gabriele Ganz, *Government and Industry: The Provision of Financial Assistance to Industry and Its Control* (Abingdon, Oxford: Professional Books, 1977).
34. A. Jacquemin, "Belgium/Luxembourg," part 1 of *Public Enterprise in the EEC,* ed. William Keyser and Ralph Windle (Alphen aan den Rijn, The Netherlands: Sijthoff & Noordhoff, 1978).
35. For details, see Gerard and Victoria Curzon, "The Management of Trade Relations in the GATT," in *International Economic Relations in the 1960s and 1970s,* ed. Andrew Shonfield (Beverly Hills, Cal.: Sage, 1976).
36. These negotiations were formally launched at a ministerial meeting convened in Tokyo in September 1973. The negotiations did not get around to serious business until the U.S. Congress gave negotiating authority to its team, and the European Commission to its side. The U.S. Congress gave such authority in the Trade Act of 1974, signed by the President on February 3, 1975. The European Commission's negotiating directives were agreed upon the following month. The actual negotiations were held in Geneva. They were known as the "Tokyo Round" and were completed by the end of 1979.
37. For details see, General Agreement on Tariffs and Trade, 1979, *The Tokyo Round of Multilateral Trade Negotiations* (Geneva: GATT, April 1979). Also see General Agreement on Tariffs and Trade, 1980, *The Tokyo Round of Multilateral Trade Negotiations: Supplementary Report,* vol. 2 (Geneva: GATT, January 1980).

7. The Limits to the Public Interest

The Delusion of a No-Risk Society

It is often argued that when optimality cannot be achieved in the market, it should be achieved by nonmarket means, usually through government. Thus, when a market failure is shown, the prescription is often for government involvement. The nonexistence of markets for bearing some risks reduces the well-being of those who would prefer to transfer those risks to others at a certain price, as well as to those who are willing to bear the risks at such a price. In unpredictable cases not under the control of the individual decision maker, the calls for such insurance come quite early: subsidies to the blind, aid to the poor, or relief against suffering caused by earthquakes or floods are some early examples. With time, the demand for public insurance has widened. Yet, risks cannot be eliminated by passing them to government. Certain risks can be insured against by government, but these entail costs, and a system for distribution of these costs must be devised and agreed on. Unfortunately, such a system has not been created, and the shifting of the problem to the public sector has not always been the optimal method.

Today, the aggregate demand for public insurance far exceeds the collective willingness to pay the insurance "premiums." Individuals trying to maximize their own utility tend to spend more time and resources in attempts to tilt governmental benefits their way and reduce the costs. Yet, the costs of all new insurance programs must be paid. In other words, as long as resources are scarce, they must be allocated. If market allocation is considered lacking, another allocation mechanism must replace it. Allocation may be based on power or on rationing. In other cases, allocation may be based on time spent in queues, in which the first to come and those willing to wait in line will be served. But, as long as resources are scarce, some mode of allocation always exists.

Each allocation mechanism involves certain problems, and each class in society would prefer a different distribution method. The rich would like a distribution based on the market; the poor may prefer a distribution based on time, which they have in relative abundance. Skilled persons would rather see a distribution on the basis of skills, and the less skilled would prefer some equality of results. Since each individual wants different things, one can easily catalog contradictions in any politico-economic system. Contradictions, in other words, are not only a capitalist phenomenon but are omnipresent in any other system too.

There are no agreed upon norms of distribution. Even if one assumes that a universal agreement may be reached on some general high-order objectives, it may still be impossible to reach a sufficient congruence of opinion on the way these objectives should be reached. Thus it may be that unanimity might be reached on the desirability of justice and equity or of equality of opportunities; there may even be a consensus on the necessity of maintaining a reasonable level of price stability or the need for growth. These agreements do not, however, include decisions about how best to ensure these objectives. Each one of a myriad of possible policies may achieve any one of the agreed upon goals. The choice of the preferred policy is not an easy matter.

Take the question of equality of opportunity. Few would disagree that it is a desirable objective. But few would agree on the policies for achieving it. Does equal opportunity mean that the amount spent on the education of each child should be the same? Is equality measured in dollars earned per capita or per family? Are we interested in equality of opportunities or of results? Is equality possible, given the differences between human beings in their abilities, aspirations, histories, motivations, and the power they possess? By the same token, agreement on the desirability of price stability is not sufficient to solve such mundane problems as whether such stability should be achieved by freezing wages, taxing capital, or some other means.

Distribution questions were solved rather more easily in the past simply because most people had no voice in the matter; they accepted the social order. As long as the black people in the United States accepted their inferior position, the "Negro problem" was dormant. It was only when blacks demanded their rights that this problem was given more attention. But trying to solve it bred more problems of quota systems and "reverse discrimination." There is no inherently "right" solution since no satisfactory way exists that can arrive at both equality of opportunity and preference for the disadvantaged at the same time.

Until an agreement is reached on distribution problems, the system can continue to function only if some are willing to accept what others dictate, either because they are unaware that they are being dictated to or because they think the dictators are superior to themselves or because they see the dicta as stemming from morally or socially justified standards or simply because they like to accept authority. Indeed, most of the contradictory arrangements made after World War II worked only because some people did not behave in the way economic theory assumed they would. Savings continued despite negative real rates of interest, and people invested in productive enterprises even when the expected rate of return was lower than what they could have received on government bonds. Today, it seems that fewer people are willing to accept an inferior position. As a result, there are demands for a complete revision of the international economic order; many countries are pressured to index savings and wages, and more and more people are unwilling to agree to let others decide on the amount of risk they should bear, the safety standards they should adhere to, or the prices they should pay.

Moderation would be the solution to many problems if only everyone would agree to be moderate. But as long as some groups push for extreme solutions, moderation as a solution is unattainable. Whenever dedication to a cause turns into intolerance for the causes of others, compromise becomes impossible. Crusaders may opt to exploit whatever powers, legal or illegal, they command to get their way; and when they do, the argument ceases to be a legitimate conflict of interest. If everyone demands a greater share of the pie and if the pie itself remains the same size, either because it is impossible or for some reason regarded as immoral to make it bigger, or if most people are unwilling to put out the effort to make it any larger, there is no way to achieve distribution that will be considered fair and equitable by all. If the demands grow too great, the contradictions become too large.

There is no price tag either in market or tax-subsidy terms for the true believer; his beliefs are both priceless and not subject to debate. Yet, what are the taboos that have to be accepted by society, and to what extent can one human being force others to accept taboos in which they do not believe? It is generally agreed that one religion should not be allowed to coerce others to believe, but that its constituents should have the freedom to pursue their own beliefs. It is also generally accepted that vegetarians should not be forced to eat meat, nor can they force others not to eat it. At the same time, the Food and Drug Administration does not allow even terminally ill cancer patients to use Laetrile. The Occupational Safety and Health Administration forces workers to use a variety of safety devices; all cars must be equipped with safety belts, and for a time the belts had to be designed so that the car would not start unless the safety belt was on. In all these instances, people obviously believed that others do not always know what is good for them. To the extent that safety features are mandatory, or pollution abatement enforced, every individual is denied the right to deal with these issues in his or her own way.

Since human beings are inherently multidimensional, it is a mistake to seek a unanimous agreement on goals to be achieved, or on the ends to achieve these goals. Agreements on the distribution of costs and benefits are based in the final analysis on ethical notions rather than questions of facts. If people disagree on the contributions each individual makes, or on the benefits individuals should receive, or on the risks each individual should bear, there is no objective test that will settle these matters to the satisfaction of everyone.

If risks are mutually exclusive, not all of them can be eliminated. A worker in a certain workplace can be protected against the risk of losing his or her job only if others are willing to bear the additional costs and additional risks; the risk of loss in social status can be eliminated only if all individuals are willing to freeze the social relationships; investors cannot be insured against the loss of a bad investment unless someone is willing to bear the risk of payment in case the investment was indeed a bad one. If all these payments are shifted to the government, they must be borne by the citizens in their capacity as taxpayers or consumers. If the citizens are unwilling to pay, the system becomes a logical impossibility. If they are willing to pay, they still bear some risks. For example, they become more dependent on the government, and this dependency increases uncertainty.

The question is often that of behavior and our inability to change it. Too many of us have a blind belief in the power of knowledge and reason. Crime control is said to be difficult because "knowledge about controlling our worst impulses has grown but little over the last few thousand years."[1] We do not know what makes a criminal behave as he does. If we did, presumably we could make him change his ways. Certainly, if we don't know how to cure a criminal, or a patient, or a lazy person, additional expenditures on crime prevention, health, or welfare are not going to help very much. But even if we did, it does not necessarily follow that the solution could be achieved, if only because telling someone what he or she is doing wrong and why will not necessarily convince him or her to act differently. People by the millions still smoke despite herculean efforts from all sides to discourage them. Of course, as we learn more about human motivation and behavior we may find out how to end the imperfections of humans and solve the social problems that grow out of them. In the meantime, some problems cannot be solved by the government or anyone else.

Of course, if killing a large number of people would be considered a solution, then the government could pass a law that all drug addicts, alcoholics, cigarette smokers, traffic violators, and underachievers would be summarily executed. This is in line with the Red Queen's edict in *Alice in Wonderland:* "Off with his head." But one hopes this "solution" is unacceptable. Barring the elimination of humans in this or some similar summary fashion, there is no way to eliminate crime, avoid death, achieve perfect equality, or live a life devoid of risk. Besides, even execution would not always be an unfailing solution. If everyone sins, who is left to be the executioner?

The importance of individual and group behavior cannot be overemphasized. If most individuals litter the public parks or streets, resources needed to clean these areas become so great that having clean public parks becomes an unattainable goal. If a large portion of the population does not comply with a government regulation, then the regulation cannot be enforced. If 70 or 80 percent of the population does not pay taxes, and if tax evasion is generally condoned, then government cannot enforce its tax laws. If the majority of the population drives faster than 25 miles per hour in a residential district, there will never be enough policemen or judges to enforce the speed limit. Legal prohibition of alcohol was unenforceable because a very large segment of the population resented that intrusion in their private lives. In general, the ability of a democratic government to enforce a certain regulation depends in some measure on consensus that the regulation is equitable, or at least justified. As long as only a small minority are criminals, society can manage to put most criminals behind bars; as soon as almost everyone becomes a criminal, jails cease to be a solution. An extreme example is the success of enraged farmers in defeating attempts by sheriffs to foreclose mortgages during the Great Depression.

In many other cases, results fall short of expectations because more is not necessarily better. More doctors do not necessarily mean a healthier population, greater wealth does not necessarily mean a happier one, and more cars do not necessarily mean a more mobile one. If people are envious, the government cannot supply harmony. If people's demands are contradictory, not all of them can be met. If each person demands to be better off than his or her neighbor, no solution is possible. Simply increasing the amount available does not solve anything.

Thus, the identification of very real unanswerable problems does not necessarily mean that solutions will be magically forthcoming once the state assumes responsiblity.

While market failures are well documented, "government failures" are often disregarded. Yet, when government takes over the insurance function, the many problems faced by private insurance firms are not necessarily solved. Moral hazard and the effect on incentives are only two of the problems that remain. Understanding the failures of government intervention will help people reach a better balance between those goods whose allocation is left to the market and those in which allocation is based on political bargaining; it will show why in many cases attempts to reduce one risk only increases other risks.

Moral Hazard

The eventuality against which insurance is taken remains, at least partly, under the control of the insured. The very existence of the insurance may reduce the incentives to avoid carelessness and, in extreme cases, create incentives to increase loss. For example, if a building is insured against fire, the insured will have less incentive to be careful or even an incentive to set it on fire to collect the insurance money. Medical insurance tends to increase the number of visits to the doctor and the use of other medical services. Unemployment insurance may reduce the incentive to stay on the job, or to look for another one, or to learn a new trade; no-fault insurance reduces the incentives for caution in the workplace. The transfer of insurance to the public sector certainly does not reduce these tendencies, and sometimes can make a bad situation worse, or at best, almost as bad as it was. The welfare program undeniably reduced suffering, but its costs zoomed and also created myriad side effects.

The case of public health may serve as an example. A national health service was recommended in various countries because it was believed that no one should be deprived of health care for want of money to pay for it. One of the finest health services in the world was installed in the United Kingdom after World War II. It was believed that the costs of health care would be reduced as a result of the nationalization of the industry because of the economies of scale. This belief was characterized by one analysis of the service as "a colossal misconception."[2]

In practice, national health service costs soared. In the spring of 1951, Aneurin Bevan, the founder of the service, resigned from the British government when his cabinet colleagues decided to establish charges for eyeglasses and false teeth. This clash was the first recognition that a totally free medical service was not feasible; the cost of a service when the population perceived it as a "free good" mounts to a degree that the government cannot cope with. Successive chancellors of the exchequer, finding they could not control the expenditures of the NHS, placed a ceiling on total costs that "threw the brunt of the saving upon those items where the consequences in the short period would be least noticeable and least likely to arouse protest."[3]

As soon as costs were controlled by arbitrary ceilings, the quality of the services deteriorated. The market mechanism was replaced by queuing: long waiting lines to doctors' services and mainly to so-called noncritical surgeries. In October 1975, Dr. David Owen, the then Labour minister in charge of NHS, in an interview in the *London Times,* talked about "quite severe areas of health deprivation" and called Newham, a town near London, "an appallingly deprived area." In the same interview, Dr. Owen said:

> The health service was launched on a fallacy. First, we were going to finance everything, cure the nation and the spending would drop. That

fallacy has been exposed. Then there was the period when everybody thought the public could have whatever they needed on the health service—it was just a question of governmental will. Now we recognize that no country, even if they are prepared to pay the taxes, can supply everything.[4]

In 1977, the total cost of the British National Health Service was less than $13 billion. The United States, with four times the size population, spent on its medical care $162 billion. Since the mid 1960s, among industrialized countries, the United Kingdom has consistently devoted the smallest share of GNP to health care. In 1960 the United Kingdom spent 3.8 percent of its GNP on health care, compared with 4.4 percent by West Germany, 3.5 percent by Sweden, and 5.3 percent by the United States. In 1975, UK health expenditure as a percent of GNP was 5.6, Germany's was 9.7, Sweden was 8.7, and the United States was 8.4. When the annual rates of growth are adjusted for the change in the consumer price index for the 1960-76 period, West Germany's annual increase in real health expenditures was 10.23 percent and that of the United States was 6.46 percent. The United Kingdom had the lowest rate of growth—5.12 percent—despite registering a higher rate of CPI increase than any other country—7.63 percent per year.

The health industry is extremely labor intensive. Wages represent 50 to 70 percent of costs. When expenditures for health care are deflated by annual growth rates in wages for the 1960-76 period, the annual rate of growth of health expenditures in the United Kingdom is still lowest—2.9 percent compared with 5.24 percent in the United States, 3.77 percent in Sweden, and 5.11 percent in West Germany.[5] The difference is so overwhelming that it reduces to insignificance the statistical cautions against such a comparison. It is clear that since the health services were governmentally financed, the ceilings put on them did not reflect needs, as originally hoped for.[6] Instead, these ceilings caused a deterioration of the value of the service. It is sometimes difficult to assess whether the heartless decisions of the market are better or worse than the heartless decisions of government bureaucracy in setting limits to a hospital budget.

From all these cases, and many others, we learn that when services are supplied as community goods, the demand for them increases and their costs mount. Multifarious demands on the limited resources of government cause an increase in the size of the public sector. To save money, government eventually has to decrease the quality of services provided.

With the wisdom of hindsight, we can see that any free social service such as the National Health Service would have foundered. First, because, in the meantime, medical breakthroughs have made health care more expensive; and their free supply increased the demands for them. As a result, the government found it had to resort to a stringent system of priorities to reduce the costs. Second, all services could be supplied free to all. This then raised the problem of equality. "There is no full equality in access to medical care anywhere, nor can there be as long as human societies must depend upon differential rewards to provide incentives."[7] Even if equality is desirable, the supply of some medical services, such as dialysis machines, is so limited as to make it impossible — some method of establishing priority has to be found. Moreover, the attempts to cut costs result in a large number of committees, absorbing an inordinate amount of professional time. Doctors and patients alike "come to spend an exhaustive, expensive and demoralizing amount of their time wrestling with a bureaucratic octopus."[8]

In many other instances, the moral hazard problem is manifested in fraud. According to a story in the *Washington Post* of February 16, 1978, of the approximately 1000 former Washington firemen currently receiving a pension, about 83 percent of them claimed disability caused by backache. "Lest you think this figure has something to do with the very real dangers of firefighting, the figure for fire chiefs is even higher. Since World War II, every single fire chief has retired on disability, proving, I guess, the perils of desk work." There is no point in singling out fire chiefs in Washington, D.C. "In fact, a whole industry has developed around personal injury claims — doctors, lawyers, and other specialists, all of it playing with the truth to extract bigger insurance claims for its clients." The same situation is reflected in the growing phenomenon of welfare claims and malpractice suits.

When government attempts to bestow benefits on a certain class of citizens, the temptation is there to get the benefits whether eligible or not. Frauds attempted under different subsidy programs result in efforts to prevent them, which then result in growing demands for certifications and in delays.

Because of the moral hazard, there is a need for increased controls, yet government cannot detect all deviations from its prescribed norms of behavior, nor can it always enforce its regulations even when it does detect a deviation. For example, a decision to declare safety standards mandatory in all places of work is not sufficient to make sure that these safety standards are actually used. Government has to create an apparatus to detect deviations and enforce its regulations. This apparatus can be very costly and create many side effects. Detection and enforcement often are limited to large firms, while small firms sometimes benefit from ignoring the laws and regulations.

Even when deviations are detected, the laws are not always enforced. Democratic governments cannot enforce laws against the will of a determined populace. An ancient dictum in the Jewish Talmud (*Avoda Zara*, 36a) states:

". . . but it is a principle not to impose on a community a decree to which the majority of the community cannot adhere." Unfortunately, when pressured to reduce risk, government sometimes ignores this wisdom. When deviations of behavior from prescribed law are not detected, the law represents an unattainable ideal rather than a reality of life. Many attempts to solve social ills are failures not because laws and regulations were not enacted but because once enacted they were not enforced.

As the rate of new and particularistic regulations increase, the possibility of actual enforcement correspondingly declines. In addition, increasing regulation clogs the availability and distribution of justice and leads to petty official tyrannies, a gradual decline in the willingness of the public to assume voluntary compliance, and a loss of respect for the law.

Private tax avoidance is one example. It has become a big business, and evasion of taxes by otherwise law-abiding citizens is said to be on the increase. In one country after another, part of the economy is based on barter exchanges where a worker is paid in goods rather than cash. Many people prefer to work, as the French call it, *en noir:* to be paid in some way that need not be reported to the tax authorities. The higher the tax rates, the more remunerative is a small cash payment relative to a higher but taxable salary. Tax avoidance and evasion have become, according to some experts, endemic to some countries. It is still much more widespread in Italy and France, for example, than in the United States or Great Britain, but it is growing throughout the Western world.[9] Whatever the exact magnitude of tax evasion, the general public feels shortchanged. Daniel Yankelovich found that 84 percent of the persons he surveyed say that people who live by the rules are shortchanged and those who flout the rules are doing just fine.[10]

Attempts to control moral hazard are common both in private and public insurance schemes. A private insurer can insist on medical checkups or on certain minimum safety standards; so can government. But since government's powers are greater and its insurance programs much more comprehensive, the controls create a correspondingly greater state of dependency.

Dependency

Life, liberty, and the pursuit of happiness are considered in the United States to be among the natural and inalienable rights. In a free political society, people have the right to vote, the right of association with anyone of their choice, and the right to form political parties. However, total political liberty is not possible without financial independence. People must have an inalienable right to earn a living without being forced to give up or to compromise political views or the right to express them. If people do not have the inalienable right to own property and consume wealth as they choose within a mutually acceptable framework, as long as others are not affected, they will also lose political freedom.

Governmental involvement creates dependency, and dependent people are not free. At the extreme, if government becomes the sole source of employment, individuals will hardly be likely to endanger their chances of making a living by voicing their displeasure with it.

Businesses whose economic success and livelihood depend on government procurement become sensitive to the whims of government executives. They are often so busy adapting to changes in policy and attempting to tilt them for their benefit that they ignore efficient operations in their business. The more government intervenes in the economy, the greater the change in the personal traits needed to manage a business successfully. The old entrepreneur is replaced by the person whose connections with government and skill in negotiation are major advantages.

In all times and all periods, leading businessmen have promoted governmental regulations to stave off what they considered to be cutthroat competition. Judge Elbert Gary, the U.S. Steel Company president, is reported to have told a congressional committee that "I believe we must come to enforced publicity and governmental control—even as to prices, and so far as I am concerned. . . . I would be very glad if we knew exactly where we stand . . . and if we had some place where we could go to a responsible governmental authority, and to say to them: 'Here are our facts and figures . . . now you tell us what we have the right to do and what prices do we have the right to charge.' "[11] The U.S. steel industry today claims that it would have accepted international competition if it had been fair but that the competition the industry is facing is unfair because it stems from differences in governmental regulations. Therefore, the steel industry is entitled to protection.

All this goes to show that businessmen are mortal and, like other people, try to avoid uncertainty and achieve legitimation. It does not follow, however, that all demands for reduction of risks should be met. Today, the evidence is overwhelming that in attempting to regulate business, governments are protecting a variety of sectors in the economy against competition. Until 1979, the Civil Aeronautics Board ensured that no new airlines would enter the field; the Interstate Commerce Commission curbs competition in transportation and reduces the risks to its owners—often at the expense of the consumer. Most governmental regulatory agencies are alleged to be servants of those they are meant to control.

The fact that businessmen want increasing government intervention to reduce uncertainty is no reason in itself to have more government involvement. Businessmen are supposed to work under conditions of uncertainty and to take risks. The essence of the capitalist system if that those who cannot produce goods efficiently for the market will go bankrupt so that other, more efficient business operations can take their place. The right to property is not a guarantee of minimum profits whatever the business might do.

Much of the increased government intervention, however, results from protection of the status quo against change and from a dependency relationship: profits can be made higher through governmental largesse than through efficient management of a business firm. Dependency feeds on itself. The more government intervenes in the economy, the less are business entrepreneurs able to compete and the more they become dependent on the discretion of government to relax some of its own regulations.

Citizens also become dependent on government help. For example, increased taxes raise costs. The higher the costs, the less the poor can afford the goods, and the more they depend on government help or subsidies so they can buy the same goods that the same government—by levying high indirect taxes —has put beyond their reach. Thus, if all building materials are taxed, and if the purchaser of a house must pay a tax, ownership of a house is placed beyond the reach of young couples. Governments then often help these couples by granting them special concessions and subsidies at the discretion of bureaucrats and politicians. At the extreme, anything can be made prohibitively expensive by indirect taxes. Should this happen, almost everyone will become dependent on government largesse to afford the goods they want.

Finally, dependency creates a dynamic demand for more government intervention: if the public pays the bill, the government feels entitled to tell the individual how to behave. The rights of the individual to make his or her own choice are constrained by the right of the public—who pay the costs—to restrict these choices to reduce the outlays of public funds. As one admittedly extreme example, David Wilkie, a recipient of old age assistance, refused to move from his place of residence and was denied assistance. In the opinion of the New York Court:

> One would admire his independence *if he were not so dependent,* but he has no right to defy the standards and conventions of civilized society while being supported at public expense. . . . After all, he should not demand that the public, at its expense, allow him to experiment with the manner of living which is likely to endanger his health so that he will become a still greater expense to the public.[12]

Thus, welfare recipients are not allowed to use the money as freely as those who earn their own income. Universities are expected to adapt their research priorities and entrance requirements to the priorities of government because they receive public funds. If a house is publicly financed, the government will dictate its size and the amenities to be installed. If health care is publicly financed, government feels that it should enforce mandatory safety and health requirements.

Rigidities

Reliance on government for protection causes many rigidities in the system. If business has the right to work in the same place and in the same position, then changes become very hard to introduce. If a more efficient producer is expected to compensate the less efficient one for the negative externality caused by driving him out of business, there is no way to ensure efficiency. In theory, social mobility and technological change mean that new forces are allowed to come in and that business firms that do not adapt to the new conditions disappear. If, however, the state is defending and protecting the status quo, no change is allowed. Indeed, if those who man the command posts of business control the government apparatus, then the same business units will continue to be protected and defended by government working for the interest of "the privileged class," and no change can ever occur.

For the radical economist, the institutions of capitalism, private property, and markets are socially wrong and economically full of irrepressible internal contradictions. Gross inequality of wealth, poverty, and racial inequality are all caused by the greed of big business controlling the political machinery. If one assumes that big business indeed controls the country, this by itself is hardly a reason for advocating more public planning and governmental involvement, since in this case, big business presumably controls the government too.

Universal suffrage prevents economic machinery from completely dominating political, social, and cultural institutions. People have some power, even if they do not own property; their power stems from the right to vote. This right is exercised to receive an increased amount of insurance from the state. The masses, who were once portrayed by Karl Marx as having nothing to lose but their chains, have considerably more to lose now, and they expect government to continue to protect them against the variety of miseries from which their like once suffered. The propertyless today have economic security, and fear of hunger rarely motivates people to work. This security has been achieved through the vote by demanding the intervention of government in the economy.

Organized labor has also acquired the power to disrupt the ordinary workings of society. Strikes are no longer limited by the short staying power of the unemployed workers because strikers enjoy unemployment benefits. Moreover, in an affluent society both the share of services in society and their indispensability increase. Commodities can be stockpiled, but an inventory of services cannot be held. Because of the increasing interdependence of urban living, small groups of workers often have the power to paralyze a community; strikes by air-traffic controllers, garbage collectors, milk distributors, teachers and firemen are familiar manifestations of this. In addition, our values—very much influenced by the miserable conditions of labor until recently—often keep us from crossing a picket line. Some striking groups can thus command higher wages because of their strategic power to obstruct services. Often, governments are left without recourse; they are reluctant to break strikes, so they appeal to reason, conscience, or patriotism and often end up paying higher wages.

One must recognize the great achievements of labor unions and voluntary movements to protect the environment. Labor leaders, environmentalists, consumer advocates, and many other groups in society support values and concerns that appeal to the moral beliefs of all of us. The misery and hardship of the technologically unemployed make us feel that such a situation is unfair and undignified, and something must be done about it. When the flooding of some beautiful countryside to make a reservoir for a city's water supply damages vegetation and wildlife, many people feel the costs are too high. These are valid interests, but at the same time, when conflicting interests carry out their causes to an extreme, the result can be that change is not allowed.

When change is not allowed, consumers pay more; and there is no incentive for anyone to do better. The defense of the status quo keeps the bottom of the ladder in its place. When the economy grows, problems of distribution seem less important because everybody becomes relatively better off. If no economic growth occurs, problems of distribution become acute and sometimes insoluble.

Yet, when each individual or group in society feels entitled to protection from any change, growth stops. When, in addition, each individual demands increasing governmentally supplied services and increased protection, the problem becomes insoluble. A fuller insurance coverage against a wider array of activities means that someone has to pay, directly or indirectly, insurance premiums that are staggering.

Unfortunately, in the political world nothing prevents the demands of interest groups from adding up to more than the total gross national product. The government apparatus itself is very rigid in its operations. Streamlining the government or amalgamating its programs has repeatedly been attempted, but with very little success. Good intentions are often translated into laws and regulations, and these new enactments are piled on top of the old ones. Old programs are rarely abolished even when their raison d'être has long since faded away. Every program has its own constituents; hence, programs are not abandoned, nor are they monitored to make them work better or adjust to new conditions. As new ones are added, government programs become a hodgepodge of accumulated laws entrusted to all varieties of governmental bureaus and full of "internal inconsistencies, numerous duplications, cross-purposes, and overlaps as well as outright conflicts and gimmickry"[13] that lead to overlapping domains, confused jurisdictions, and dispersed accountability. The more government attempts to mitigate conflicting risks, the more it faces insurmoutable difficulties in implementation. In politics, however, temporary gains are often more important than long-run solutions; success is measured in terms of a very short time horizon.

Short Time Horizon

Politicians are elected for relatively short terms and prefer objectives and programs that can be accomplished within a short period of time so that they can point to accomplishments before the term is over.[14] This preference is reinforced by constant exposure to the press and television. While the business executive functions in near anonymity and works on the basis of long-term goals, the public executive must immediately respond to pressing problems. The media's treatment of issues has a pernicious impact on policy. Television news brings issues into every family's living room. Once the issues are brought to public attention, public managers can no longer afford to ignore them. At the same time, by its very nature, the press generally does not present basic issues but highlights the unusual and timely. Broad long-term social problems are neglected; time, effort, and other resources are concentrated on short-term solutions and crash programs.

Modernization of an industry is a better long-term solution than protection, but protection has immediate results. The devastating long-term effects of a short-term policy can be discounted because politicians may well be out of office before they begin to be manifested. Closing an unneeded army base may reduce the burden of the defense budget, but it creates unemployment and causes political disaffection. Hence the tendency to avoid such acts.

Political control of the economy tends to discourage long-range planning and to create a quick-fix, crisis mentality. Incumbent politicians determine the location and timing of economic benefits to win elections. According to Paul McCracken: "The whole process of economic policy decision-making has such a short-run focus . . . [the] political calendar does not mesh well with the time required for economic processes to work themselves out. This makes for disinterest in programs with a payoff beyond one or two years. And it creates a great temptation to embrace programs that in the short-run might be popular even if they are inimical to the longer-run economic vitality of the country."[15]

Delays

Essential to democracy is public debate. Public resources are supposed to be allocated among different projects only after issues have been aired in the public forum. Essential though this is, it is also time-consuming; governments sometimes resort to the use of independent public authorities because these authorities can do the job faster, free of the hindrances of the political arena.

The delays that occur both in the initiation of a new policy and in the implementation of an existing one become especially prolonged and uncertain when a number of governmental agencies are involved. Congressional delays in the implementation of the three major tax bills of the 1960s, for example, were eighteen, thirteen, and eighteen months.[16]

The greater the government intervention, the longer the delays. The construction of a nuclear plant at Seabrook, New Hampshire, has been delayed for many years as a result of indecision and conflicts among various governmental authorities. After six years of hearings, demonstrations, regulatory rulings, and judicial decisions, there is still no final decision on the suitability of the site for a nuclear reactor in which ocean water will be used to cool the plant and then put back into the sea. In the course of the proceedings, many decisions were reversed and reversed again by various levels of governmental authorities. The New Hampshire Public Service Company began construction on the basis of the first approval, taking the risk of subsequent reviews. The utility had to periodically stop construction and wait for various governmental authorities to make up their mind. Throughout that period, several antinuclear groups raised objections, appealed to the court, or—as the Coalition for Direct Action did—tried to occupy the site. In the meantime, construction costs increased.

In many similar cases, the need to achieve a compromise among the demands of workers, the protests of environmentalists, and the pressures of businessmen means that no decision is made for a very long time, for hearings must be held, courts deliberate, and other democratic political processes take place. Small groups of vocal citizens learn to use delaying tactics for the advancement of their cause.

In such a litigious environment, public managers give high priority to "legal sufficiency." In the absence of a supportive consensus about either ends or means, public managers tend to avoid a controversial exercise of discretion. They have to take into account the conflicting demands of legislators, dozens of different interest groups, representatives, other public officials, and the media. The result often is procrastination and the postponement of decisions. This is a further irritant to business managers, who are faced with increasing uncertainty regarding governmental decisions on environmental protection requirements, construction standards, safety regulations, and so on. Moreover, each decision may be challenged by one group or another or contested by public-interest lawyers utilizing every procedural opportunity to slow down the decision process if they disagree with the probable decision.

Thus the demands for regulatory protection from risks of technological development cause pervasive uncertainty to investors as well as increasing costs because of delays due to the postponement of decisions. Sohio efforts to move oil from the West Coast inland may serve as an example. The company began the process of securing the necessary permits and government approvals for its pipeline project in January 1975. Approximately 700 different permits were required from 140 federal, state, and local agencies in order to construct the pipeline. On May 13, 1979, the company decided to abandon the project. Over these fifty months, it spent $50 million, or $1 million a month, in the approval process, and managed to secure only 250 of the 700 permits required.[17]

Delays in the administration of governmental programs result not only in increasing costs but in petty official tyranny and improper pressures to expedite matters. Long delays may also dampen the public's willingness to comply with the laws and regulations. As government regulation reaches out to cover more and more forms of citizen conduct, as delays in receiving a variety of required licenses increase, the tendency to circumvent or simply ignore the regulations grows. Delays also retard innovation.

As an example, Southern Railway introduced in the 1960s "Big John" grain hoppers. These were specially designed high-capacity lightweight aluminum hoppers to move grain at sharply reduced costs. Southern had to spend four years taking its case to the Supreme Court in order to counter ICC objections to its reduced freight rates before final approval was granted.

Finally, delays entail risks of their own. The case of the drug lag is one example. Every drug has some side effects, and the use of any drug therefore entails certain risks. At the same time, drugs can be beneficial in reducing the risk of death and curing disease. The problem is thus not the total avoidance of risks but the careful balancing of one risk against another. If one decides not to use a drug because of its probable side effect, one simultaneously makes the decision to accept the risk that some beneficial drugs will not be approved or that the approval will be delayed until extended testing can be done. This risk is known as the drug lag.

It is claimed that the United States errs in the direction of caution, and the delay in the use of beneficial drugs has become too great. In 1962, Kefauver-Harris amendments to the Food, Drug and Cosmetics Act added the requirement that a firm must provide documented scientific evidence that new drugs are effective as well as safe. These amendments also gave FDA discretionary power over the clinical research process and imposed controls on the promotion of prescription drugs. Recent studies have concluded that these amendments not only have reduced research and development efforts below what they would have been otherwise but also have sharply increased the time and cost of meeting all FDA requirements or approval. Multinational firms diverted their research efforts abroad. As a result, the number of new prescription drugs currently being introduced has been reduced below what it would have been otherwise.[18] A change in the system is therefore recommended: "a more permissive policy toward the marketing of new drugs coupled with a more rigorous program of postmarketing surveillance."[19] It was found, for example, that in the period from 1962 to 1971, "nearly four times as many new drugs became exclusively available in Great Britain as in the United States"[20] and that "Britain probably did not lose appreciably from the introduction of ineffective drugs, nor from the fact that a greater number of new drugs were made available. . . . Conversely, Britain experiences clearly discernible gains by introducing useful new drugs."[21]

Inefficiencies and Increased Risks

In the final analysis, attempts to correct market failures are designed to increase the efficiency of operations. Natural monopolies are regulated to capture the efficiencies of scale economies without the costs associated with monopolistic attempts to reap monopolistic profits; and natural resources are regulated to achieve more efficient exploitation and to avoid excessive utilization of the resource. When information is unavailable, the government supply of information improves the efficiency of the markets. If government does not intervene in the market, private firms tend to use the environment as a free input in the production process. Intervention is needed to ensure that these private firms take into account the full costs of their operations. In many cases, government intervention is called for to avoid the imposition on the community of intolerable levels of risks, in particular when these risks are not taken voluntarily by individuals but are imposed on them by a third party. For example, the risk of a nuclear coremelt is imposed on those living in the vicinity of a nuclear plant and is not borne by those owning and operating the facility. This is, therefore, a "market failure" whose correction is called for.

Yet the correction of many market failures results in other inefficiencies. When the government attempts to regulate monopolies, the result is sometimes insurance against any changes. Competitors are not allowed to enter the market, and introduction of new technology is hampered. The regulations, when they are not properly designed, may in fact cause disincentives to innovation. As one example, in the early 1960s there were two alternative satellite technologies; the random-orbit system of fifty satellites was more costly and more capital-intensive than the alternative synchronous-orbit system designed to use a small number of high-altitude synchronous-orbit satellites with much less complex ground stations. The Bell system is alleged to have preferred the first and more costly alternative because it would have expanded the system's rate base.[22] In this instance, the least expensive system was eventually adopted, but only because it was developed by a nonregulated firm—Hughes Aircraft—for a different use.[23]

Government intervention of the wrong kind may create many other problems. To the individual citizen, a major consequence of the attempts to reduce risk has been persistent and debilitating inflation and the grim prospects of increased unemployment.

Inflation is one of the most pressing problems of the 1970s and '80s. At bottom, inflation was caused by the inability of our political institutions to restrain the growth of insurance within tolerable limits. The increased insurance necessitated much higher costs, both in the public and private sectors. It also reduced competition and innovation.

Because of the nature of democracy, competitive behavior in the market has been replaced by competitive vote bidding. Voters do not spend much time informing themselves and do not take the trouble to learn the problems and the limits to their solutions. A small, determined group can therefore utilize the political machinery to advance its own self-interest and receive from the state much more than the average individual. Politicians find it easier to take a little from many and give a lot to the few who are able to pressure the government to work in their interest.

Government legitimacy is based on the belief in mass democracy and the myth of the "intelligent" voter. At the same time, it is faced with pressures of small interest groups and the apathy of most citizens. Government may want to achieve equality, but it also must provide incentives, usually in the form of material rewards. It must allow changes because economic, social, and technological conditions are, and should be, in a state of constant flux. At the same time, it is expected to shield individuals from risks and not allow changes. In short, government is faced with conflicting and therefore unattainable goals.

Faced with insoluble problems and hampered by the short time horizon allowed for operations, government tends to buy time and gloss over the conflict. The result is a combination of stagnation through arresting change, rampant inflation because of a growing invisible government, and a deterioration of the international economic situation through increasing demands for protection. The attempts to achieve a no-risk society in fact increase the long-term risks faced by individuals; they see their savings wiped out by inflation and their future as largely insecure. Yet social attitudes change at a much slower pace than reality. The rhetoric of the 1940s and '50s is still believed, although it has long been discredited by the facts. Lofty ideals on the ability of society to shield each and every individual from all kinds of risks are still adhered to, and are, cynically perhaps, exploited by strong pressure groups to tilt benefits to themselves.

Economic Change without Risk?

The capitalist system is founded on the assumption that human beings are selfish hedonists combined with the belief that they have a natural right to pursue their own interests without interference; a society composed of individuals in pursuit of their own self-interest is assumed to promote the common weal if it relies on perfect competition.

But, as we all know, it does not work that way. In practice, large enterprises and huge trade unions hold sufficient power over the market to prevent the automatic adjustment of prices and wages. When conditions are uncertain, it is impossible to assume maximizing behavior. Resources are not easily transferred from one industry to another; and economies of scale, indivisibilities, externalities, and lack of information all make the perfect competitive view of the world an unattainable ideal.

The rigidities in the system, however, do not result only from the market power of large enterprises and trade unions or from bottlenecks in resource transfer. They result from the nature of human beings. Openly to force a worker to change his or her profession or admit that his or her skills are obsolete is no longer acceptable in Western society. Considerable socioeconomic pressure must be used to persuade workers to leave one town where no work is available for another where it is. Neither necessity nor authority can make workers leave; they can apply for government aid instead. Others, too, want protection against a growing variety of risks. As a result, change becomes increasingly difficult to achieve. Yet economic order, particularly international economic order, cannot be established unless some tacit or overt agreement can be reached on the rules for an equitable coordination and just distribution of the costs of adjustment.

"Economic adjustment" cannot be achieved in a laboratory. It involves human beings: people who are unemployed because their skills are no longer needed; people who are uprooted from the village or town of their ancestors and moved to cities to join the anonymous masses; people who have to learn a new profession at an advanced age; or people who must begin life over again at a time when they would have liked to begin to enjoy the fruits of their earlier labors. But people who find themselves in predicaments such as these are no longer entirely powerless; they are also voters. When they rebel against bearing the costs of progress, governments are often forced, and sometimes choose, to arrest economic progress and subsidize an obsolete industry; in short, to preserve some parts of the status quo and prevent too rapid a change. Change is an essential ingredient of economic growth. If workers are guaranteed jobs in outmoded industries and employers are guaranteed a market for outmoded products, new products, new technologies, and new professions are not apt to be developed, or not apt to be successful if they are developed. At the same time, if economic growth is not achieved, economists know of no way to maintain full employment.

Capitalism, when left to the discipline of the marketplace and the invisible hand, has been found to be too harsh and heartless. The sufferings during depressions and the inhuman conditions of work in British nineteenth-century factories have been considered too high a price to be paid for an unfettered operation of the market. With the increased interdependence of the world, these problems have grown too, and their magnitude is such that few people today believe in complete laissez-faire. It should be recognized that government's involvement in the economy is sometimes indispensable to avoid a vast wreck, alleviate extreme social injustices, and avert calamities including rapid exhaustion of resources.

Governments, however, cannot solve all problems; they cannot rescue all business firms nor guarantee prosperity to all. When the discipline imposed by the market mechanism is lost, for whatever laudable reason, the problem of setting limits remains to be solved by some other mechanism. Governments can shift the burden of risk from certain individuals to others or else divide the risk among many. Nevertheless, the insurance premium must be paid. At the same time, each individual feels entitled to more guarantees, more income, and the supply of more services. The individual does not have to decide who will pay. Therefore, the demand for protection increases and, often, the budgetary deficit of the country increases as well. Most people, however, know little or nothing about balance of payments deficits or the national debt. Each government is increasingly hemmed in by decisions made by previous governments and tends to postpone unpopular decisions as much as it dares, which often means until it is too late.

This is not meant to imply that all progress ended in the last few decades or that once government intervenes in the economy, everything automatically goes wrong. Some decisions certainly should not be left to the vagaries of the market. But when public expectations are aroused that cannot possibly be fulfilled, and goals are set that are sometimes not even attainable, feelings of frustration and failure result that are not so much a reaction to our realization that the earth's resources are limited, though we may think that is the case. Rather, these feelings result from the fact that governments are confronted with objectives that are almost always unattainable.

Specifically, the elimination of all risk is impossible. This is so not only because the distribution problems are yet unsolved but mainly because the exact causes of social problems are often unknown, let alone their solutions. Moreover, insurance is not always efficient because the roots of most social problems lie in individual or group behavior; government cannot change behavior, at least if it wants to maintain a modicum of individual liberty. The moral hazard problem remains, and it causes an increase in direct controls. Insurance also involves administrative and other costs, and the reduction of risk to one individual can be achieved only by an increased risk somewhere else or to someone else. If one avoids nuclear reactors, one is exposed to the risks of mining coal; if one avoids dangerous drugs, one must accept the risk of pain or death; if one wants to protect people through welfare payments, one must accept the risks of disrupted family life, less willingness to work, fraud, and bureaucracy that has a stake in the perpetuation of the apparatus on which it depends.

U.S. legislation regulating pension funds is designed to assure workers a secure income when they reach retirement. This legislation has also led many small companies to eliminate pension plans. The more government attempts to mitigate risks, the higher the costs to the private sector and the less money left for future investments that would create additional jobs.

The risks to one group of individuals often can be eliminated or reduced only by increasing the risks to others. Licensure statutes have been explained by the need to protect the public from incompetent practitioners, but medical licenses also increase medical costs and restrain innovation. An army paramedic who attempts to practice his profession in the civilian market faces the risk of criminal prosecution for practicing without a license. The worker who is able to shift the risk of unemployment in a steel or textile factory is also a taxpayer sharing the costs of all different insurance programs and a consumer paying higher prices as a result of risk-shifting schemes. He or she can also be the owner of capital, directly in the stock market or indirectly through a pension fund. The net impact on this individual of all these programs of risk reduction is extremely difficult to calculate. However, it is almost sure that he or she suffered at least the additional risk of inflation caused by the widening gap between wants and willingness to pay.

When government reduces risk, it creates dependence. This dependence becomes a source of uncertainty about a change of government's policy. A firm whose sole customer is government is largely immune from risks of changes in the cost structure during the development of a new product. Nevertheless, it faces a considerable risk of not having any contract at all or of having the contract being made smaller than a firm supplying products to private consumers. Many large firms that have been totally dependent on government contracts make heroic efforts to diversify into other markets in order to reduce this risk. In general, the more an individual or a firm is dependent on government, the larger the risk from a change in government policy. Even pension rights of federal employees or rights granted by the social security laws can be changed by Congress. If one is totally dependent for one's future income on government, one bears much higher risks from a change in policy or law.

The demand for a reduction of risk changes behavior. To the degree that management attention is diverted from its traditional role of concern for efficient production and marketing to that of meeting governmentally imposed risk-reduction requirements, efficiency of operation is hampered. In the long run, the ability of the firm to compete in world markets can be weakened, and the risk of loss of employment made greater. Attempts to reduce risks may reduce pollution or product hazards, but they may also retard innovation; the introduction of a new product becomes more uncertain, and the additional costs of getting an approval of a government regulatory agency for the innovation reduces the forecasted revenue. As a result, the hidden costs reduce the rate of innovation, which may in turn reduce the rate of increase of the gross national product and cause increased risks of unemployment.

It may also be that voluntary organizations for many worthy causes lose much of their appeal. Since people are to some extent benevolent, a society based on market exchange and property rights will always have voluntary organizations that attempt to help the poor or subsidize the arts. If, however, government is expected to take care of the poor, the needy, the artists, the lonely, and all other members of society, the propensity to volunteer may decline. The poor are left to the cold and faceless bureaucracy, and the needy must comply with the rules of the administration. Such a system may be efficient and may even increase somewhat the income of the poor. What will be missing is the human element, the love and compassion.

But the most important added risk is that of a major change in the fabric of society, and possibly of the collapse of the system. In a private insurance scheme equal premiums are usually avoided; individuals with a high incidence of risk rarely pay the same premiums as those with a low incidence. If the latter were not charged lower premiums, they would find the insurance too expensive and decide to withdraw from the insurance scheme. This withdrawal would increase the risk the insurance company faces. The insurance company then would respond by increasing premiums, causing the next group of lesser risk to leave.[24] In practice, of course, insurance companies attempt to avoid this by dropping or rejecting high-risk candidates or, in the case of mandatory insurance, through the assigned-risk mechanism.

In compulsory insurance administered by government, however, a "premium" is often equalized. This constitutes, in effect, a redistribution of income from the low-risk to the high-risk group similar to what would otherwise happen in private insurance. Since the insurance is compulsory, low-risk individuals cannot cancel the insurance policy. They can leave the system only by moving to another territory, changing their behavior and becoming higher risks, or using their political power to fight for a change in the system. There are instances of the first solution being chosen, for example, in the movement of production to places where governmental regulations are less severe; of the second, in the reduced productivity of workers; and of the third, in the changing attitude of the middle class toward taxes and the social programs they pay for.

NOTES

1. Statement of Gerald M. Caplan, of the Law Enforcement Administration of the Department of Justice, before the House Committee on Science and Technology, 18 July 1975. A similar tone is reflected in the report of the Vera Institute for Criminal Justice on violent delinquents. After an ambitious attempt to survey the literature on violent crimes by minors, the report's main findings are that in trying to deal with juvenile crimes, there are no simple answers, and not even simple questions. See Paul A. Strassberg, "Violent Delinquents," as quoted in the *New York Times,* 9 July 1978. For a discussion of different approaches to crime policy, see James Q. Wilson, *Thinking About Crime* (New York: Basic Books, 1975); and Larry J. Cohen and David C. Paris, "Crime, Punishment, and Human Nature," *Policy Sciences,* April 1978, pp. 329-43.
2. John and Sylvia Jewkes, *Value for Money in Medicine* (Oxford: Basil Blackwell, 1963), pp. 59-60.
3. R. E. Tyrell, Jr., *The Future That Doesn't Work* (Garden City, N.Y.: Doubleday, 1977), p. 55.
4. The *Times* (London), 12 October 1975, p. 6. Quoted in Tyrell, *The Future That Doesn't Work,* pp. 22-23.
5. Joseph G. Simanis and John R. Coleman, "Health Care Expenditures in Nine Industrialized Countries, 1960-76," *Social Security Bulletin* 43, no. 1 (January 1980): 5.

6. Harry Schwartz, "The Infirmity of British Medicine," in Tyrell, *The Future That Doesn't Work,* p. 40.

7. Ibid.

8. *The Economist,* 21 July 1979, p. 16, summarizing the findings of the Royal Commission on the health services (Cmnd. 7615).

9. See, for example, "Tax Dodgers: Growing Worry the World Over," *U. S. News and World Report,* 9 April 1979, p. 86.

10. *Time,* 25 September 1978, p. 59.

11. Quoted in Gabriel Kolko, *The Triumph of Conservatism* (Glencoe, Ill.: Free Press, 1963), p. 174.

12. *Wilkie v. O'Connor,* 25 N.Y. Supp.2d 619 (1941). Italics added.

13. *Housing in the Seventies: A Report of the National Housing Policy Review* (Washington, D.C.: U.S. Department of Housing and Urban Development, 1974), p. 22.

14. Joseph L. Bower, "Effective Public Management," *Harvard Business Review,* March-April 1977, pp. 131-40.

15. Paul McCracken, as quoted in Edward R. Tufte, *Political Control of the Economy* (Princeton: Princeton University Press, 1978), pp. 147-48. See also William D. Nordhaus, "The Political Business Cycle," *Review of Economic Studies* 42 (April 1975): 169-90; and Assar Lindbeck, "Stabilization Policy in Open Economies with Endogenous Politicians," *American Economic Review* 66 (May 1976): 1-19.

16. Paul R. Portney, "Congressional Delays in U.S. Fiscal Policy Making," *Journal of Public Economics* 5 (April-May 1976).

17. See George P. Shultz, "The Abrasive Interface," in John T. Dunlop, ed., *Business and Public Policy* (Boston: Division of Research, Graduate School of Business Administration, Harvard University, 1980), p. 17.

18. Henry G. Grabowski, *Drug Regulation and Innovation* (Washington, D.C.: American Enterprise Institute, 1976).

19. William M. Wardell, "Therapeutic Implication of the Drug Lag," *Clinical Pharmacology and Therapeutics* 15, no. 1 (January-February 1974): 73-96, as quoted in William L. Lowrance, *Of Acceptable Risk* (Los Altos, Calif.: William Kaufmann, 1976), p. 145.

20. William W. Wardell, "Introduction of New Therapeutic Drugs in the United States and Great Britain: An International Comparison," *Clinical Pharmacology and Therapeutics* 14, no. 5 (September-October 1973): 773-90.

21. Wardell, "Therapeutic Implication of the Drug Lag."

22. The rate base is the depreciated value of the capital used. Regulatory commissions allow a certain rate of return on that base. The higher the base, the bigger the return.

23. William G. Shepherd, "The Competitive Margin in Communications," in *Technological Changes in Regulated Industries,* ed. W. M. Capron (Washington, D.C.: Brookings Institution, 1971), p. 106.

24. For a technical discussion, see George Akerlof, "The Markets for Lemons: Quality, Uncertainty, and the Market Mechanism," *Journal of Political Economics* 84, no. 3 (August 1970): 488-500.

8. Toward an Age of Humility

As the 1960s drew to a close, economists and politicians alike were congratulating themselves on their ability to "fine tune" the economy. They had achieved high productivity and stable prices, high levels of employment, and sustained economic growth. The long period of prosperity that had followed World War II fooled many into believing that depressions, unemployment, rampant inflation, and economic trade wars were things of the past.

This period of self-congratulation and self-satisfaction proved short-lived. By the middle of the 1970s, economists were hard at work searching for an explanation to a new phenomenon, a combination of inflation and recession that had acquired the name "stagflation." The value of the U.S. dollar deteriorated from 4.30 Swiss francs to less than 1.7; the rate of unemployment in many developed countries was on the increase; and most of the industrialized nations had production capacities that were underutilized. The oil-producing countries quadrupled the price of oil, causing havoc to the balance of payments of many countries. The international monetary order—the postwar Bretton Woods system—was in a shambles, and no agreement on what to do about it was in sight.

At the same time, despite the fact that the magnitude of international production (in the form of offshore industries managed by affiliates of corporations owned and controlled by another country's nationals) outstripped international trade, almost no international rules and certainly no enforceable international agreements governed either direct investment flows or the operations of these enterprises. Host countries have been trying to legislate constraints on international production, as have home countries. These efforts will probably intensify over the next few years. Host countries are using national measures to tilt the advantages of direct foreign investment in their favor, while the investment exporting countries are trying to draw the benefits back toward themselves. Examples can be found in legislation requiring a certain proportion of value added to be produced in the country, or the prohibition of the export of know-how, or restrictions on the free flow of foreign investments. These signs and others suggest that the major industrial countries are ready, unilaterally, to start to curb the free flow of trade, labor, and investments in the world.

In the 1960s economists were not the only ones to assume that they had reached the promised land of known solutions. Social reformers were also touting a bold new world with less crime, more equality, better transportation, lasting security, fewer slums, increased health care, guaranteed income, clean water, purified air, more leisure, and more varied recreation. The myth of the self-regulating market was replaced by the myth of the power of humankind to solve all problems by declaring "war" against them, armed with public funds, government regulations, and battalions of civil servants.

The forecasts since then have been more gloomy about the American social system. George Cabot Lodge has described "America in the mid 1970s [as] an apprehensive nation, lacking a sense of direction and control on the part of politicians, business managers, and the American people at large";[1] Douglas Dowd has suggested, as have many of his fellow radical economists, that "the United States is in the midst of a developing social crisis, at once economic, political and moral, simultaneously domestic and international";[2] Charles Reich has written that America has become "one vast, terrifying anticommunity";[3] its confidence drowned in aimlessness and malaise; Fred Hirsch has enumerated "the social limits to growth";[4] and others have discussed the alarming and perplexing prospect of "a finite earth."

These people and others find the only solution to lie in government intervention. Some say so explicitly; some are more apt to talk in terms of what "society" should do, without admitting that government is society's active agent. Some optimistically count on a change in human character through an education that would teach people to put the demands of the state or community or "society" above individual interests.

It is abundantly clear that governments have been asked to achieve the impossible, prevent the inevitable, and reconcile the irreconcilable. Many of our problems have been with us for centuries and are yet to be "solved" now that the responsibility for their solution has been placed on the shoulders of government. With the realization that government is not the omnipotent saviour of the human race, there has come an increased feeling of disenchantment, disillusion, and frustration.

In particular, younger men and women, who attempted in the 1960s to change or "revolutionize" what they considered to be an unjust society, have joined the "establishment" or succumbed to despair and a growing nihilism, caused in part by a belief that "the system" is unchangeable, corrupt, and controlled by "big business" or the Mafia or the "establishment." Collective action, they say, in an interdependent world, is essential; but all our institutions are corrupt and "the public interest" is abused. While enjoying the fruits of economic growth, they worry lest the price tag become unbearable. While benefiting from the manifest ability of big corporations to raise large aggregations of capital and utilize resources efficiently, they are afraid that the power of big business is excessive and that its values are incompatible with the enlightened ideals of Western tradition. So the power of large organizations, whether business or government, must be tamed. Some are trying to find their own solutions, either within themselves or in varieties of philosophical or religious movements. Few recognize that some problems cannot be solved and that a no-risk society is a contradiction in terms because any remedy for one problem always generates new problems.

Have We Gone Too Far?

In the new social order, some members of society feel they have lost rights as others have gained them. Management is less free to hire and fire workers or behave as if pollution had no costs. Workers who tend to be risk-takers may have found that their rights to take risks for extra compensation have been reduced through social and regulatory legislation. Young men who would rather spend today than save for tomorrow are constrained from doing so. On the other hand, equal opportunity for women and minority groups and access to health care for the poor are increasing, though many would say that the present equality of opportunity is not enough and others that it has already been carried too far.

The right to private property is no longer accepted as sufficient justification and legitimation of private business interests. Today's business leaders stress their contributions to society—innovation, efficiency, zeal, ability to coordinate—and the services they render to economic growth. Workers demand fewer managerial prerogatives and full recognition of their rights to equality. Both groups demand more protection.

These growing demands, the complexities of a highly technological dependent urban society, and the increasing participation of people in political decisions have led inexorably to a bigger governmental role.

By now, a growing number of people feel that society has gone too far. Big government, mounting regulations, and ever higher taxes lead them to complain that governments "route too much of income away from productive private uses, . . . high tax rates destroy the rewards of production, and capricious economic policies and tenacious inflation destroy the climate for investment to produce jobs and income."[5]

Many are concerned about ubiquitous government influence and the diminishing arena for individual decision. As they see it, the new trends will end by destroying both individual liberty and productive power. They believe that it is the private or the so-called free enterprise sector that continues to be the source of real value, the distribution of whose products makes government policies possible. They are also much afraid that the government will kill the goose that lays the golden egg. For them, the time has come to revive the old laissez-faire and return to the days of rugged individualism. They are concerned with what they see as the excessive and irresponsible power of the unions. Workers demand more wages to offset more taxes, which are the results of demands for lifetime security; when demands are met, they create inflationary pressures. Union powers must be curbed. Others feel that unions can and should use pension funds to prevent factories from moving from the Northeast to the South and to achieve a variety of other objectives for the workers.[6] Still others, alarmed by our apparent inability to cope with myriad new problems caused by the rapid advance in science and technology, would return to a Rousseauan world of small-scale enterprise and abandon technological change, economic growth, and the scientific discoveries that have caught civilization unprepared.

Some people call for a new philosophy in which individual demands will be replaced by communitarian needs. John Kenneth Galbraith expresses this view. Okun[7] similarly justifies a variety of acts as called for by "society." The problem is that most people do not always behave in cooperative, harmonious ways; and social, economic, and aesthetic values are always in a state of flux. A major dilemma of the modern world is how to allow for changes in technology, products, and sometimes values without destroying the basic fabric of the society in which we live. At the same time, self-interest does not govern all private behavior. If it did, social systems would not operate. Most people have some sense of duty and obligation, loyalty, benevolence, and morality that leads to self-restraint. One can rely also on social conventions, norms, and pressures. Any extreme position, be it total reliance on the vagaries of the market or a complete confidence in governmental omnipotence, will not work. This leaves us with various vital philosophical questions that have to be thoroughly examined: Who can determine what is socially beneficial and by what means? Who has the right to shape the attitudes and norms of young minds, and how?

The Need for Balance

Luckily, there seems to be an increased understanding that government is not the omnipotent saviour of the human race, that some problems are insoluble, and that a no-risk society is impossible. There seems to be a more realistic appraisal of what is possible and an understanding that neither competitive individualism nor benevolent management by governments can deliver the necessary goods and services that will solve all problems. As a result, there is a growing acceptance of the need to live with unsolved problems and unsatisfied human desires, while never losing hope that a solution might ultimately be found.

A system best maintains its components by not overworking them.[8] Hence, one cannot place too much confidence in government, nor in any other link in the system. Once it is recognized that all solutions are imperfect, one can begin to look for a solution that may be less imperfect than the rest. If no one is allowed to impose any particular religion, doctrine, or belief on others, it then becomes possible to devise rules, both for the allocation of scarce resources and the distribution of risk based on considerations of efficiency, justice, equity and, in some very important ways, a certain amount of skepticism regarding the altruism of others. The pull of human greed requires limits on the power of any group through constant vigilance over the system of checks and balances.

Is such a system possible, or will present trends eventually stifle initiative and thwart scientific and technological progress? Are we doomed by an ever expanding government, reduced productivity, elimination of incentive, and the ability to work and produce? Are we to suffer from a continuous inflation? Not necessarily. As meeting old problems generates new ones, and as objectives are found unattainable, methods and goals will change. Sociologists hold to the theorem that agencies unable to achieve certain goals will replace them with goals they can reach; and individuals will tend to do the same things. Our next advance should not be yet another technological breakthrough or wonder drug, but the realization of our socially limited possibilities. This does not necessarily mean a limited or zero-growth society, but rather a careful analysis of the various alternatives: a better balance of growth and no growth, risk-bearing and risk-avoidance, market exchange and government support.

It is unrealistic to place all our faith in "market solutions." By the same token, it is unrealistic to rely solely on government for answers. Political allocation creates its own problems, not to mention the ever-present danger of a totalitarian state. The real challenge for economists and other social scientists is not to attempt to reach an unattainable general equilibrium, rely completely on either market exchange or government leadership, or manipulate markets or plan society. It is simply to decide how much market and what kind of government. As long as some people are malevolent, defense is necessary. The question is, how much ? As long as criminals exist, police are necessary. The question is, how many? As long as society refuses to accept misery, welfare is necessary. The question is, for whom?

The results will almost by definition not be efficient or optimal in the narrow economic sense of these terms, nor will they make everyone happy or abolish poverty, crime, maladies, or, ultimately, death. A new attitude toward reality is both necessary and possible. A system of moderate risk-protection against catastrophic change, of reduced inequality but not a fully egalitarian society, of human rights legally defined and scrupulously enforced without choking the legal system is both a possible and a desirable goal.

Nor should one analyze each and every government action as if it were a distortion of the equilibrium to be achieved in a perfectly competitive market economy. The propensity of economists to label certain phenomena as "imperfections of the market" leaves people with the impression that a perfect world lies out there somewhere, a world in which imperfections don't exist. But not every move away from an idealized market economy is a "distortion." In the interdependent world of the 1980s, many externalities exist. The behavior of the individual often is sensible, but the sum of many identical sensible behaviors is senseless. Owning a car is often a perfectly rational solution to a transportation problem. But when everyone owns a car, the roads become clogged and building more roads brings out more cars. An individual buys a house in a suburb to have both the advantages of the city and privacy from neighbors. But if enough individuals move to the suburbs, the suburbs become a city, and the city can't function. In both instances, "the tyranny of small decisions"[9] produces a result unanticipated and unwanted by those who caused it.

In other cases, the possibility of a mishap imposes a cost on all those who might be injured. Certain possible mishaps cannot be taken into consideration in the market because no information is available to assess probabilities. Sometimes there is no alternative to governmentally imposed standards. Latent health hazards in the workplace or the risk of a nuclear coremelt are two obvious examples. The real challenge is to find the right blend of individual freedom and societal rights—efficiency, justice, and equity. Much more must be known about human behavior before we can determine the degree to which reliance can be placed on selfishness or benevolence, and the degree to which power must be checked. This much is already known: The individual cannot always be trusted to pursue his or her self-interest without doing irreparable damage to others, the physical environment, and society. Nevertheless, the greater the control and surveillance we hand over to the government to check the individual, the less compatible is government with individual freedom and the greater the probability of repression for all. Government, too, cannot always be trusted to pursue its own self-interest unfettered.

By now, we all recognize that perfect competition cannot exist in practice, and a capitalist economy must be a mixed one. It is also well known that an excessive concentration of power, whether in industrial private management or in the hands of the state bureaucracy, is dangerous. The specter of too much concentration of unanswerable power must serve as a check on our desire for a no-risk society. Again, this does not mean an opposition to any government intervention, but a call for a reduction of too obtrusive policies of intervention, as well as a plea for moderation in the entitlements to which individuals lay claim from their government and a hope for a stronger sense of civic enterprise and allegiance to a fellow human being. To the extent that decisions are made by units controlled by the state, these units must be accountable to the public and controlled by its representatives. At the same time, it might well be that in guiding economic activities and attempting to reduce different risks, democracy can be preserved if different government agencies are not too well-coordinated, maintaining alternative diffused and conflicting power centers within the state apparatus.

We have also much more to learn about the impact the various methods of government intervention have on individual and corporate behavior. The choice is not simply one between public regulation of the market and private decisions, but between different methods of command and control. What form of regulatory apparatus, what kinds of information handed out, what institutional structures or incentive patterns should be used? Government could attempt to cure a social ill, for example, by command and control or through a voucher system distributed to eligible recipients that allows private and public institutions to compete for clientele. Before deciding the most appropriate method to be used, much more must be known about the respective roles of individuals and society, about incentives and how they work, and about the influence of techniques of intervention on allocation and distribution. The challenge is to devise methods that allow the maximum feasible amount of individual choice while still taking into consideration the pitfalls of an increasingly interdependent world.

Individual rights have always been connected with individual obligations. In precapitalist societies, rights and privileges were based on inheritance and could not be changed by individual initiative. That status carried with it both privileges and commensurate obligations. In the early days of capitalism in England, freedom and property were generally considered inalienable natural rights, even though the crown or the state did grant some property rights. Although these rights were considered "natural," the possession of them imposed on their holders some minimum obligations. A major principle of the Western way of life has been that the individual is a better judge and protector of his or her interests than is the state. The state has been expected to protect the individual's rights of freedom, property, and the pursuit of happiness; in return, individuals have been expected to support the social order, avoid inflicting harm on other people, and bear the consequences of their own decisions.

In the emerging social order, some individuals have more rights, others less; but their obligation to bear the consequences of their own freely chosen acts has declined materially. The insurance state is expected to compensate the individual for almost any loss he or she sustains and to shield the individual against almost any risk he or she may face.

The 35 million Europeans who emigrated to the United States during the nineteenth century certainly were more adventurous and greater risk-takers than those who chose to stay in the Old Country. Today, however, many private risks have become unacceptable; individuals have been calling on government to eliminate some risks and insure them against others.

Indeed, some of the risks in a technologically complex society are of such magnitude that prudence calls for their reduction. Often people do not have enough information about the magnitude of the risk. In fact, what is accepted in the marketplace may not accurately reflect the public preferences for safety. At least according to one study, individuals feel that technological risks in many activities today are unacceptable; they would prefer serious action, such as legislation to restrict the practice, to be taken. This is true not only for nuclear reactors, but also for all sorts of risks: alcoholic beverages, motor vehicles, pesticides, spray cans, and cigarette smoking.[10]

There is some evidence that individuals tend to feel that risks are less acceptable when they are taken involuntarily or when the consequences are unknown to science, uncontrollable, unfamiliar, or delayed. There is also some ground to suspect that individuals tend to ignore the benefits in their reaction to risks, or at least that those who weigh the benefits perceive the acceptable risks to be higher than those who do not.[11] Much more scientific exploration is needed before we can fully understand the behavior of individuals and their reaction to risks.

Certain things, however, seem to be clear. First, most individuals, even though they are risk-averse, choose not to take the trouble to protect themselves. Flood insurance, even when it was available at highly subsidized rates, was not taken until it became compulsory. Perhaps individuals believed they would be relieved from suffering the consequences even if they were not insured; if so, the behavior of Congress after the disaster of Hurricane Agnes proved them right. However, in many other instances, individuals prefer not to inconvenience themselves. When the National Highway Traffic Safety Administration (NHTSA) proposed in September 1974 a bill according to which cars would not start without seatbelt hookup (the so-called interlock ignition), the opposition at the grass roots was so strong that the bill sent to the President did not make the requirement mandatory. Instead, the bill made a sequential warning system mandatory; a series of buzzers and lights would remind the driver to buckle up if he or she so desired. According to the calculations of the NHTSA, the interlocking system would have cost $100 per car to install, and it was estimated it would save 7000 human lives a year in addition to reducing the number of traffic injuries by 340,000. Yet the nuisance of the interlocking system was considered too great.[12]

Second, most of the risks insured by government are not involuntary and are not catastrophes (at least if a catastrophe is defined as the sudden death of thousands of persons). Instead, most attempts to reduce risks and insure against their consequences were in such areas as premature death and old age, unemployment, and competition. In many of these cases, the government insures certain individuals or groups at the expense of consumers and taxpayers. Moreover, this insurance often starts, like the Social Security System, on a small scale, attempting to offer a minimum of insurance. With time, zealous bureaucrats and interest groups increase the coverage. In addition, the costs of most of these insurance programs are invisible, and the public is not aware of them. Third, many of the consequences of the increased insurance were unintended. As a result of attempts to insure individuals against risks, American leadership in new technologies has been eroding; annual productivity gains in 1965-75 averaged about half the rate achieved in 1950-65, and further deteriorated over the last few years to the lowest level of annual growth among the noncommunist economies.[13] The ability of the United States to generate cheaper or better production processes has been dwindling. Many U.S. firms seem to have lost their willingness to engage in risk-taking and their ability to deal with unpredictability; they would rather attempt to manipulate the rules of the game to allow them to survive under government protection. Much of the attempt to reach an insurance state shelters producers from the competitive consequences of lassitude and inefficiency.

There are various ways of setting up systems of pooled risks or insurance. The most primitive form is the pooling of risks within the family unit. Children are taken care of by parents until parents grow old, then parents are taken care of by their children. The loosening of family ties, at least in the developed countries, may be one explanation for the expansion of insurance schemes beyond the family unit.

In a society based on individual decisions and transactions in a market system, any costs of risky events are borne by individuals. If complete information about all hazards were free, the decisions of individuals in the market would force the wages of hazardous employment to be higher than safer alternatives, the costs of hazardous products would be lower, the return on risky projects higher, and so on. If there were such a thing as a perfect market economy with perfect information, risks would be compensated for, or preventive measures taken, depending on which alternative minimized the costs. Under these circumstances, a reduction in the level of acceptance of risks would result in an increase in the compensation paid for carrying out hazardous tasks, an increase in insurance coverage, and a voluntary increase in preventive measures to avoid the costs of litigation or the need to pay higher compensation. In practice, however, these adjustments may not occur for many reasons.

For example, people may not buy insurance out of ignorance—either of the hazard or of the availability of the insurance. Again, no private insurance firm can organize the insurance because losses cannot be anticipated since they are a function of unknown governmental activities. Thus, it is almost inconceivable that a private firm, however large, can offer unemployment insurance, partly because the probability of unemployment is a function of governmental policies. More often, the insurer cannot define his risks, partly because the existence of the insurance causes a change in the behavior of the insured and therefore in the probabilities upon which the insurance company has hitherto relied. This, of course, is the moral hazard problem already mentioned.

In practice, therefore, the range of possible contingent contracts is limited to those in which events are easily verifiable to both parties. The possibility that only high-risk individuals will insure reduces the availability of such insurance for everyone, as does the probable change of behavior of an insured person.

In some of these situations, a case could exist for public insurance. If the tastes of all individuals were homogeneous, the costs of acquiring and processing information could be reduced by delegating the decision to a single body. Thus, if all persons are equally interested in avoiding the consumption of a product proved to have certain carcinogenic properties, the costs of generating, processing, and evaluating information could be reduced without loss of efficiency by delegating the decision on whether that product is safe for consumption to a regulatory agency. But, when tastes are not the same, as they usually are not, the cost saving of a standard-setting regulatory agency with respect to the generation and dissemination of information has to be measured against the costs it imposes when its standards go against the preferences and perceptions of risks of those it is trying to protect.

Nevertheless, people have found it more expedient to use their political clout to receive additional protection against risks, shifting the payment for additional protection to society at large. The flurry of activity in the creation of new regulatory agencies and other forms of governmental intervention, particularly in the last two decades, is partly the result of increased pressures by a growing number of individuals to shift risk-bearing to others. As a result, laws have been enacted and policies have been formulated that expanded and amplified the role of government in matters related to the pooling of risks. At the same time, the collective willingness to pay the costs of the additional insurance premiums has not kept pace with these demands. As a result, the gap has been widening between the demands for risk reduction and the willingness to pay for it.

Inflation, it should be noted, is largely a result of the increased costs of compulsory insurance. Many insurance programs reduce the competition that could keep prices in line. The list is long and growing. Thus, the Civil Aeronautics Board did not allow any competition among airlines for years. Even when some competition was allowed, the entry of new airlines was restricted and fares were regulated. To a large extent, it might be said that the Civil Aeronautics Board operated a cartel for the benefit of the airlines, the Federal Communications Commission for the benefit of existing broadcasting companies (resisting competition of pay television), and so on. The ICC licensing arrangements and route restrictions drastically curtailed competition in the trucking industry. Import quotas, "trigger prices," "orderly marketing agreements," and price supports have been used to "protect" the steel industry and the sugar manufacturers, and have limited the supply of imported cars, television sets, and textiles. Federal and state regulations restrict entry to many occupations and industries, thus reducing competition and increasing prices. The higher costs of other regulations increase the costs of production, and the increased payroll base of social security raises the cost of labor, and hence, of prices.

The changing demographic structure will make it increasingly expensive to maintain the levels of benefits promised by the Social Security Act; the payroll tax must rise to more than 20 percent in the next twenty-five years to maintain the benefits specified in the existing legislation.[14] These and other problems should make Americans reflect on the level of insurance they really want and are really willing to pay for. It should also make us realize that an essential part of any attempt to assess the costs and benefits of insurance is to identify them and then make them visible. Innovations in the way insurance is organized often can save much unnecessary cost, but this can be found out only if every cost—visible and invisible—is identified and justified by a comparison to the benefit. Certainly, the review itself will be found to yield more benefits than costs.

As shown, there are many problems in shifting risk-bearing to the public sector. First, the moral hazard is not reduced by the institution of government insurance. When the government gets into the business of insuring people, there is usually no visible link between payments and benefits. But the lack of a visible link between behavior and payment tends to increase the cost of the system, since the moral hazard becomes more important. The existence of the insurance may change the behavior of citizens because they are protected against loss and have less incentive to be cautious. Second, to reduce the moral hazard problem, government, not unlike a private insurance firm, has to resort to direct controls over the insured; the latter must agree to have his or her premises inspected or to take certain precautions. If the public pays the costs of medical treatment, a case can be made for enforcing precautions against falling sick, from the compulsory use of safety belts to the elimination of cigarette smoking. Third, when a government agency is responsible for risk-reduction, it does not have to calculate the cost of its efforts. To be sure, the agency does take into account direct costs of operation. But it often ignores the total costs to society of imposing the risk-avoidance or the insurance scheme. Thus, the Federal Aviation Administration is expected to protect people against the hazards of flying when a plane is not airworthy, not to calculate the total costs of its regulations. For the agency, the natural reaction to a crash of one DC-10 airplane was to ground all DC-10s until it was sure about the cause of the accident.[15]

The Occupational Safety and Health Administration is responsible for increased work safety, not to calculate the costs of its regulations and compare them to the benefits. Theoretically, it is possible to calculate the costs of the increased protection against the number of lives saved or diseases avoided. Indeed, many such calculations have been attempted, and the costs of lives saved have been imputed from the costs of the regulations. They vary widely, and in some instances are high to the point of absurdity. For example, a noise-level standard of 85 decibels in factories requires companies to spend an estimated $31 billion on noise abatement. In another example, the Occupational Safety and Health Administration coke-oven standards were estimated to cost $240 million by the agency and $1.3 billion by the industry. Since these standards have saved an estimated 27 lives, they value life at $9 million if the agency is right or at $48 million if the industry is right.

Richard Wilson calculated that the Occupational Safety and Health Administration proposal for the regulation of exposure to benzene would require, based on the agency's own figures for the cost of regulation, an expenditure of $300 million to save one hypothetical life. On that basis, the whole of the U.S. GNP of $2 trillion would have to be spent to save 6000 hypothetical lives. But lives would still be lost in the manufacture of the control equipment. According to Professor Wilson's calculations, four lives will be taken in the manufacturing process for each life saved.[16] Again, however, the agency is not expected to gauge its regulations according to such calculations, and this frame of reference may have caused regulations whose costs are much higher than their benefits. Being part of government, these agencies tend to "follow the rules" and cannot tolerate uncertainty in their operations. Their monitoring activities are designed to detect hazards that are easier to detect rather than those that represent the greatest risks.

Most of the additional insurance programs were forced on the government by interest groups. Farmers forced a crop-buying program and the maintenance of crop prices, businessmen secured themselves against failure and against the unpredictability of competitive markets, and workers secured themselves against work hazards and the risks of unemployment. In the United States, it was mainly the Great Depression that started the trend toward insurance. In the 1930s, businessmen forced on the government the Reconstruction Finance Corporation, and the deep anxiety of the depression changed the attitude of the legislature toward other insurance programs. With time, these insurance programs covered more and more individuals against more and more risks. The consequences we have already discussed: higher costs, rampant inflation, reduced competitiveness in world markets, the uncertainty as to whether these insurance programs can continue, and the increased dependence of individuals on the government. Today, many would argue, government is reaching into every nook and cranny of modern life.

In all these cases, the bill is paid by the entire population in terms of higher taxes, higher prices of goods and services, as well as out-of-pocket expenditures and foregone opportunities for increasing growth. As employers pay higher fringe benefits or part of the social security payroll tax, they certainly take these costs into account when they negotiate wage agreements. When the cost of manufacturing increases because of various risk-reduction regulations or higher rates of insurance, the producer attempts to shift these costs to consumers. There also may be less capital for investment in the creation of new jobs and less willingness to develop new products. The exact distribution of these costs is not easy to calculate, but they certainly are not the same as the payments made in the first round.

Too many predictable elements in society may make planning easier, but they also do not leave any place for innovation. In attempting to reduce the agony and the suffering of the poor and the needy, we do not have to insure against all possible hazards and reduce all changes. If we do, we create predictable bureaucracies. In addition, the value of our individual assets is daily ripped away by inflation, and spending power is transferred to government. The engine of inflation is budgetary deficits and newly created money, all caused by good intentions. Inflation is simply a tax paid to cover the costs of the insurance state.

It is time to reconcile the demands of political participation and the calls for more and more public insurance with the needs of the individual for a little more competition in the marketplace, a little lower cost of living, and a stability of prices. Obviously, when markets slacken, competition becomes fierce. In periods of flagging demand, many firms find it more convenient to turn from rivalry in the marketplace to a manipulation of the political machinery and greater demands for security for themselves. The longer the government sustains such firms against competition, the more they become accustomed to the easy life without competition, and the higher the price paid by the consumer.

Once it is found that government has a cause for intervention, one should make sure, (1) that the correction of a market failure would not result in a greater and costlier government failure; (2) that the methods of intervention would be the most suitable for the case; and (3) that the operations will be visible. An attempt to correct a market failure often causes high costs, and the situation may get worse rather than better.

Much more work on innovation in organizations and government methods of intervention is necessary. Too often, government has attempted to reduce risk by imposing unattainable or unenforceable standards when a change in the tax law could have achieved the same level of risk-reduction in a much more efficient way. The U.S. government aids many charitable institutions by allowing contributions to these institutions to be deductible from taxes. This way, the government in fact pays part of the costs of maintaining these organizations, but decisions about which of the tens of thousands of organizations are to be aided are left to individual taxpayers. In other countries, aid is given directly by the government, causing official petty tyranny and allowing a government official to be the only judge of worthy causes. The same methods of manipulating the tax can be used to enhance innovation or reduce risk and insure against its consequences.

Individual Americans are frustrated by what they perceive as a hopeless mess: exorbitant taxation, rampant inflation, and ever increasing governmental dictation of their way of life. The average American pays almost half his income in direct taxes, and much more in hidden taxes. One can easily hit hard on what's gone wrong and demand that the government get off the individual's back. One can easily persuade the reader that taxes are too high. Yet individuals who want a tax cut, the millions of people who are stifled by government regulations, the citizens who are frustrated by roaring inflation, are also the voters who elect the government. They accept less private risk and demand more social protection.

If we really want more growth, more employment, more freedom, and less government intervention, we should better understand the myriad ways, visible and invisible, in which the government is protecting us. It is essential that all governmental regulations and the variety of the means used to protect all sorts of interest groups be fully exposed and periodically examined. The official budget of the United States is subject to a close scrutiny and annual debate. The invisible budget is rarely discussed, and once a tariff or a regulation has been established, there is little chance that it will be reexamined. Once all these invisible methods are brought to the public attention, individuals will have to decide how much risk they are willing to take and to what extent they want government protection.

It is easy to blame the government, or the "system," but the government is elected by the people, and the "system" is us. If all of us agree that a no-risk society is an impossible dream, if we all feel that the willingness to take risks in the marketplace is what made America a great society, if we really and honestly want less intervention and not merely the protection of our own petty interests, then it is up to all of us to change the rules of the game. Politicians are elected today because they promise more insurance, more protection, and more benefits. They also promise lower taxes. Yet it is impossible to insure all of us unless we are willing to pay the premiums. If Americans want fewer regulations and lower taxes, they should be willing to receive less protection, less public insurance, and less benefits. If Americans want their government to stop printing more dollars that merely deteriorate in value, they should also be willing to bear the burden of moving from old and obsolete industries to new ones; they should be willing to learn new jobs; they should be ready to take more risks. In short, they should be willing to reduce the size and the scope of the public insurance.

It might be argued that the public has voted lately against economic efficiency and for an insurance state. However, these votes, if indeed they were cast, were not based on full information of the costs involved. The increasing use of invisible methods indeed reduces the choice of the intelligent voter.

Slogans are important for exciting the people, but in the end harsh realities always rein-in flights of fancy. In their day-to-day decisions, government officials seldom think in terms of zero pollution or full employment or the total elimination of mental retardation, any more than businessmen who hail the free enterprise system really try to foster competition. There is a huge gap between intention and act. Reality leads us to less than perfect solutions and widens the gap between promises and delivery. When these disparities are noticed, they are attributed to a lack of money, the interference of vested interests, and inept bureaucracy, or poor analysis, depending on one's point of view. In time, at least some of us possibly realize that the reason is much simpler: there was no solution in the first place, largely because people are too complicated. People are selfish but also willing, altruistic, sometimes paternalistic but also self-centered, cooperative and sociable but individualistic. They sometimes want to be dependent on charismatic leaders, but they like to feel responsible for their own destinies. Any theory based on only one of these contradictions is bound to fall short. Any wise person knows it is impossible to do everything and achieve every goal.

People will continue to count on the great answers, the miracle breakthroughs, and the single equitable solutions. One can only hope that these dreams will not end in totalitarian solutions; that a place will be left where each individual can dream his or her private dreams; and that eventually people will learn to accept the inevitable, achieve the possible, and tell the difference between the two.

In fact, in the coming age of humility, there should be a healthy skepticism toward "one and only" answers. To live in an interdependent world, a moderate balance must be struck between private rights and social obligations, between individual freedom and societal restraint.

NOTES

1. George Cabot Lodge, *The New American Ideology* (New York: Knopf, 1975), p. 3.
2. Douglas F. Dowd, *The Twisted Dream: Capitalist Development in the United States Since 1776* (Cambridge, Mass.: Winthrop, 1974), p. 5.
3. Charles Reich, *The Greening of America* (New York: Random House, 1970), p. 3.
4. Fred Hirsch, *The Social Limits to Growth* (Cambridge, Mass.: Harvard University Press, 1976).
5. Editorial, *Wall Street Journal,* 7 September 1977.
6. Union-managed pension funds own a growing share of U.S. equity capital. For suggestions on how to use pension funds to achieve union-desired objectives, see Jeremy Rifkin and Randy Barber, *The North Will Rise Again: Pensions, Power, and Politics in the 1980s* (Boston: Beacon, 1978).
7. Arthur M. Okun, *Equality and Efficiency: The Big Trade-Off* (Washington, D.C.: Brookings Institution, 1975).
8. Martin Landau, "Redundancy, Rationality, and the Problem of Duplication and Overlap," *Public Administration Review,* July-August 1969, pp. 346-58.
9. Alfred E. Kahn, "The Tyranny of Small Decisions: Market Failures, Imperfections, and the Limits to Economics," *Kyklos,* 1963, pp. 23-46.
10. In the study, subjects were asked to rate thirty items according to risks, other items according to benefits. They were to assess the acceptable level

that is "good enough," where "good enough" meant that the advantages of increased safety are not worth the costs of reducing risks or otherwise altering the activity. At least in that group, subjects thought most items should be made safer. See Baruch Fischhoff, Paul Slovic, Sarah Lichtenstein, Stephen Read, and Barbara Combs, "How Safe Is Safe Enough? A Psychometric Study of Attitudes Toward Technological Risks and Benefits," *Policy Sciences* 9 (April 1978): 127-52.

11. Ibid.

12. See different issues of *Automotive News,* August-November 1974.

13. See Campbell R. McConnell, "Why Is U.S. Productivity Slowing Down?" *Harvard Business Review,* March-April 1979, p. 36. In 1978, the growth in productivity in the United States was 1.1 percent compared with 8.3 percent in Japan, 5.5 percent in Sweden, and 4.9 percent in France.

14. Martin S. Feldstein, "Social Security Hobbles Our Capital Formation," *Harvard Business Review,* July-August 1979, p. 6.

15. After an American Airlines DC-10 crashed in Chicago on 25 May 1979, and 273 persons were killed, the FAA suspended certificates of all 139 DC-10s flying in the United States on 6 June 1979. The suspension was lifted 17 July 1979. The daily revenue of DC-10s is $7 million a day, $4.5 million of which was picked up by other aircraft. The net direct loss of revenue to the airlines was $93 million. See *Aviation Week,* 23 July 1979.

16. Richard Wilson, "A Rational Approach to Reducing Cancer Risk," *New York Times,* 9 July 1978, p. E17.

Appendix

Operating Revenues, Expenses, and Profits or (Loss) of Selected Federal Insurance Agencies, 1973-81
(in millions of dollars)

	1973			1977		
	Revenue	(Actual) Expenses	Profit or (Loss)	Revenue	(Actual) Expenses	Profit or (Loss)
Insured Loan Agencies						
1. Rural Development Insurance Fund	11.3	25.5	(14.2)	102.2	245.4	(143.2)
2. Agricultural Credit Insurance Fund	55.0	605.8	(550.8)	272.1	587.8	(315.7)
3. Federal Deposit Insurance Corporation	503.2	51.6	451.6	820.6	128.1	692.5
4. Veterans Loan Guaranty Revolving Fund	81.9	103.5	(21.6)	92.6	117.2	(24.6)
Student Loan Insurance Fund						
5. Federal Insurance	4.5	23.6	(19.1)			
6. Federal Reinsurance	.8	12.4	(11.6)			
7. Federal Savings and Loan Insurance Corporation	352.5	93.6	258.9	604.2	131.9	472.3
Federal Housing Administration						
8. Mutual Mortgage Insurance Fund	360.7	246.3	114.4	404.4	250.9	153.5
9. General Insurance Fund	120.4	332.8	(212.4)	143.9	508.0	(364.1)
10. Cooperative Management Housing Insurance Fund	5.8	.9	4.9	5.4	1.3	4.1
11. Special Risk Insurance Fund	77.0	271.4	(194.4)	71.0	352.7	(281.7)
12. Rural Housing Insurance Fund	37.3	436.6	(399.3)	473.9	1,074.6	(600.7)
13. Federal Ship Financing Fund	6.6	1.5	5.1	23.6	2.8	20.8
14. Credit Union Share Insurance Fund	13.3	2.7	10.6	30.4	8.5	21.9
15. Indian Loan Guaranty and Insurance Fund	—	—	—	.4	4.7	(4.3)
SUB-TOTAL	1,630.3	2,208.2	(577.9)	3,044.7	3,413.9	(369.2)
Property Insurance Agencies						
16. Aviation War Risk Insurance Revolving Fund	2.2	.1	2.1	1.0	.1	.9
17. War Risk Insurance Revolving Fund	.1	.1	.1	.1	.1	.0
18. Federal Crop Insurance Corporation	42.0	29.9	12.1	91.7	157.6	(65.9)

	(1)	(2)	(3)	(4)	(5)	(6)
National Insurance Development Fund						
19. FAIR (Riot Reinsurance)	7.4	1.4	6.0	7.1	1.2	5.9
20. Crime Insurance	1.3	2.3	(1.0)	6.6	15.3	(8.7)
21. National Flood Insurance Fund	1.5	30.2	(28.7)	9.9	91.6	(81.7)
SUB-TOTAL	54.5	63.9	(9.4)	116.4	265.9	(149.5)
Life Insurance Agencies						
22. Service-Disabled Insurance Fund	18.2	31.7	(13.5)	25.5	40.8	(15.3)
23. Veterans Reopened Insurance Fund	49.8	48.0	1.8	50.8	44.4	6.4
24. Veterans Special Life Fund	61.0	53.0	8.0	82.8	76.9	5.8
25. Servicemen's Group Life Insurance Fund	79.4	79.4	–	118.1	118.1	–
26. National Service Life Fund	798.0	518.9	279.1	912.8	697.6	215.2
27. U. S. Government Life Insurance Fund	39.1	66.3	(27.2)	37.4	71.1	(33.7)
SUB-TOTAL	1,045.5	797.3	248.2	1,227.4	1,048.9	178.4
28. Unemployment Trust Fund	6,690.7	5,353.8	1,336.9	14,986.0	14,103.0	883.0
TOTAL, 1-28	9,421.0	8,423.2	997.8	19,374.5	18,831.7	542.7
29. OASDHI						
Old Age and Survivor Insurance Trust Fund	43,439.3	43,622.5	(183.2)	71,795.6	73,478.6	(1,683.0)
Disability Insurance Trust Fund	5,946.5	5,467.3	479.2	9,374.2	11,589.7	(2,215.5)
Hospital Insurance Trust Fund	8,351.6	6,841.7	1,509.9	15,374.0	15,207.1	166.9
Supplemental Medical Insurance Trust Fund	2,902.1	2,636.9	265.2	7,382.6	6,341.6	1,041.0
TOTAL OASDHI	60,639.5	58,568.4	2,071.1	103,926.4	106,617.0	(2,690.6)
GRAND TOTAL, 1-29	70,060.5	66,991.6	3,068.9	123,300.9	125,448.7	(2,147.9)

SOURCE: Budget of the U.S. Government for different fiscal years. Totals may not add precisely due to rounding. .0 signifies less than .1 million.

	1978			1979		
	Revenue	(Actual) Expenses	Profit or (Loss)	Revenue	(Actual) Expenses	Profit or (Loss)
Insured Loan Agencies						
1. Rural Development Insurance Fund	147.2	252.4	(105.2)	190.5	406.5	(216.0)
2. Agricultural Credit Insurance Fund	437.7	739.4	(301.7)	765.5	1,355.5	(589.9)
3. Federal Deposit Insurance Corporation	924.0	149.5	774.5	1,067.7	81.1	986.6
4. Veterans Loan Guaranty Revolving Fund	90.2	115.2	(25.0)	102.2	102.9	(.7)
Student Loan Insurance Fund						
5. Federal Insurance	33.4	61.5	(28.0)	37.8	66.5	(28.7)
6. Federal Reinsurance	20.9	64.2	(43.3)	25.4	71.5	(46.1)
7. Federal Savings and Loan Insurance Corporation	668.5	136.0	532.4	784.7	154.9	629.8
Federal Housing Administration						
8. Mutual Mortgage Insurance Fund	438.5	252.1	186.4	488.1	282.6	205.5
9. General Insurance Fund	158.7	431.6	(272.8)	183.3	404.4	(221.1)
10. Cooperative Management Housing Insurance Fund	5.8	1.0	4.8	5.6	1.8	3.8
11. Special Risk Insurance Fund	71.0	291.9	(220.9)	72.6	304.3	(231.7)
12. Rural Housing Insurance Fund	687.2	960.0	(272.8)	849.0	1,764.6	(915.7)
13. Federal Ship Financing Fund	.7	.5	.2	34.3	18.8	15.5
14. Credit Union Share Insurance Fund	37.4	8.3	29.0	45.9	12.2	33.7
15. Indian Loan Guaranty and Insurance Fund	.2	.6	(.4)	.2	.7	(.5)
SUB-TOTAL	3,721.6	3,464.3	257.3	4,652.8	5,028.3	(375.5)
Property Insurance Agencies						
16. Aviation War Risk Insurance Revolving Fund	1.2	.0	1.1	1.4	.1	1.3
17. War Risk Insurance Revolving Fund	.0	.1	(.1)	.0	.1	(.1)
18. Federal Crop Insurance Corporation	102.7	168.9	(66.2)	93.8	65.6	28.2

National Insurance Development Fund						
19. FAIR (Riot Reinsurance)	5.8	1.6	4.1	6.9	3.2	3.7
20. Crime Insurance	6.5	20.2	(13.7)	13.0	25.5	(12.4)
21. National Flood Insurance Fund	71.3	179.6	(108.2)	125.6	463.0	(337.4)
SUB-TOTAL	187.4	370.5	(183.0)	240.8	557.5	(316.7)
Life Insurance Agencies						
22. Service-Disabled Insurance Fund	27.3	32.4	(5.1)	28.3	43.0	(14.7)
23. Veterans Reopened Insurance Fund	53.0	46.1	6.9	55.5	60.0	(4.5)
24. Veterans Special Life Fund	95.2	92.2	3.0	102.1	107.6	(5.4)
25. Servicemen's Group Life Insurance Fund	118.7	118.5	.1	105.5	105.6	(.1)
26. National Service Life Fund	939.7[1]	667.8[2]	272.0	982.5[1]	785.4[2]	197.1
27. U. S. Government Life Insurance Fund	36.2[1]	67.0[2]	(30.8)	38.3[1]	70.8[2]	(32.5)
SUB-TOTAL	1,270.0	1,024.0	246.0	1,312.3	1,172.4	139.9
28. Unemployment Trust Fund	15,160.9	11,169.1	3,991.8	15,888.8	11,173.0	4,715.9
TOTAL, 1-28	20,340.0	16,027.9	4,312.0	22,094.7	17,931.3	4,163.3
29. OASDHI						
Old Age and Survivor Insurance Trust Fund	76,811.4	81,205.4	(4,393.9)	86,893.3	90,128.7	(3,235.4)
Disability Insurance Trust Fund	12,783.8	12,655.3	128.5	15,876.0	13,944.0	1,252.0
Hospital Insurance Trust Fund	18,514.0	17,832.7	681.3	21,876.7	20,310.0	1,566.7
Supplemental Medical Insurance Trust Fund	9,045.5	7,356.5	1,689.0	9,839.1	8,813.6	1,025.5
TOTAL OASDHI	117,154.7	119,049.9	(1,895.2)	133,805.1	133,196.3	608.8
GRAND TOTAL, 1-29	137,494.7	135,077.8	2,416.9	155,899.8	151,127.6	4,772.1

	1980			1981		
	Revenue	Estimated Expenses	Profit or (Loss)	Revenue	Estimated Expenses	Profit or (Loss)
Insured Loan Agencies						
1. Rural Development Insurance Fund	234.0	526.6	(292.6)	285.4	633.0	(347.6)
2. Agricultural Credit Insurance Fund	1,064.4	1,846.1	(781.7)	1,347.4	2,090.1	(742.7)
3. Federal Deposit Insurance Corporation	1,175.2	121.8	1,053.4	1,404.0	132.0	1,271.9
4. Veterans Loan Guaranty Revolving Fund	103.4	121.6	(18.2)	88.8	131.7	(42.9)
Student Loan Insurance Fund						
5. Federal Insurance	36.8	33.5	3.3	..	..	..
6. Federal Reinsurance	31.5	102.5	(71.1)	..	..	..
7. Federal Savings and Loan Insurance Corporation	851.1	143.4	707.7	911.4	118.3	793.2
Federal Housing Administration						
8. Mutual Mortgage Insurance Fund	533.0	300.6	232.4	549.9	229.5	320.4
9. General Insurance Fund	190.6	448.7	(258.1)	207.2	435.8	(228.5)
10. Cooperative Management Housing Insurance Fund	5.6	1.7	3.9	5.5	1.9	3.6
11. Special Risk Insurance Fund	72.5	323.9	(251.4)	76.7	317.0	(240.3)
12. Rural Housing Insurance Fund	965.1	2,197.5	(1,232.4)	1,112.7	2,666.5	(1,553.8)
13. Federal Ship Financing Fund	31.0	4.2	26.8	31.4	4.4	27.0
14. Credit Union Share Insurance Fund	51.4	17.2	34.3	57.7	19.2	38.5
15. Indian Loan Guaranty and Insurance Fund	.6	4.6	(3.9)	1.4	5.0	(3.6)
SUB-TOTAL	5,346.3	6,193.9	(847.6)	6,079.6	6,784.4	(704.7)
Property Insurance Agencies						
16. Aviation War Risk Insurance Revolving Fund	1.5	.2	1.3	1.6	.2	1.5
17. War Risk Insurance Revolving Fund	.3	.3	(.0)	.3	.3	(.0)
18. Federal Crop Insurance Corporation	105.8	120.7	(14.9)	110.8	136.0	(25.2)

National Insurance Development Fund						
19. FAIR (Riot Reinsurance)	4.6	1.5	3.1	4.2	1.0	3.3
20. Crime Insurance	15.7	29.0	(13.3)	15.3	29.7	(14.4)
21. National Flood Insurance Fund	144.7	272.7	(128.0)	161.7	275.5	(113.9)
SUB-TOTAL	272.6	424.4	(151.8)	293.9	442.8	(148.8)
Life Insurance Agencies						
22. Service-Disabled Insurance Fund	29.7	46.2	(16.6)	30.8	48.0	(17.2)
23. Veterans Reopened Insurance Fund	58.1	70.0	(11.9)	61.0	73.8	(12.8)
24. Veterans Special Life Fund	106.7	96.5	10.2	111.5	109.0	2.4
25. Servicemen's Group Life Insurance Fund	104.1	104.1	–	104.1	104.1	–
26. National Service Life Fund	1,029.1[1]	803.0[2]	226.1	1,060.2[1]	931.0[2]	129.2
27. U. S. Government Life Insurance Fund	35.9[1]	68.7[2]	(32.8)	34.3[1]	63.6[2]	(29.3)
SUB-TOTAL	1,363.6	1,188.5	175.1	1,401.9	1,329.6	72.2
28. Unemployment Trust Fund	17,400.0[3]	15,851.7[2]	1,548.3	19,300.0[3]	18,700.0[2]	600.0
TOTAL, 1-28	24,382.5	23,658.5	724.0	27,075.4	27,256.7	(181.3)
29. OASDHI						
Old Age and Survivor Insurance Trust Fund	99,525.3[1]	104,029.2[2]	(4,503.9)[4]	111,883.6[1]	121,163.0[2]	(9,279.4)[4]
Disability Insurance Trust Fund	17,406.7[3]	15,364.9[2]	2,041.7	20,581.4[3]	17,399.0[2]	3,182.4
Hospital Insurance Trust Fund	25,517.2[3]	23,219.3[2]	2,297.8	32,539.1[3]	26,313.0[2]	6,226.1
Supplemental Medical Insurance Trust Fund	10,405.0[3]	10,321.1[2]	83.9	12,468.0[3]	12,111.6[2]	356.4
TOTAL OASDHI	152,854.2	152,934.5	(80.5)	177,472.1	176,986.6	485.5
GRAND TOTAL, 1-29	177,236.7	176,593.0	643.7	204,547.5	204,243.3	304.2

NOTES: 1. Total income. 2. Total outlay. 3. Budget authority. 4. Social Security Administration's estimates.

Index

Accidents, 65; industrial, 51; nuclear, 53-60, 97-98; traffic, 39, 42, 44-45, 56
Accountability, 114
ACEC, 163
Ackerman, Bruce A., 60, 74
Adolescent Health Services, 89
Advertising, 19-20, 34
Aerospace industry, 156
Agricultural Credit Insurance Fund, 90
Aid to Families with Dependent Children, 67, 99
Airline industry, 2, 39, 129, 133, 178, 203, 204
Akerlof, George, 192
Alfasud, 115
Alford, Robert, 37
Alienation, 34-35
Allocation, resource, 169-70
American Council on Education, 126
AFL-CIO, 52
Andersen, Kristi, 34, 38
Arrow, Kenneth J., 72
Asia, 152-53, 158
Atomic Energy Commission, 53, 121
Australia, 2, 105, 142
Austria, 88
Authorities, public, 118
Automobile industry, 145, 147-48, 163
Averch-Johnson effect, 129
Aviation insurance, 92

Bank failures, 76-77
Baran, Paul, 16, 36, 37
Barber, Randy, 208
Barker v. Lull Engineering Co., 74
Barro, Robert J., 108
Barter exchanges, 177
Baumol, W. J., 139
Beagle Aircrafts, 162
Becker, Gary S., 72
Belgium, 38, 88, 99, 102, 105, 163
Bell, Daniel, 37

Bernstein, George K., 96, 109
Bettmann, Otto L., 46, 72
Bevan, Aneurin, 174
Bianchi, Patrizio, 168
Bieber, R. M., 74
Bismarck, 51
Bjork, Gordon, 20, 36
Blackhurst, R., 166, 167
Bonds, tax-exempt, 118
Boulding, Kenneth, 134, 139
Bower, Joseph L., 192
Boyle, Robert H., 73
Brazil, 69-70
Breckenridge, Adam C., 36
Breton, Albert, 27, 37
British Airways, 68
British Leyland, 148, 162
Brittain, John A., 108
Brittan, Samuel, 37
Broker state, 24-26
Brookings Institution, 130
Buckley, Robert M., 139
Budd, Edward C., 37
Budget, federal, 100-106; off-budget items, 118-21
Bupp, I. C., 73
Bureaucrats, 26-27, 182-83
Bureau of Economic Analysis, 127
Burton, Ian, 38

Cable and Wireless, 162
Caldicott, Helene, 73
California, 58, 62-63, 96
Canada, 88, 99, 115-16, 142, 145, 161
Capitalism, 11, 15-16, 25, 160, 180, 188
Caplan, Gerald M., 191
Capron, W. M., 139
Cardozo, Judge, 62
Carson, Rachel, 55, 73
Carter, Jimmy, 57-58, 89
Chamberlain, John, 24, 37
Check Forgery Insurance Fund, 96

Child Health Assurance Program (CHAP),
    89
Chrysler Corporation, 121, 163
Civil Aeronautics Board, 129, 178, 203
Civil disorders, 94-96
Civil service, 23, 26-27
Civil Service Retirement Act, 82
Class struggle, 6, 9
Coalition for Direct Action, 183
Cohen, Larry J., 191
Coleman, John R., 108, 191
Collard, David, 36
Combs, Barbara, 73, 209
Commodity Credit Corporation, 121
Communist Manifesto, 25
Competition, 186-87, 198-99, 203, 206
Compliance costs, forced, 124-33
Congressional Budget Act (1974), 134
Consolidated Rail Company (Conrail),
    115-16
Consumer price index, 80, 83, 88, 175
Consumer Product Safety Act (1972), 63, 102
Consumers, 9, 34, 62-63, 125, 128, 151, 153,
    181
Contracting, government, 10, 121-24
Cooper, Richard N., 166
Cooperative Management Housing Insur-
    ance Fund, 91
Corden, W. M., 168
Cornwall, John, 167
Corporations, 29, 71, 117
Cost-of-living index, 69-70
Council of Economic Advisers, 130
Council on Environmental Quality, 127
Credit programs, 119-21, 122-23
Credit Union Share Insurance Fund, 92
Crime, 19, 172, 191; insurance against, 94-96
Crop insurance, 92, 97, 205
Curzon, Gerard, 168
Curzon, Victoria, 168

DC-10, 204, 209
DDT, 40, 50, 55
Defense expenditures, 99, 101-3, 105, 121-23,
    145
Defense Plant Corporation, 116
DeFina, Robert, 127
Delays, program, 183-85
Denmark, 85, 99
Dennison, Edward, 130
Dependency, social, 177-80, 190

Detroit, 145
Devlin, Patrick, 36
Dickerson, Reed, 74
Disability benefits, 80-81
Disaster Relief Act (1974), 94
DNA, 57, 60
Domestic International Sales Corporations
    (DISC), 158-59
Douglas, George W., 138
Douglas, Mary, 36
Dow Chemical, 126
Dowd, Douglas, 194, 208
Downs, Anthony, 27, 37
Drug industry, 8, 19, 97, 133, 184-85

Earthquake Hazard Reduction Act (1977),
    94
Economic(s): change, 187-90; classical,
    15-17; Keynesian, 23-24
Education, 3, 16, 105, 126-27
Edwards, Anthony, 166
Ehrlich, Isaac, 72
Eisenhower, Dwight D., 55, 124
Elites, 24-26
Employee Retirement Income Security Act
    (1974), 119
Employment, guaranteed, 4, 66-69, 75,
    149-50
Energy policy, 54-59, 71, 148-49
England. See United Kingdom
Environment, protecting, 34-35, 40, 51, 127,
    129-30, 181, 183, 185
Environmental Protection Agency (EPA), 51,
    102, 129
Epstein, Samuel S., 73
Equality of opportunity, 170, 195
Equal rights, 14-15, 24
Ethics, 59; markets and, 17-20, 22
Europe, 10, 47, 48, 50, 67, 142, 146-47, 161
European Economic Community, 85, 142,
    147, 152-53, 154, 158
Expectations, rising, 12, 32
Export-Import Bank, 117, 120
Exports, world, 143-48
Externalities, 21-22

FAIR, 94
Farm Credit Administration, 119
Farmers, 9, 25, 33, 92, 117, 119, 173, 205
Farmers Home Administration, 121
Featherbedding, 68

Federal Aeronautics Administration, 128
Federal Aviation Agency (FAA), 92, 121, 204
Federal Bureau of Investigation (FBI), 95
Federal Communications Commission
(FCC), 203
Federal Crop Insurance Corporation, 92
Federal Deposit Insurance Corporation
(FDIC), 76, 90, 92, 107, 119, 131
Federal Emergency Management Agency,
93-94
Federal Employees Health Benefits Program,
65, 89
Federal Fire Prevention and Control Act
(1974), 94
Federal Home Loan Bank Board, 91
Federal Housing Administration, 91, 131
Federal Insurance Administration, 93, 94-95,
96
Federally Funded Research and Develop-
ment Centers, 124
Federal National Mortgage Association, 117,
120, 132
Federal Reserve System, 84, 90
Federal Savings and Loan Insurance Corpor-
ation (FSLIC), 91, 92, 131
Federal Ship Financing Fund, 91
Federal Trade Commission (FTC), 19
Federal Water Pollution Control Act (1972),
60
Feld, Werner J., 167
Feldstein, Martin, 68, 75, 108, 209
Fillmore, Charles J., 19
Finland, 88
First Amendment, 15
Fisher, Charles, 108
Fishhoff, Baruch, 73, 209
Fitzgerald, A. Ernest, 123, 138
Flood Disaster Protection Act (1973), 28, 93
Flood insurance, 28, 35, 42, 92-94, 97, 200
Florida, 95
Food and Drug Administration (FDA),
50-51, 133, 171, 185
Food, Drug and Cosmetics Act (1962), 185
Ford, Gerald, 63
Ford, Kristina, 130-31, 139
Ford Motor Company, 161
Foreign aid, 163
Fox, Ronald, 114, 137
France, Anatole, 66
France, 99, 115-16, 144, 153, 156-59, 163, 177
Fraud, 176

Friedland, Roger, 37
Friedman, Milton, 20
Fringe benefits, 33, 89
Furstenberg, George M. von, 108

Galbraith, John Kenneth, 36, 37, 196
Galileo, 59
Gans, Herbert J., 37
Ganz, Gabriele, 168
Gary, Elbert, 178
General Agreement on Tariffs and Trade
(GATT), 142, 145, 152, 154, 158-59, 162,
164
General Motors, 74, 126
Genetics research, 56-57, 59-60
Germany (Federal Republic), 51, 85, 88, 99,
115, 116, 140-41, 145, 147, 153, 154-56, 158,
162, 175
Gibson, Robert M., 108
Gilpin, Robert, 142, 166
Glaverbel, 163
GOGOs, 124
Government Corporation Control Act, 117
Government-sponsored enterprises, 115-17
Government Student Loan Association
(GSLA), 91
Grabowski, Henry G., 192
Graham, Otis L., Jr., 37
Great Britain. *See* United Kingdom
Grebler, Leo, 139
Greene, Mark R., 107, 109
Guest workers, 147-48

Hall, Charles P., Jr., 74
Harris poll, 79
Hart, H. L. A., 36
Hayek, F. A., 37
Hazard(s): moral, 33, 45, 89, 106, 173-77,
202; natural, 42, 65, 97; radiation, 56-57;
work-related, 7, 34, 54-55, 97
Health care, 17-18, 33-34, 47, 60-61, 65, 80,
85-90, 174-76, 195, 204
Henderson, Dale W., 74
Hennigsen v. *Bloomfield Motors,* 62
Hilferding, Rudolph, 7
Hirsch, Fred, 194, 208
Hitler, Adolf, 47
Homeowners, 42, 91, 117, 134, 136
Home Ownership Assistance Program, 91
Hoover Commission, 116
Housing Act (1949), 91, 131

Housing industry, 131-33
Housing and Urban Development Act
    (1968), 92-93
Huntington, Samuel P., 37, 38
Hurricane Agnes, 42, 93, 200

Illegal markets, 18-19
Immigration, 142, 166-67
Immorality, 18-19
Income: maintenance programs, 85; mini-
    mum, 3; redistribution, 20, 34-35
Indexation, 70, 80, 82
Indian Loan Guaranty and Insurance Fund,
    92
Indian Financing Act (1974), 92
Individualism, 3, 7, 9-11, 20, 30-31, 79, 173,
    195, 199-200; market system and, 15-17;
    society and, 13-15
Industrial Development Authority (IDA), 159
Industrialization, 40
Industrial policies, 148-52
Inflation, 2, 5-6, 10, 35, 45, 49, 66-67, 69-70,
    80, 82, 141-42, 148, 186, 203, 205-6
Insurance state, 32-36, 76-109
Interdependence: nation-state, 10, 140-43;
    social, 8, 33
Interest groups, 14, 24-26, 145, 184
International Monetary Fund (IMF), 142
International Trade Commission, 77, 150,
    151
Interstate Commerce Commission (ICC),
    129-30, 178, 184, 203
Ireland, 88
IRI, 115, 162
Israel, 69-70
Italy, 115-16, 145, 159, 162-63, 177

Jacquemin, A., 168
Japan, 88, 99, 144, 145, 146, 148, 151, 152,
    153-56, 158, 161, 164
Jasinowski, Jerry J., 138
Jefferson, Thomas, 125
Jencks, Christopher, 37
Jewkes, John, 191
Jewkes, Sylvia, 191

Kahenman, Daniel, 72
Kahn, Alfred E., 208
Kales, Robert, 38
Keohane, R., 167
Keynes, John Maynard, 23
Keyser, William, 137

Khorana, Har Gobind, 57
Kindleberger Charles, 167
Kirkland, Edward Chase, 73
Kissinger, Henry, 71
Kneese, Allen V., 74, 138
Kolko, Gabriel, 192
Kunreuther, Howard, 38, 72
Kurth, Wilhelm, 167

Landau, Martin, 208
Law, Sylvia, 74
Law enforcement, 22-23, 49, 100
"Legal sufficiency," 183-84
Leveson, Irving, 168
Levhari, David, 75
Levine, Robert A., 36
Liability cases, 62-65
Licensure statutes, 189-90
Lichtenstein, Sarah, 73, 209
Lindbeck, Assar, 192
Lipschutz, Ronnie D., 73
Little, Paul, 167
Liviatan, Nissan, 75
Living standards, 20
Lockheed Aircraft, 163
Lodge, George Cabot, 73, 194, 208
Long Term Textile Agreement (1962), 153,
    163-64
Loopholes, tax, 2, 134, 177
Lowi, Theodore, 37
Loxley, Colin, 126

MacAvoy, Paul, 37
McConnell, Campbell R., 209
McCracken, Paul, 182, 192
McPherson v. Buick Motor Company, 62
Madison, James, 14
Malmgren Harald B., 168
Malpractice suits, 63-65, 176
Mandel, Ernest, 36
Manley, John F., 137
Mansfield, Mike, 96
Marian, N., 166, 167
Maritime Administration Ship Construction
    Guaranty Program, 119
Maritime Appropriation Authorization Act
    (1979), 91
Market system, 9, 180, 198; ethics and,
    17-20; failures in, 20-24, 169; individuals
    and, 15-17; inefficiencies in, 185-87
Marsh v. Alabama, 36
Marx, Karl, 25, 48, 180

Maryland, 96
Massachusetts, 59, 95
Materne, 163
Media, 182
Medicaid, 88, 99
Medicare, 47, 81, 88, 99
Mehr, Robert I., 107
Melman, Seymour, 32, 38, 138
Mercantilism, new, 160-66
Middle Ages, 18
Mill, John Stuart, 23
Miller, Arthur S., 137
Miller, James C., III, 138
Miller, S. M., 37
Milwaukee Railroad Restructuring Act
   (1979), 116
Mine Safety and Health Administration, 102
Minimum wage, 49
Minority groups, 3, 26, 195
Mishan, E. J., 12
Mitchell, Broadus, 73
Modernization, industrial, 182
Moral hazard factor, 33, 45, 89, 106, 173-77,
   202
Moral rules, 18-19
Mortgages, 91, 119-20, 131-34, 173
Multi Fibre Agreement (1974), 153
Multinational firms, 5, 8, 146-48, 150, 185
Munnell, Alicia H., 107, 108
Musgrave, Peggy, 108
Musgrave, Richard, 108
Mutual Mortgage Insurance Fund, 91

National Aeronautics and Space Administra-
   tion (NASA), 121
National Association of Manufacturers, 116
National Center for Health, 39
National Consumers Safety Council, 128
National Flood Insurance, 28, 42, 93
National Health Plan, 89
National Health Service (British), 174-76
National Highway Traffic Safety Adminis-
   tration, 128, 200, 201
National Housing Policy Review, 132
National Institute of Health, 57, 59
National Insurance Development Fund, 94
National Investment Company, 163
Nationalized industries, 67, 68, 162-64, 168
National Park Foundation, 117
National Park Service, 64
National Resources Defense Council, 58
National Science Foundation, 124

National Transportation Safety Board, 100
Negligence, 51, 64
Nelson, James C., 138
Netherlands, 99, 102, 105, 115, 116, 145, 153
New Deal, 76, 131
New Hampshire Public Service Company,
   183
New Jersey, 62, 97
New Mexico, 58
New York, 46, 95, 96, 111, 121
New York Times, 54
New Zealand, 2, 85
Nie, Norman H., 34, 38
Nihilism, 194-95
Niskanen, William A., Jr., 26, 37
Nixon, Richard, 63
Nold, R. G., 139
Nordhaus, William D., 192
Norway, 99
Nuclear industry, 53-60, 97-98, 183
Nuclear Regulatory Commission, 102, 128
Nye, J., 167

Occupational Safety and Health Act (1970),
   63
Occupational Safety and Health Administra-
   tion, 52, 102, 128, 130, 171, 204
O'Connor, James, 12, 25, 37
OECD, 85, 88, 149, 151, 152-53
Ohio, 96
Oil crisis, 8, 54, 71, 144, 148-49, 163, 184,
   193
Okun, Arthur M., 196, 208
OPEC nations, 71, 193-94
"Orderly adjustment," trade and, 152-58
Owen, David, 174

Papier, William, 68, 75
Paris, David C., 191
Paris, S. J., 74
Paris Commune (1873), 48
Payroll tax, social security, 80-85, 203, 205
Peck, Morton J., 138
Pennsylvania, 95, 161
Pension Benefit Guaranty Corporation, 119
Pension funds, 97, 189
Periasamy, Palani G., 167
Pfaff, Martin, 134, 139
Pike, David F., 74
Pirenne, Henri, 74
Polan, Steve, 74
Polanyi, Karl, 167

Pollution control, 19, 60-61, 114, 127, 129-30
Poor, the, 3, 48-49, 134, 190
Poor Laws, Elizabethan, 134-35
Portney, Paul R., 192
Pregnancy Prevention Program, 89
Price agreements, 2
Price-Anderson Act (1957), 97, 98
Privity of contracts, 62
Productivity, 106, 151
Product-liability cases, 8, 62-65, 97
Property, 20, 45, 47, 180, 190, 195; insurance, 90-94; quasi rights, 111-14
Prosser, William L., 74
Protectionism, 77, 136, 142, 145-46, 149, 154-55, 158-61, 163-66; rigidities of, 180-82
Protestant ethic, 31
Public interest, 2, 20, 25; limits to, 169-92

Quasi property rights, 111-14
Quotas, 77, 154, 163

Racial discord, 34-35, 170
Railroad industry, 115-16, 129-30
Railroad Retirement Act (1974), 96, 116
Rainwater, Lee S., 37
Rasmussen, Norman C., 53
Rates of exchange, international, 151-52, 164, 193
Read, Stephen, 73, 209
Reconstruction Finance Corporation, 205
Regional Rail Reorganization Act (1973), 116
Reich, Charles, 194, 208
Responsible Genetic Research, 59
Retirement programs, 78-85, 97, 189
Rifkin, Jeremy, 208
Risk, passim; avoidance, 44-46; decision process under, 41-44; demands for protection against, 46-50, 65-69; in international perspective, 140-68; meaning and measurement, 39-41; pooled, 201-2; "private," 41; reduction by decree, 50-53; shifting responsiblity for, 61-65; unknown events and, 53-61
Robertson, L., 137
Roby, Pamela A., 37
Rokkan, Stein, 37
Rolls Royce, 162
Rose-Ackerman, Susan, 74
Rowe, W. D., 72
Rudman, R., 72
Rural Development Insurance Fund, 90

Rural Electrification Administration, 119, 121
Rural Housing Insurance Fund, 91, 132

Safety standards, 2, 31, 33, 44, 50-60, 112, 128, 171, 176, 200-201
Samuelson, Paul A., 30, 38
Savings, 76-77, 84, 106, 108, 132-33, 171
Sawyer, James W., 74
Schafer, Stephen, 38
Scherer, Frederick M., 138
Schultze, Charles L., 74, 138
Schwartz, Harry, 192
Securities and Exchange Commission (SEC), 61, 125
Securities Investors Protection Corporation, 117
Seidel, Stephen, 130, 139
Self-interest, 15-16, 30-31, 196
Severance pay, 69
Shapo, Marshall S., 74
Shepherd, William G., 192
Shipbuilding industry, 119, 157-58
Shoe industry, 77, 136, 151
Shonfield, Andrew, 37
Shultz, George P., 192
Silent Spring, 55
Simanis, Joseph G., 108, 191
Sjöström, H., 73
Slovic, Paul, 72, 73, 209
Small Business Administration, 42, 93, 119
Smith, Adam, 15, 23, 71, 112
Social Security Act (1935), 67, 78, 84, 89, 203
Social Security Amendments (1977), 80
Social Security System, 28, 47, 78-85, 99, 113, 201
Social welfare programs, 80-81, 86-87, 102, 156, 174
Society: evolving social order of, 6-12; individuals and, 13-15; models of humanity in, 30-32; uncertainty and choice in, 27-30
South Africa, 147
Southern Railway, 184
Soviet Union, 32, 147
Spain, 116
Stagflation, 5, 193
Starr, C., 72
State government insurance, 77-78, 162-64
State-owned enterprises, 10, 115-18, 124
Statsförtag, 162
Steel industry, 126, 136, 145, 153-56, 163

Stigler, George J., 37
Stobough, Robert, 73
Strange, Susan, 167
Strassberg, Paul A., 191
Student Loan Insurance Fund, 90-91, 121
Student Loan Marketing Association (SLMA), 91, 121
Subsidies, 2, 3, 11, 21, 25, 114, 116, 120-21, 132-33, 136, 158-61, 171
Suffrage, universal, 7, 33, 49, 180
Supplemental Security Income (SSI), 81
Sweden, 88, 99, 115, 116, 157, 158, 175
Switzerland, 71, 147

Taboos, 18-19, 31
Tariffs, 27, 136, 142, 150-51, 156
Taxes, 10, 27, 33, 99-100, 109, 124-25, 133-37, 150, 173, 177, 196, 205-7; disguised, 111-14
Tax Reform Acts (1962, 1969), 131
Tax-transfer systems, 81, 99-100, 113, 133-37
Technology, 8, 10-11, 21-22, 33, 59, 142-43, 147, 151, 181, 184, 186, 195
Textile industry, 152-53, 164
Third World, 142, 144, 151
Thirteenth Amendment, 48
Three Mile Island, 55, 98
Times (London), 174
Titmuss, R., 18, 36
Tokyo Round (trade negotiations), 164, 168
Trade, international, 77, 143-48; adjustments, 152-55; industrial policies and, 148-52; liberalization, 155-57; and new mercantilism, 160-66
Trade Act (1974), 77, 96, 150
Trade Expansion Act (1962), 96
Travel, international, 8, 146
Treaty of Rome, 142
Tuccillo, John A., 139
Tufte, Edward, 137
Tullock, Gordon, 36
Tumlir, J., 166, 167
Turner v. *General Motors*, 74
Tversky, Amos, 72
Tyrell, R. E., Jr., 191
Tyrrell, C. Merton, 138

Uncertainty, 41, 43, 70-71; social class and, 27-30. *See also* Risk
Unemployment, 3, 7, 42, 47, 49, 65-69, 77, 96, 115, 116, 156, 158-59, 174, 181, 186, 193

Unemployment Trust Fund, 96
Unions, trade, 7, 66, 115, 158, 180-81, 196
United Auto Workers, 145
United Kingdom, 17, 51, 69-70, 88, 99, 102, 115-16, 144, 147-48, 153-60, 162, 174-76, 177, 185
UN Industrial Development Organization, 67, 75
Upper Clyde Shipbuilders, 162
U.S. Chamber of Commerce, 116
U.S. Department of Agriculture, 92
U.S. Department of Commerce, 127, 144
U.S. Department of Defense, 92, 123
U.S. Department of Education, 91
U.S. Department of Energy, 58
U.S. Department of Health and Human Services, 90, 121
U.S. Department of Housing and Urban Development, 91, 121
U.S. Department of Labor, 119
U.S. Department of Transportation, 112, 121
U.S. Postal Service, 117
U.S. Steel Company, 178
U.S. Supreme Court, 36, 58, 98, 184
U.S. Treasury Department, 96, 117, 164
Urbanization, 21-22
Urban Property Protection and Reinsurance Act (1968), 94

Vaccination program, 97
Val-Saint Lambert, 38, 163
Value systems, 13-14
Vera Institute for Criminal Justice, 191
Veteran Loan Guaranty Revolving Fund, 90
Veterans benefits, 85, 96
Vietnam war, 32
Villani, Kevin, 139
Volcker, Paul, 117
Volkswagen, 147, 161
Vorhes, J. G., 126
Votaw, Dow, 37

Walker, William, 74
Walsh, Annmarie, 121, 138
Wardell, William W., 192
Washington, 96
Washington Post, 176
Waste Isolation Pilot Plant (WIPP), 58
Wealth, distribution of, 17, 20, 35, 180
Weaver, Robert, 117

Weidenbaum, Murray L., 127, 138

Weiss, Harry, 73

Welfare recipients, 179-80

Welfare state, 1

Wheeler, Jimmy, 168

Whipple, C., 72

White, Gilbert, 38

Wilensky, Harold L., 12

Willkie, David, 179

Wilkie v. *O'Connor,* 192

Wilson, James Q., 191

Wilson, Richard, 204, 209

Windle, Ralph, 137

Women, 3, 33, 195

Work Incentive Program, 67

Workmen's compensation, 51-52, 77-78

Work-related hazards, 7, 34, 54-55, 97

Yankelovich, Daniel, 177

Yarborough, Ralph, 95

Yergin, Daniel, 73

Zetten, Robert A., 108

Zoeckler, Major General, 123